D0837649

50 Hikes

In Ohio

Day Hikes and Backpacks throughout the Buckeye State

RALPH RAMEY

Second Edition

Backcountry Publications

Woodstock, Vermont

An Invitation to the Reader
Over time trails can be rerouted and signs and landmarks altered. If you find that changes have occurred on the routes described in this book, please let us know so that corrections may be made in future editions. The author and publisher also welcome other comments and suggestions. Address all correspondence to:

    Editor
    50 Hikes Series™
    Backcountry Publications
    PO Box 748
    Woodstock, VT 05091

Library of Congress
Cataloging-in-Publication Data

Ramey, Ralph.
50 hikes in Ohio : day hikes and backpacking trips throughout the Buckeye state / Ralph Ramey. —2nd ed.
    p. cm.
Includes index.
ISBN 0-88150-401-7 (alk. paper)
1. Hiking—Ohio—Guidebooks.
2. Backpacking—Ohio—Guidebooks.
3. Ohio—Guidebooks.
I. title
GV199.42.03R35   1997
917.7104'43—dc21   97-18838
                          CIP

Text and cover design by Glenn Suokko
Cover and interior photographs by Ralph Ramey
Maps on pages 32–33, 39, 65, 70, 94, 115, 119, 150–151, 155, 160–161, and 248–249 by Hedberg Maps, © 1997 The Countryman Press
All other maps and map overlays by Dick Widhu

© 1990, 1997 by Ralph Ramey

Second Edition; Third Printing 1999

All rights reserved. No part of this book may be reproduced in any form or by any electronic or mechanical means including information storage and retrieval systems without permission in writing from the publisher, except by a reviewer who may quote brief passages.

Excerpt from *Idle Weeds,* copyright © 1980 by David Rains Wallace, is reprinted with permission of Sierra Club Books.

Published by Backcountry Publications
An imprint of The Countryman Press
PO Box 748
Woodstock, Vermont 05091

Distributed by W. W. Norton & Company, Inc.
500 Fifth Avenue
New York, NY 10110

Printed in Canada
10 9 8 7 6 5 4 3

To Carolyn Louise Ramey (1954–1997), who was unable to hike with me during her lifetime but will now be by my side on every trail.

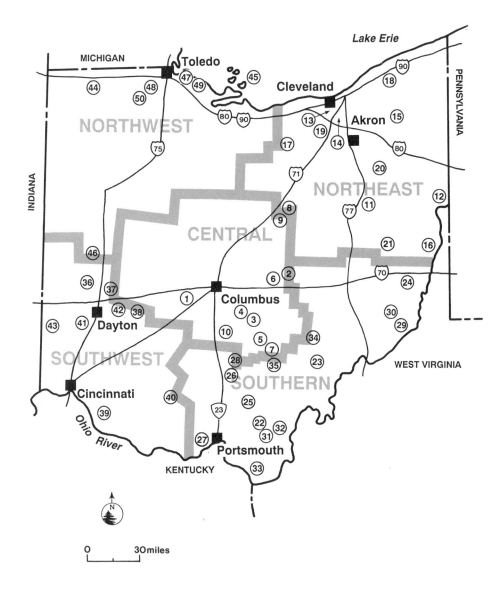

MICHIGAN

Toledo

⑰ ㊼ ㊺ ㊻ ㊺ ㊹ ㊺

Lake Erie

PENNSYLVANIA

⑨⓪

⑱

Cleveland

⑱

Akron ⑮

NORTHWEST

㊻ ㊹ ㊺

⑳

⑧⓪

⑬

⑲

⑭

⑰

NORTHEAST

⑫

INDIANA

⑮

⑯ㄱㄴ

⑪

⑦⑦

CENTRAL

⑧

⑨

㊻

㉑

⑯

㊱

㉚

⑥ ②

⑦⓪

㉔

① Columbus

④ ③

⑫ ㊳

⑪ Dayton

⑩

⑤

㉚

㉙

SOUTHWEST

⑦

㉞

㊸

㉘

㉓

WEST VIRGINIA

㉖

SOUTHERN

Cincinnati

㊵

㉕

Ohio

River

㉓

㉒ ㉜

㉗ Portsmouth

㉛

KENTUCKY

㉝

N

0   30 miles

Contents

Acknowledgments

My special thanks to the personnel of the Ohio Department of Natural Resources, both in the Columbus office and in the field, for sharing their knowledge and providing maps and literature. Also, thanks to the folks at the metropolitan parks, the federal facilities, the conservancy districts, the Ohio Historical Society, the privately owned areas, and the Buckeye Trail Association who readily gave the same kind of help.

I will forever be indebted to the late Bill Cohn and the late Mac Henney, who as the Scoutmasters of my youth in Troop 3 in Bexley started me hiking Ohio's trails; and to the Scouts and Scouters of Troop 417 in Upper Arlington who, when I became a Scoutmaster, shared with me the joy of exploring the Ohio countryside on foot. Thanks to the staff and volunteers at Antioch University's Glen Helen nature preserve, where I was employed when I wrote the first edition, for graciously accepting weekend program duties in my stead while I trekked Ohio's trails. Like-wise, my gratitude goes to friends throughout the state who offered advice and encouragement.

I could not have done without the support of my family. My sons, John and Jim, provided hiking gear, and John got me started on the computer and bailed me out when I got in trouble. My daughter Carolyn's cheerful "How you doing with your hikes, Dad?" urged me on. Most important of all has been the support and encouragement of my loving wife, Jean, who kept the home fires burning on the dozens of weekends that I spent away from home on the state's footpaths.

Lastly, the gentle and thoughtful criticisms and suggestions given by the editor of the first edition, Jane McGraw, and the folks at Countryman Press, made my first publishing adventure both pleasant and productive. I am especially indebted to Helen Whybrow of Countryman Press for tolerating my slippage on deadlines during a time of family crisis.

Introduction

Hiking opportunities in Ohio are as varied as its topography. From the once mighty Ohio River on the southern border (tamed long ago by navigation locks and dams) to the "reborn" Lake Erie on the northern, the state hosts trails through deep forests or open meadows in country ranging from nearly flat to very hilly. Trails are found in state forests, wildlife areas, parks, nature preserves, and memorials. Walking paths also crisscross national forests and recreation areas. Park district preserves and reservations offer some of the best hiking in the state, and privately owned nature centers have well-developed trail systems. In the eastern part of the state, the lands of the Muskingum Watershed Conservancy District beckon hikers, and at least one utility company has opened its landholdings to recreation. There are trails that follow lakeshores, streams, old canal towpaths, interurban and railroad rights-of-way, abandoned country roads, Native American trails, early wagon roads, game paths, and much more. Lastly, there are trails that form part of the National Trail System and paths used by the statewide Buckeye Trail system.

This great breadth of hiking opportunities is a result of the natural diversity of the Buckeye State. Its exposed bedrock is all sedimentary, laid down by successive warm seas, inland embayments, river deltas, and swamps. From the Cincinnati arch, which runs from Lima to Cincinnati, the bedrock dips gently as you travel both east and west. The edges of successive layers of bedrock are thus exposed, the oldest visible along the arch, the younger strata visible as you go east or west. In eastern Ohio the exposures are mostly sandstone, shale, and coal, the materials from which acid soils are derived. In the western part of the state, limestones and dolomites prevail—the building blocks of sweet soils. Several ice advances reshaped the northwestern half of the state, leaving boulder fields, kames, eskers, outwash plains, reversed streams, fossil beach ridges, filled valleys, and the like. The southeastern half was carved into hills by erosion, partly from glacial meltwater, forming a succession of major river systems to carry water to the ocean.

The hikes in this book visit many of the places across Ohio where the geological processes that shape the land are exceptionally well illustrated. One trail passes the world-renowned glacial grooves on Kelleys Island. At Oak Openings, you will walk on sand that was once on the bottom of an ancient lake. In Hocking Hills State Park, the trail follows the bottom of a deep gorge carved in the sandstone by meltwater; and at Clifton Gorge, you will walk on the rim of another meltwater-carved gorge, this one of limestone and dolomite.

Before the arrival of white settlers, most of Ohio was covered by eastern hardwood forest. There were also unforested areas occupied by prairie, fen, bog, and coastal marsh. Here and there across the state are relict plant communities from times when the general climate was much different, preserved from earlier eons by microclimatic or edaphic conditions.

Bison, wolf, elk, passenger pigeon, Carolina parakeet, and other species of animals that were common prior to settlement are now gone. When drained with ditches and tile, the extensive prairies that once supported big bluestem and baptisia became fields of corn, soybeans, and wheat. Where native herbivores once grazed in the summer on the native warm-season grasses of the prairies, cool-season grasses from Eurasia were planted to support cattle and sheep. Swine were turned loose in the woods to eat whatever they could. Rivers and streams that supported dozens of species of fish and mollusks in clear, well-oxygenated water were dammed to provide for power and navigation, and polluted with chaff from mills. The industries, towns, and cities that grew along the watercourses added their waste to the streams and rivers. Virgin forests were cleared to open areas for cropland and pasture and to provide construction material and fuel. Much of southeastern Ohio's timber was cut to make charcoal for use in iron furnaces. Extractive industries mined iron, coal, sand, gravel, stone, clay, and more. Wells pumped gas and oil from below the surface. After a series of treaties, the Native Americans were driven completely from the area. In less than a century, the farmers, canallers, railroaders, road and bridge builders, and ditch diggers had brought civilization to the rough Ohio wilderness.

Hiking Trails in Ohio

Though Ohio ranks 36th in size among the 50 states, it is 7th in population. A major agricultural state, it is also heavily industrialized, with most of its 11 million people living in one of six urban areas. Shortly after World War I, civic leaders recognized a need for large, publicly owned natural places for outdoor recreation near the cities. Thus was born the system of local park districts, one of the nation's finest. There are now metropolitan park systems in all of Ohio's urban areas and in many rural counties as well. Most operate on a philosophy that calls for retaining 80 percent of the land in a natural state. They have many miles of trails and are great places to hike. This book includes a selection of hikes in parks with especially nice natural features from several districts.

In 1918 Ohio began systematically to acquire state forest land. Though originally established to preserve (or perhaps restore) the timber resources of the state, the 173,415-acre system now includes an area designated as wilderness where no timber-management activities occur. The federally operated Civilian Conservation Corps (CCC) of the 1930s built many recreation facilities, including trails in the state forests, and many of these still provide great pleasure to hikers. New trails, including two backpacking trails, have been added in recent years.

In 1949 a unified Ohio Department of Natural Resources (ODNR) was created that established, for the first time, a state park system. Publicly owned lands that were being used as parks or that had the potential to be developed into parks were put under the control of the ODNR, and they became the nucleus for the present 200,884-acre state park system. Nineteenth-century canal feeder lakes, scenic areas of state forests, and lakes created for fishing, flood control, stream flow augmentation, or water supply were among the diverse areas brought into the system. As major flood-control projects were built in the 1950s and 1960s, they joined the fledgling park system. Today, virtually all of the 72 state parks have some foot trails.

A direct descendant of the earlier Division of Conservation and Natural Resources of the Department of Agriculture, the Division of Wildlife manages areas large and small across the state that provide places for the public to hunt and fish. Though paid for with fees and taxes collected from sportsmen, state wildlife areas are now being managed for overall biological diversity as well as for fish and game production. Some offer good opportunities for hiking, and one such area has been included in this book, although hikers will want to explore these areas during the times when hunting is not permitted. A complete list can be obtained from the ODNR publications office.

The newest agency within the ODNR with land holdings attractive to hikers is the Division of Natural Areas and Preserves. Since 1971 it has acquired 110 parcels totaling over 20,000 acres in all corners of the state. These areas preserve habitat for threatened and endangered plant and animal species and are examples of the wide variety of ecosystems that made up Ohio prior to settlement. Hemlock-filled sandstone ravines, fern-lined limestone gorges, fens, bogs, mature upland woods, swamp forests, and prairie are but a few of the special places now under public ownership. Hikes in a few of these areas that have good trail systems have been included here. A directory of Natural Areas and Preserves can be purchased from the division. A list of natural areas and preserves—and, often, brochures describing individual areas—is available free from the same source.

The Ohio Historical Society (OHS) has long been guardian of the state's treasury of old forts, battlefields, historic homes, and prehistoric mounds and earthworks. Explore the two state memorials included here, then seek out others on your own. Some include small, on-site museums (often with restricted months and hours of operation) as well as developed trail systems. The state travel and tourism office will send you a free list of the properties operated by the OHS along with information about the society.

The federal government also plays a role in providing hiking opportunities in Ohio. The United States Army Corps of Engineers (USACE), charged with responsibility for flood control on navigable streams of the nation, has built dozens of reservoirs in all parts of the state. These are managed by a variety of agencies, including the corps itself, local park districts, and the Department of Natural Resources. In eastern Ohio, the Muskingum Watershed Conservancy District (MWCD), a local political subdivision of the state organized to control flooding, owns and manages the land behind the dams the corps built there. Hikes in two MWCD parks are included here, but there are trails in others. Information about this agency's other facilities is available from the MWCD office.

The National Park Service (NPS) operates several areas in Ohio, including the Cuyahoga Valley National Recreation Area (CVNRA), which preserves the pastoral beauty of that northeastern Ohio river corridor. The CVNRA is already a good place to hike and new facilities continue to be opened. The North Country National Recreational Trail is also a responsibility of the NPS, but development of the trail is up to local jurisdictions. A section of this congressionally authorized trail uses one of the Wayne National Forest trails included in this book.

The United States Fish and Wildlife Service manages many acres of wildlife refuge in Ohio, principally along the southern shore of Lake Erie and around the Erie islands. A walk through the one area open to the public is included here. The United States Forest Service (USFS) has been present in Ohio in a quiet way for many decades. In recent years, it has consolidated land-holdings and aggressively pursued the development of recreational trails. It offers some of the best wilderness hiking in the state in its Wayne National Forest. Six trails suitable for backpacking or day hiking in the Wayne are included here.

One privately owned and two university-owned nature preserves have been included, but there are many other nature centers around the state, all with good trail systems aimed at helping the visitor learn more about the natural world. Self-guided, interpretive trail guides are available for many.

The American Discovery Trail, a footpath across the nation, passes through Ohio. For the most part, it uses already existing trails on federal- or state-owned land or rural roads. When hiking some of the trails in this book, you may see symbols indicating that the trail is part of this system.

The Nature Conservancy (TNC) has been active in protecting natural areas in Ohio for nearly four decades. It owns and manages more than 13,000 acres of good wild land in all parts of the state, operating some in conjunction with other agencies and organizations such as the Museum of Natural History and Science of the Cincinnati Museum Center. A call to TNC's Ohio office will get you a list of its areas and information about visiting them.

With the continuing consolidation of the country's railways, many miles of rights-of-way have been abandoned. The Rails-to-Trails Conservancy (RTTC) has worked closely with many local and state organizations to convert these corridors to recreational use. To date, nearly 250 miles of such trails have been developed in Ohio. Since all of them allow bicycles and in-line skates, they are more congested than most hikers prefer. Information about such facilities in the Buckeye State is available from the Ohio office of the RTTC.

No discussion of trails in Ohio would be complete without mention of two organizations: the Buckeye Trail Association (BTA) and the Boy Scouts of America (BSA). The BTA was established in 1959, originally to complete a trail from the Ohio River to Lake Erie. The trail now links the four corners of the state and is over 1200 miles in length. It crosses both public and private land and, when an off-road route cannot be found, uses lesser-traveled rural roads. Maintained almost entirely by volunteers, the Buckeye Trail takes the hiker through some of Ohio's most spectacular countryside. Though there are many loop trail opportunities along its circuitous route, it is essentially a linear path. Many of the hikes in this guide are partly or totally on the Buckeye Trail.

Over the years, a number of active Boy Scout troops around the state have established officially sanctioned Scout hiking trails. Often these are 10 miles in length, with 5-mile options to allow Scouts to complete requirements for the hiking merit badge. Unfortunately, because of their locales, many of these trails are on paved roads and city streets. Four long-established and well-maintained off-road Scout hiking trails are included.

About This Book

Most of the hikes in this book are 1-day outings, but nine, all located in southeastern Ohio, offer overnight backpacking trips of 2 to 9 days, as well as day walks. Nearly all of the 50 hikes are loop hikes, allowing you to finish where you started. There are two end-to-end trails, where you must either hike in both directions, use a two-car shuttle, or follow the other creative suggestions I have offered in those chapters. It is always a good idea to hike with one or more companions, but many hikers prefer to travel alone, while recognizing the added risks of doing so and preparing for them. Whether you hike alone or with companions, be sure to tell someone your destination, planned route, and expected time of return. I have hiked alone for more than 50 years and, with two exceptions, I walked all of the Scouting trips for the trails in this book alone. When I day-hike, I usually carry a fanny pack with some basic emergency supplies and, in recent years, a cellular phone (though I doubt if I could reach a cell from many of the southeastern Ohio valleys and ravines).

Maps

The maps that accompany the trail descriptions in this book are all based on United States Geological Survey (USGS) 7½' quadrangles. (Such maps are available for the entire state.) These "topos" have all been prepared since World War II, but changes that have occurred since they were prepared mean that they don't always exactly match man-made features. You can gain insight into the early character of an area by studying the earlier 15' quadrangles, most prepared around the turn of the century. Though these can no longer be purchased from state or federal map agencies, many can be found in the federal document repositories and map rooms of libraries, colleges, and universities. They can often be copied to carry on the trail. They are a great help in identifying old trolley and railroad lines, long-gone homesites, industrial complexes, cemeteries, roads, bridges, and even

entire communities. Clues to the presence of early human activity are the presence of fruit trees, plantings of ornamental bulbs and shrubs, and fallen-down buildings and dumps. Other guides for the curious hiker are the inexpensive folders sold by the OHS that show the locations of early canals, covered bridges, and iron furnaces.

Many of the managing agencies have trail maps available for their areas. These can be good supplements to the maps in this book, as they sometimes reflect changes made during the current season. They can usually be obtained at no charge by writing or calling the appropriate agency. In some places they are available at the trailhead, but don't depend on it. Buckeye Trail section maps can be purchased from the BTA. It will send you a list of maps available and information about the association upon request.

Hike Statistics

The *hiking times* shown for suggested routes are based on my experiences when surveying the trails and on a speed of no more than 2 miles per hour on flat terrain, less in hill country. Always allow ample time for both road and trail travel. In both cases, expect and be prepared for the unexpected. The *vertical rise* calculation is the difference between the highest and the lowest points on the trail; there will never be a single climb of that amount. The *mileage figures* are from measurements made on the topographic maps and/or from figures provided by the managing agencies.

Equipment

There are many good books on the subject of hiking and backpacking, so there is no point in covering that material here. In my opinion, no hiker should be on the trail without at least a copy of the map as presented in this book (if not the USGS quad-rangles), a compass and knowledge of how to use it, a Swiss army knife, a thunder whistle, sunscreen and insect repellent if needed, and a pocket first-aid kit. A good pair of broken-in hiking shoes and socks of a weight and material appropriate for the season are a must. Though many people hike in sneakers, I prefer an ankle-high boot of either leather or nylon. A twisted ankle can ruin a hike. Dressing in layers makes the most sense for hiking, since clothing can be adjusted for the temperature during the course of the day. A day pack or fanny pack with a poncho and a water bottle of adequate size are always in order. No surface water is safe to drink *anywhere* in the state.

Pocket-sized tree, flower, berry, animal track, and fern identification books, such as the "Finder" series published by the Nature Study Guild, can help you learn more about the nature of things seen along the trail. A pocket magnifying glass and a pair of lightweight binoculars allow a closer look at plants and animals large and small. The currently available lightweight point-and-shoot 35 mm cameras (some water resistant and many with telephoto or zoom lenses) allow you to capture special sights and moments. A walking staff (homemade or otherwise), to the top of which has been added a ¼-inch-by-20-thread bolt, will serve as a third leg when crossing creeks or climbing hills, and as a monopod (really the third leg of a tripod when added to your two legs) to stabilize a camera in the low-light situations often found on woodland trails.

Accommodations

Ten of the trails in this book can accommodate backpackers, and 17 hikes are located in recreation areas where there are family campgrounds. Many of these areas offer boating, fishing, swimming, and interpretive programs. Most are near other suggested hikes or close to recreational or tourism resources such as amusement parks, museums, festivals, or crafts shops. Call 1-800-BUCKEYE for information on places and events in the area you are planning to visit. Local convention and visitors bureaus (CVBs) can also supply useful information on area attractions. The official "Ohio Tour and Highway Map," available from the same source, lists the names, addresses, and phone numbers of all Ohio CVBs.

Much has been written about the desecration of outdoor recreation resources by careless users. The special places covered by the 327 miles of trails suggested in this book deserve the best stewardship by those who use them. Practice minimal-impact hiking and camping as advocated and described in many books and periodicals: "Pack it in; haul it out." As I used to tell the Boy Scouts of Troop 417 in Columbus, "Let no one say unto your shame, all was beauty here until you came." Go home with good pictures and wonderful memories and leave behind only light footprints. Happy hiking!

Information Resources

Acorn Naturalists
17300 East 17th Street
#J-236
Tustin, CA 92780
Catalog of resources—books, etc.—for the trail and classroom

Brukner Nature Center
5995 Horseshoe Bend Road
Troy, OH 45373
513-698-6493

Buckeye Trail Association
PO Box 254
Worthington, OH 43085
(Enclose a stamped, self-addressed,
business-sized envelope)

Cleveland Metroparks System
4101 Fulton Parkway
Cleveland, OH 44144
216-351-6300

**Columbus and Franklin County
Metropolitan Park District**
PO Box 29169
Columbus, OH 43229
614-891-0700

**Cuyahoga Valley National
Recreation Area**
15610 Vaughn Road
Brecksville, OH 44141
216-526-5265

Five Rivers Metroparks District
1375 East Siebenthaler Avenue
Dayton, OH 45414
513-275-7275

Glen Helen/Antioch University
405 Corry Street
Yellow Springs, OH 45387-1895
513-767-7375

Hamilton County Park District
10245 Winton Road
Cincinnati, OH 45231
513-521-7275

Kelleys Island Chamber of Commerce
PO Box 783M
Kelleys Island, OH 43438-0783
419-746-2360

Lake County Metro Parks
11211 Spear Road
Concord Township, OH 44077-9542
216-639-7275

Metropark District of the Toledo Area
5100 West Central Avenue
Toledo, OH 43615
419-535-3050

Miami County Park District
2535 East Ross Road
Tipp City, OH 45371
513-667-1086

**Muskingum Watershed Conservancy
District**
PO Box 349
New Philadelphia, OH 44663-0349
216-343-6647

Ohio Biological Survey
1315 Kinnear Road
Columbus, OH 43212-1192
614-292-9645
*Catalog of available publications on
Ohio flora, fauna, and biodiversity*

**Ohio Department of Natural Resources
Division of Geological Survey**
4383 Fountain Square Drive
Columbus, OH 43224-1362
614-265-6576
*Catalog of maps and other resources on
Ohio geology*

**Ohio Department of Natural Resources
Division of Natural Areas and Preserves**
1889 Fountain Square Court
Columbus, OH 43224-1331
614-265-6453

**Ohio Department of Natural Resources
Public Information Center**
1952 Belcher Drive
Columbus, OH 43224-1386
614-265-6605

Ohio Division of Travel and Tourism
PO Box 1001
Columbus, OH 43216
1-800-282-4393

Ohio Historical Society
1985 Velma Avenue
Columbus, OH 43211
1-800-282-5393
Site information

Patricia Ledlie Bookseller, Inc.
One Bean Road, PO Box 90
Buckfield, ME 04220
207-336-2778
*Purveyor of books on natural science and
conservation biology*

Shelby County Park District
9871 Fessler-Buxton Road
Piqua, OH 45356
513-773-4818

Wayne National Forest
Athens Ranger District
219 Columbus Road
Athens, OH 45701
614-592-6644

US Forest Service
Athens Ranger District—Marietta Unit
Route 1, Box 132
Marietta, OH 45750
614-373-9055

Wayne National Forest
Ironton Ranger District
Route 2, Box 203
Pedro, OH 45659
614-532-3223

Key to Map Symbols

— — — main trail

• • • • • alternate or side trail

(P) parking

(T) trailhead

(R) rest rooms

(W) water

lookout

bridge

1

Battelle–Darby Creek Metro Park

Total distance: 4½ miles (6.7 km)

Hiking time: 2½ hours

Maximum elevation: 920 feet

Vertical rise: 90 feet

Maps: USGS 7½' Galloway; MPDCFC Battelle–Darby Creek Metro Park map

The Darby Creeks are considered to be among the finest of Ohio's streams. The Nature Conservancy designated them and their riverine environment as one of the nation's Last Great Places. They receive virtually no industrial and very little municipal effluent as they flow from the Darby Plains area of Madison and Union Counties to their confluence with the Scioto River just north of Circleville. Designated as a State Scenic River for many years, in the early 1990s the (Big and Little) Darby Creeks were added to the National Scenic River System. The Big Darby is a stream of pristine beauty as it passes below the high bluffs in Battelle–Darby Creek Metro Park in southwestern Franklin County.

A facility of the Metropolitan Park District of Columbus and Franklin County, this lovely metro park has public and reservable picnic areas as well as a winterized meeting lodge. There is a year-round program of nature interpretation conducted by a park naturalist. An ongoing project to restore large areas of native tallgrass prairie within the park boundaries will add a new dimension to the park in years to come.

How to Get There

To reach Battelle–Darby Creek Metro Park, travel 14 miles west of downtown Columbus on I-70 to exit 75. Travel 2.5 miles south on OH 142 to US 40, then 1.5 miles east (left) to Darby Creek Drive. Turn right and drive 3 miles south to the park entrance on the right. It is open every day during daylight hours.

Big Darby Creek from an overlook along the trail

➤ What Is a Metro Park?

Ohio's metropolitan parks are the result of legislation passed at the close of World War I that allowed the establishment of special districts for the conservation of the natural resources of the state. The Cleveland Metropolitan Park District was the first created and set the standard for the others that followed. Most important was their determination to keep 80 percent of the land within the park in a wild, undeveloped state; no more than 20 percent could be used for playgrounds, picnic areas, ball fields, parking lots, and reservoirs.

Park districts have been leaders in environmental interpretation and education, many building nature centers and hiring staff naturalists even in the late 1930s. In more recent years, they have led the way in restoration management, using controlled burning, alien plant eradication, and other techniques to reestablish original ecosystems. They have also led the way in creating facilities for "under your own power" outdoor recreation opportunities, providing hundreds of miles of footpaths through field and forest, beside lakes and streams, and along old railroad and canal towpath rights-of-way.

There are Metro Parks within an hour's drive of virtually every Ohioan, providing places for many quick walks on short notice. For a brochure with the names and addresses of 55 park districts around the state, write to the Ohio Parks and Recreation Association, 1069A West Main Street, Westerville, OH 43081-1181. The phone number is 614-895-2222.

The Trail

The 4¼-mile Indian Ridge Nature Trail starts behind the park office/concession building. It becomes a gravel trail when it leaves the picnic area, heading due west toward the bluffs overlooking Big Darby Creek. The woods on the thin-soiled uplands are oak/hickory, and those in the river bottom are a typical floodplain hardwood mixture. *Note:* The Cedar Bluff Lookout Trail is now a separate trail. The bridge, steps, and trail connecting it with the rest of the trail system have been removed.

The trail turns south to follow the stream over a series of steps and bridges. Benches located along the trail provide opportunities to stop and enjoy the quiet woods and nearby creek. After dropping to a ravine and crossing a stream, the trail emerges onto a hillside below a meadow, then follows the contour of the land close to the river before passing beneath two new concrete bridges.

Once south of Alkire Road, the trail passes paths to the nearby parking lot and to the canoe-launching area at stream's edge, then returns to the riverbank, where it heads south to pass under the railroad bridge. One hundred yards beyond the bridge a sign, BEGIN LOOP, points left for a 2-mile round-trip. Turn left and go upslope on what appears to be an old road. There is a picnic area through the trees to the right where drinking water and rest rooms can be found. Old concrete fence posts mark the edge of the railroad right-of-way. Staying left at an intersection, the trail heads uphill where it crosses a bridge before swinging right, all the time in young oak-hickory woods. At one place, the present trail deserts the old road, leaving the water-filled ruts of the former track as good spawning areas for frogs and toads. Continuing through more woods, the trail finally reaches the mowed parkway. After

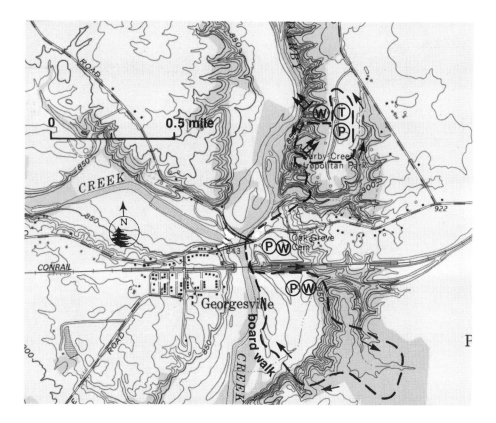

entering a wet woods beyond the road, it crosses a number of obviously man-made ditches, early attempts to make this poorly drained land productive. Here grow pin oaks, good indicators of the acidity of the soil in this part of the park. Some stretches of the trail are covered with wood chips, others with gravel. There are a few places where the trail is soggy a good bit of the year. Not far off the trail lie the rusting bodies of a 1950s-era Chevy truck and some farm equipment. As the trail turns west parallel to a ravine, some great old, open-grown trees can be seen.

The trail now descends toward the river bottom, where, for several hundred feet, it is on a boardwalk made necessary by the constant drainage of water across the area from the hills to the east. A side trail to the right leads to play and picnic areas, but the Indian Ridge Trail completes its loop by returning via a riverside trail to the intersection where the sign was seen earlier.

Return to the northern part of the park over the same trail, except take the first trail to the right after entering the woods past Alkire Road. That trail goes up another set of steps to an overlook, then to another picnic area. As it passes through a wooden fence into the picnic area, the trail once more becomes a blacktopped walk. To return to the trailhead, cross the road and follow the trail as it loops east, then north, through young woods and shrubland. It emerges from the woods opposite the parking lot where it began.

2

Blackhand Gorge State Nature Preserve

Total distance: 5 miles (8 km)

Hiking time: 3 hours

Maximum elevation: 1000 feet

Vertical rise: 197 feet

Maps: USGS 7½' Toboso and Hanover; ODNR/DNAP Blackhand Gorge Nature Preserve brochure

When on July 4, 1825, at a site near the present city of Heath, Ohio, New York's Governor De Witt Clinton turned the first shovel of dirt to start the construction of the Ohio and Erie Canal, a massive public works project was born that would forever change the shape of Ohio's lakes and rivers.

To get from the Muskingum River drainage system to that of the Scioto, it was necessary to bring the canal up the valley of the Licking River to the divide, where Governor Clinton had broken ground, so that it could then descend toward Portsmouth. Just beyond the glacial border and east of Newark, the Licking River passed between vertical cliffs of sandstone. On one cliff face, Native Americans had carved a large hand. Since it was on a well-traveled canoe route to the nearby flint ridge area where flint was quarried for arrow and spear tips, many people believed the hand signified that the land beyond this point was neutral ground for all tribes. At any rate, the name Black Hand Gorge had been applied to this area, as well as Licking Narrows.

The cliff face where the hand was painted was blasted away to allow construction of a towpath. Though the black hand was gone, early geologists had already seen it and named the particular sandstone exposed there Black Hand sandstone.

A coarse-grained, well-cemented, massive sandstone with some iron impurities and often with quartz pebbles embedded in it, the Black Hand sandstone is a prime player in the creation of some of Ohio's most scenic areas. Laid down perhaps 325 million years ago as a delta of outwash from

The Black Hand that was once etched into this rock was blasted away when a ledge was built for canalboat-pulling mules to traverse the north bank of the Licking River.

eroding mountains to the southeast, Black Hand sandstone is present in a band 20 to 30 miles wide from the Ohio River to Wayne County. The rock shelters of the Hocking Hills region are all eroded from Black Hand sandstone, and Lancaster's Rising Park is of the same rock.

For nearly a century, Blackhand Gorge echoed to the "gees" and "haws" of mule-skinners as they towed canal packets north and south on the Ohio and Erie Canal. The 1913 flood brought that era to an end, but a new form of transportation had already entered the gorge. The Central Ohio Railroad had acquired a right-of-way through Licking Narrows and was operating a steam-powered railroad.

In the early part of the 20th century, yet another form of transportation came to the narrows—the interurban. Instead of using the narrow ledge of the towpath, this elec-tric railroad system chose to blast a tunnel through the Black Hand sandstone bedrock on the north side of the river. For nearly two decades, traction cars carried passengers from Newark to Zanesville through the Blackhand Gorge. The place was one of such natural beauty that a recreation area known as Rock Haven Park was developed there, attracting revelers from far and wide. The interurban made a regular stop at Rock Haven Park and ran specials to the area on weekends and holidays.

By 1929, traction cars had given way to buses and, more important, to Henry Ford's mass-produced, inexpensive motorcars. The interurban right-of-way became a road-way, and Rock Haven Park continued as an attraction for many years. The old narrow road was finally closed to traffic when mod-ern highways were built.

In 1975, recognizing the natural beauty

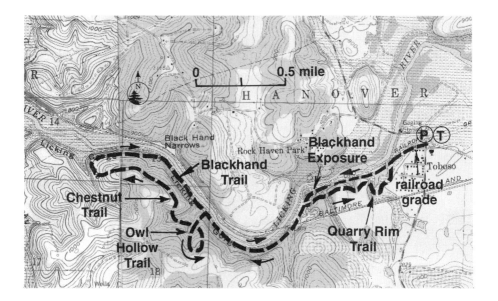

of Blackhand Gorge, the state of Ohio set it aside as a state nature preserve. The boats, interurban cars, steam locomotives, and automobiles are all gone; only remnants of the artifacts remain. Nature is being allowed to take its course as the area returns to its original natural vegetation.

Most of the artifacts of early transportation through the gorge lie on the north side of the river, and some of them can be seen from the Canal Lock Trail, which can be reached by crossing the river on the highway bridge and turning left (west). Unfortunately, the state does not own all of the land through which the interurban trail travels, nor even the Black Hand Rock, so hiking opportunities are limited on the north side of the river. There are, however, many miles of trail through the gorge along the south bank.

If you are a bicyclist, you may want to bring your bike with you and explore the 4-mile North Central Bikeway upstream to where the town of Claylick once stood on the floodplain of the Licking River. Motorized vehicles of any sort are prohibited.

Cross-country skiing is permitted when the snow falls.

How to Get There

This 981-acre nature preserve is easily reached from the Columbus area by traveling approximately 10 miles east of Newark on OH 16, then turning right on OH 146 and, very shortly, turning right again on County Road 273. The preserve is located about 1.5 miles south on County Road 273 on the right. The driving time from downtown Columbus is about 1 hour. The hike at Blackhand Gorge combines well with the walk at Flint Ridge State Memorial, which is located only a few miles to the south.

The Trail

A walk through Blackhand Gorge starts at the parking area along County Road 273 just outside the village of Toboso. This community was moved from the low land along the Licking River to its present site when Dillon Reservoir was built downstream. Begin by looking over the pioneer log house that has been moved to the entrance for use in interpretive programs. Then pass through the opening in the stone wall across the drive from the cabin, and turn right onto the blacktopped railroad right-of-way, part of the North Central Bikeway. Two primitive latrines sit to the right of the trail. The large amount of bush honeysuckle in the area gives evidence to this having once been close to homes and yards.

Shortly you will pass a sign on the left indicating the route of the 1¼-mile-long Quarry Rim Trail. Sandstone from these quarries was crushed and shipped by rail to Newark to be used to produce beer bottles. Star Glassworks and American Bottle Company were among the enterprises of Edward H. Everett, "The Bottle King," but the enactment of the alcohol prohibition law in 1920 brought on the demise of his bottle business. On either your outward- or inward-bound trip, you should follow that path as it winds its way around the rim of several abandoned quarry pits. Buttonbush now fills much of the first quarry, and amphibians and birds such wood ducks utilize the ponds in their respective seasons.

There is a shortcut that will bring you back to the blacktop between the two major quarries, but don't take that; go the full distance on the interesting rim trail. Then, back on the blacktop, continue west with the river on the right and the woods and occasional outcrops on your left. Not long after passing under the active railroad bridge, there is another sign along the left side of the trail. Turn left there to follow the Owl Hollow and Chestnut Trails. If you are there in a wet season, you will face a gently cascading waterfall, but two bridges and two sets of steps will bring you to the dividing point between the two trails.

Explore the mile-long Owl Hollow Trail by turning right, then following the trail marked by white triangles. I took it counterclockwise, first crossing the creek and climbing the right side of the hollow, then crossing over to the rock-strewn left side to return to the trail junction. There are some good-sized hardwoods near the high point on the trail, and the north-facing slope should be a good place for spring wildflowers.

Back at the trail junction, turn left to cross the stream on a boardwalk, then follow the Chestnut Trail as it climbs the right flank of the valley on what looks like an old roadway or logging skid. Near the head of valley, the trail hooks right to rise to the high ground; then for the next mile it follows the contour through the deciduous woods above the Licking River. If you see hemlocks through the woods to the right, it is likely there is a Black Hand sandstone cliff below them. There are great patches of Christmas fern in the woods in places along here. Chestnuts have been gone from the Ohio forest for decades, so I wondered how this trail got its name. Just before the trail begins its descent to the river, past sandstone cliffs and hemlocks, there are some rotting chestnut boles and a decaying chestnut stump. Chestnut is a very durable wood, and it can still occasionally be seen in the forests of eastern Ohio nearly three-quarters of a century since it died and fell to earth.

The trail returns to the bike path at a point where the distance between the blacktop and the river is widening. Upon reaching the blacktop, turn right to head back toward the Black Hand Rock and the trailhead. Notice the abundance of scouring rush growing in the strip between the path and the river. A handful of that silica-laden plant, a little water, and lots of elbow grease got many an iron skillet clean on the Ohio frontier.

In the winter, the new railroad cut is

➤ Black Hand Sandstone

The presence near the surface of the Mississippian-aged Black Hand sandstone is responsible for some of eastern Ohio's most magnificent scenery. In places this fine-grained, buff-colored rock with its layers of pea-sized quartz pebbles can be as thick as 200 feet. Where did it come from? How did it get its name? Why does it make such striking features where it is exposed?

About 325 million years ago, much of what is now Ohio was covered by a shallow sea. Erosion in the upland to the southeast created a huge delta, much like that of the present-day Mississippi River. These sediments were later consolidated and became the formation known as Black Hand sandstone. For thousands of years the area of the delta sank so that it was completely covered by sea, with finer-grained sediments deposited over it. After millions of years, the area became a swampy coastal plain with dense vegetation, the source of later coal deposits. About 230 million years ago, the area was uplifted and tilted and stream erosion began to shape it. Coal beds and other rocks were eroded away, eventually exposing the Black Hand sandstone in the valleys and gorges. About 1 million years ago, ice advances across Ohio nearly reached Hocking and Licking Counties, where the rock was exposed, causing damming of streams that flowed northwesterly from those areas. The scenic features of Hocking and Licking Counties acquired their present forms over the last million years as the result of stream erosion and weathering. It is the high erosion resistance and the vertical and horizontal cross-bedding of the Black Hand sandstone that make vertical cliffs, overhanging promontories, re-entrant caves, and large slump blocks. And its surface, when moist, makes a good substrate for mosses, lichens, and liverworts—the green of the sides of the gorges.

clearly visible on the hillside on the far side of the river. Except when a freight train is rumbling through the gorge, this is a very quiet place. There is no car noise, and the preserve does not appear to be on any airline flight pattern. The loud call of an occasional pileated woodpecker or the rattle of a kingfisher may break the silence. Here and there are sections of the river where rocks in the stream add the sound of riffles and rapids to the silence.

Shortly after passing under the railroad and after passing the Quarry Rim Trail entrance, you will see a sign on the stream side of the trail pointing to the Black Hand Rock. Take a side trip to see the sheer cliff where the black hand once was. Notice the sandstone blocks neatly laid up at the base of the cliff. When the Ohio and Erie Canal came this way, there was slack water here backed up from a dam farther downstream, and the canalboats used the river for navigation. Above the stone wall, there is a ledge where the mules and their skinners walked as they pulled the boats through the Licking Narrows.

Now, return to the blacktopped path and head east to return to the parking lot.

3

Clear Creek Metro Park

Total distance: 4½ miles (7.24 km)

Hiking time: 3 hours

Maximum elevation: 1100 feet

Vertical rise: 225 feet

Maps: USGS 7½' Rockbridge; MPDCFC Clear Creek Metro Park brochure

The narrow, forested valley of the small Hocking River tributary called Clear Creek has been a magnet for central Ohio naturalists for more than a century. I was first introduced to it in 1948 when I was invited to attend the annual weekend "hegira" of the Wheaton Club, a Columbus-based men's naturalist group. They gathered each year on the first weekend in June at a place called Neotoma (for the Eastern wood rat that once inhabited the rock ledges of the area), then owned by the late Edward S. Thomas, at the time curator of natural history at the museum of the Ohio Archaeological and Historical Society. The late-spring flora was at its peak and the trees were full of migrating warblers, vireos, thrushes, and the like. My eyes were opened to orchids and trilliums; lizards, salamanders, and snakes; toads and frogs; and much, much more—all new to a kid who grew up with the paved streets, storm sewers, and vacant lots of the city.

In the 50 years since, I have explored much of the Clear Creek valley in search of things that creep, crawl, sing, fly, and bloom. It is a place of splendid natural beauty where there is always a sight, sound, or smell to delight the senses and boggle the mind. In the early 1970s I played a small part in helping fend off the threat of a Corps of Engineers dam in the valley; later, I urged public officials and private landowners to preserve as much of the valley as possible in a natural state in some sort of public or quasi-public ownership.

Scientists of many disciplines have explored the Clear Creek valley over the years.

It's been many years since this barn housed livestock.

Many theses have been written and papers delivered about the natural history of the valley at conferences and meetings. The two best-known studies, published by the Ohio Biological Survey 35 years apart, are "A Botanical Survey of the Sugar Grove Region" by Robert Griggs and "Microclimates and Macroclimate of Neotoma, a Small Valley in Central Ohio" by Wolfe, Wareham, and Scofield. Both are still excellent references on the nature of this treasured place.

Today, probably no one knows the valley better than Tom Thomson of Columbus, whose book, *Birding in Ohio,* extols the diversity of bird life that can be seen there. What the book does not reveal is the hundreds and hundreds of birding trips Thomson made to the valley over the course of several decades to compile what must be one of the most complete records of breeding birds made for any such area anywhere. We can all hope that Thomson publishes his

observations and data someday. It is a special treat to join him for one of the birding trips through the valley that he occasionally leads for the Columbus Audubon Society. Attesting to the special nature of this place is the fact that most central Ohio birders, when setting out to take a "big day" bird count, jump-start their list by birding the Clear Creek Road at the crack of dawn on a May morning.

Fortunately, today most of the 7-mile-long Clear Creek valley is in public ownership, thanks to the foresight of Edward F. Hutchins, retired director of the Columbus Metro Parks. With patience, perseverance, and persuasion, he acquired for the park district the tracts that make up the Clear Creek Metro Park. Now 3200 acres in size, the park was opened to the general public for the first time in 1996. The trail system was still a work in progress during the months I spent rewalking trails for the new edition of this book, and I am pleased to be able to include them. On my last walk there, I came upon a work crew adding one more bridge, and I know that you will find additional changes when you walk the new trails. What will not have changed is the beauty of fern-covered sandstone, the towering hemlocks, or the call of the wood thrush, ovenbird, or pileated woodpecker. Walk on a weekday and you may be the only person on the trail. Even on the weekend, few people have discovered the Metro Park, two counties away from the core of Columbus.

How to Get There

To reach Clear Creek Metropark, take US 33 southeast from Columbus through Lancaster. About a dozen miles beyond Lancaster, you will find Clear Creek Road leaving US 33 to the west (right). There is a gasoline station/convenience store there. The trailhead for the park is located at the Creekside Meadows parking lot along Clear Creek Road, about 2 miles from US 33.

The Trail

Begin walking by heading downstream on the east spur of the Creekside Meadows Trail. After leaving the mowed grass area and entering an old field that glows with goldenrod in the fall, turn left at your first opportunity, heading toward the road. Across the tarmac, a sign introduces the Cemetery Ridge Trail. Climbing an old driveway below a grove of spruce, the trail soon ascends the ridge and heads west on what looks like partly old township and partly gasline service roads. The south-facing slope holds a good mixture of hardwoods, including several species of oak. An occasional non-native white pine appears along the trail, the results of human effort to reclaim abandoned hilltop farm fields of yore. Native hemlock and Virginia pine also show up among the dominant hardwoods of the ridge.

After traveling just over a mile, look for the skeleton of an old cattle barn to the left of the trail. It is quite obvious when the leaves are down, but may be well hidden during the summer. Explore cautiously if you wish, but leave it the way you find it, so others may also enjoy this remnant of the old ways of agriculture. If there was at one time a house nearby, its setting is not clearly evident.

At the barn you are at an 1100-foot elevation, about 325 feet above the elevation of the Ohio State House lawn in downtown Columbus, and you still have another 20 feet or so of rise to the top of the trail. After swinging north, the trail heads west again following the gas-line road on the side of the hill. The deeply cut route of the old rural road is quite evident uphill to the right. To this naturalist, the crushed limestone the gas company uses to fill soft spots in the trail looks out of place in sandstone country. Incidentally, most of the gas wells of this area are not in production, but are being used for underground storage of gas piped in from outside Ohio.

As the trail returns to the ridgetop, the trees are especially grand. In the head of valley to the right is a nice stand of mountain laurel. And as I walked the trail among the large white oak and tulip poplars on an early November day, a monarch butterfly flew up from the leaves. What do you suppose its chances were of staying ahead of winter's arrival long enough to make it to the monarch overwintering roosts of central Mexico?

After crossing a narrow saddle while still in the woods, the trail soon emerges at a meadow where the gravel gas-well service road heads north and the trail heads south, a juncture marked by an arrow on a 6 x 8

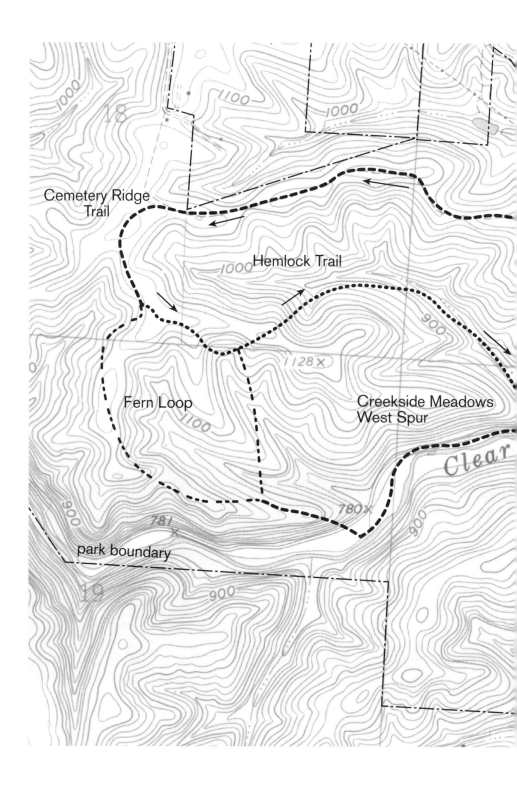

Cemetery Ridge
Trail

Hemlock Trail

Fern Loop

Creekside Meadows
West Spur

Clear

park boundary

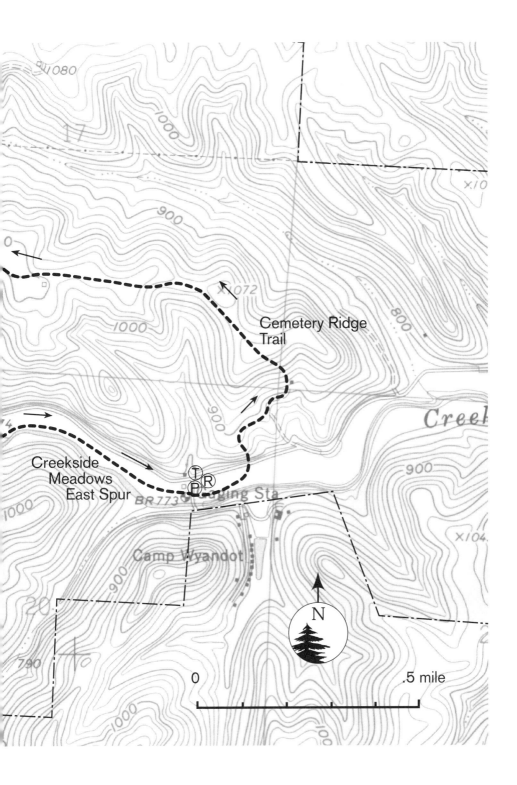

Cemetery Ridge
Trail

Creekside
Meadows
East Spur

Camp Wyandot

BR773

Creek

N

0   .5 mile

➤ Peculiar Pollination

The mountain laurel (Kalmia latifolia) is one of America's most beautiful shrubs. (In the southern Appalachian Mountains, where rainfall may reach 200 inches annually, it can appear somewhat treelike, reaching heights of 30 to 35 feet. Natives there refer to it as ivy.) Growing native in 25 or so counties in unglaciated southeastern Ohio, it is usually found on moist slopes, often near exposed sandstone outcrops. One look at its beautiful flower will tell you why mountain laurel is sometimes called calico bush.

According to the pioneering plant ecologist and botanist E. Lucy Braun, the pollination mechanism of the mountain laurel is particularly interesting. In fresh flowers, the anthers (the pollen-sac-bearing structures at the end of the stamen—the male organ) lie in the concavities of the corolla (the flower petals). In this position, the filaments (the slender structures of the stamen that terminate in the anthers) are under tension. When the tongue of a bee is inserted in the crevice between ovary and stamens, the tension is suddenly released, changing the position of the stamens and causing pollen to be thrown onto the head of the bee. The bee then moves on, carrying the pollen to the stigma (the female organ) of the next mountain laurel flower visited, thus effecting pollination—an out-crossing rather than a self-pollination. Braun says this trigger-release can be effected by a pin.

post. Following alongside the thicket of abandoned pasture, the trail next crosses a nice high meadow, complete with bluebird boxes, before reaching its end. With the 2½-mile Cemetery Ridge Trail behind, you now are traveling on the Fern Loop. A short distance farther, the trail splits. Going right will carry you around the hillside in a gentle descent toward the creek. Before reaching the road, you will have the option to turn left and ascend a valley and rejoin the Hemlock Trail or to continue to the west spur of the Creekside Meadows Trail.

If you turn left here, as I did, you will travel through young hardwoods and soon reach another juncture, where there is a sign introducing you to the 1½-mile-long Hemlock Trail heading off to the left. This is an unimproved trail that may find you hanging onto the side of the hill, and at times walking it requires scrambling over blocks of sandstone. Suddenly the forest changes, and you are in the soft shade of a hundred hemlocks with the rustle of deciduous trees left behind. The trail drops off the nose of a point of land and switches back to cross the creek on a bridge that was under construction the day I walked it. With a ravine to the right, the trail follows the contour of the land, winding in and out before climbing steeply over a ridge. Quartz pebbles in the trail are evidence of a Black Hand sandstone outcropping above, and large oblong holes chiseled near the bases of less-than-healthy trees give away the presence of pileated woodpeckers, the "cocks-of-the-woods." The stump of a long-gone chestnut remains visible alongside the trail, and mountain laurel can be seen in this cool, moist environment. Passing large sandstone slump blocks and great patches of Christmas fern, the trail makes its slow descent through the hemlock forest toward the valley floor. As I reached what looked like an old logging skid or road, I stood quietly as two yearling does moved through the forest close by ... one of the rewards of walking alone.

The trail crosses and recrosses a small stream as it passes through the white oak, beech, and hemlock woods, and soon reaches a trailhead sign at Clear Creek Road. From there, it is ½ mile of hoofing to the east on the west spur of the Creekside Meadows Trail before you cross Starner Road and arrive at the parking lot. Among the many wonders of the Clear Creek valley is Leaning Lena, the huge, leaning sandstone block that you must pass under on your way back to US 33. And be sure to enjoy the beauty of the roadside wildflowers as you leave the park.

4

Chestnut Ridge Metro Park

Total distance: 2 miles (3.2 km)

Hiking time: 1 hour

Maximum elevation: 1060 feet

Vertical rise: 150 feet

Maps: USGS 7½' Canal Winchester; MPDCFC Chestnut Ridge Metro Park brochure

Fall trees line the trail at Chestnut Ridge Metro Park.

A hike, a walk, or a stroll along the trails of Chestnut Ridge Metro Park will be rewarding in many ways. This is a trek through a moderate but not overwhelming variety of habitats. The near views, as well as those to the far horizon, can be spectacular at any time of the year. Chestnut Ridge is situated on a narrow outcropping of a sandstone resistant to weathering, the Black Hand—the same sandstone responsible for the beauty of the rock shelters of Hocking Hills and the glory of the gorge that bears its name along the Licking River (see Hike 2). But this time, instead of being on the hillsides, it *is* the hill. The high connected hills that make up the ridge cover only a few square miles, but they stand out on the landscape like a scene from an early western. In truth, in a state where the maximum elevation is just over 1500 feet, the 410-foot difference between the lay of the land where US 33 crosses Big Walnut Creek 2 miles east of the park entrance and the peak of the ridge is striking: from 780 feet at the highway bridge to 1180 feet on the highest peak. Though downtown Columbus is about 19 miles away, it is easily seen from an overlook on Chestnut Ridge.

This very special place is the result of the foresight of Walter A. Tucker, the first director-secretary of the park district. He purchased the land in the 1960s, more than two decades before funds became available to open it to the public. He was truly a visionary, to whom the people of Ohio owe a great debt of gratitude.

➤ A Year on Chestnut Ridge

In his 1980 book Idle Weeds *(Sierra Club Books), naturalist-writer David Rains Wallace tells of life through the year on Chestnut Ridge. His story, which blends the largest cataclysmic events and the smallest nuances of nature as he observed and was part of them, takes the reader to a new level of understanding of life on earth. The Chestnut Ridge that Wallace describes is the Chestnut Ridge of this hike. He writes, "The ridge might even be said to have a soul, at least a place that is always beautiful, from which beauty radiates." He goes on to describe "a little grove of sugar maples on the upper west slope just below the spring-wildflower-covered mound. The maples are young, no more than sixty years old, but something about the place makes them seem venerable. A quiet emerald light plays on the slope in summer, and in autumn the crisp sunbeams that stream through the golden canopy make the grove sparkle like cloisonné. In winter the trees stand as gracefully against the snow as in those leafless woods through which knights hunt wild boar in a medieval book of hours."*

How to Get There

To reach Chestnut Ridge Metro Park, drive southeast from Columbus on US 33. At the traffic light at Carroll, make a hard right onto Winchester Road NW. The entrance to the park is approximately 3 miles from the traffic light on the left (west) side of Winchester Road.

The Trail

A good place to begin hiking is from the first parking lot on the left after you pass the ranger station. There are rest rooms and drinking water there. The trail leaves from the far end of the parking lot and heads for the wooded hillside. In August, both pale and spotted jewelweed bloom at the wood's edge to the left. You will find a map of the trails of the park at this intersection. Note that an oak leaf marks the Ridge Trail. Turn right under the tall trees and follow this trail as it begins its gradual ascent to the ridge. It's only about a 150-foot rise from the trail entrance to the ridge, so don't sweat it. Enjoy the beauty of the deep, mixed mesophytic woods as the large trees give way to younger growth. About halfway along this reach of the trail, there is a boardwalk and a bench. Trailside interpretive signs about the trees were in place when I traveled this trail, but there was no mention of what looked like an old chestnut stump on the hillside below. Signs regarding the history of the area are still to come. I believe the story of the sandstone quarry on the slope below will eventually be told along here. Around 1830, hundreds of huge blocks of sandstone were taken from the hillside quarry to be used for the construction of locks on the nearby Ohio and Erie and Hocking Canals. There were six massive lock chambers in Lockville, less than 2 miles away, and others up and down both canals. Where could there be a more economical source of building stone?

From here, the trail returns to gravel surface and continues uphill, making a hard turn to the left past some old fruit trees and a meadow managed for grassland birds. Reentering woods, the trail crosses over the ridge to the west side, where there is an observation deck. On a clear day you can't see forever, but you can certainly see down-

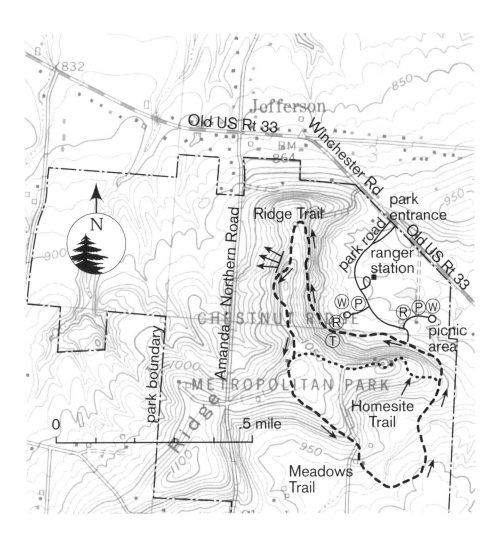

town Columbus 19 miles to the northwest. Beyond the overlook, the trail continues to climb and soon levels out on the ridge where a deck protrudes into the woods to the right. This is the grove of maples that David Rains Wallace writes about in *Idle Weeds,* and some of his words, quoted above, will be put on a sign here. Indeed, it is a good place to pause and reflect upon the beauty of the world of plants in which we animals reside.

The trail crisscrosses the ridge, soon arriving at its juncture with the Meadows and Homesite Trails. The latter goes left and leads along the ridge to a former homesite. The male and female holly trees growing in my yard started out many years ago as seedlings from hollies planted around the house that once stood here, the gift of a former resident. Beyond the obvious home garden and house area, the trail follows the high ground for a while, then drops to meet the other trails in the valley to the east to eventually join the Meadows and Ridge Trails.

I prefer following the Meadows Trail as it traces the edge of a high meadow just inside the woods. The last time I passed this way I looked to the meadow and saw 10 cabbage butterflies doing an aerial dance together in almost perfect synchrony, a sight I had never seen before and have not seen since. The trail now passes some apple trees and a planting of blight-resistant hybrid chestnuts. The American chestnut trees that originally grew in great profusion on the ridge, and from which the area got its name, died out in the 1930s when a chestnut blight swept across the country. A turn to the right takes the trail through the woods to join what remains of the driveway that served a farmhouse of the now relocated Far View Farms on the ridge. Along this trail there are some large trees, including a sycamore that seems out of place this far from a stream, and a hackberry, a tree usually found on neutral to alkaline soil but here growing within 10 feet of a sassafras—a tree that is an indicator of acid soil. But seeds don't read books, they just put out a seed root and start growing if the moisture conditions are right. There is also an awesome growth of wild black cherry trees along the trail as you approach the driveway.

Turning right, the trail moves downhill alongside open meadow. I have fond memories of spending time here many years ago, photographing a female red admiral butterfly as it deposited eggs on a nettle plant in the field near the creek below. Beyond the shade of a nice maple tree, the trail heads toward a bridge over a small stream. There is a cattail wetland to the right where dragonflies hover awaiting prey, then a meadow managed for dickcissels and other grassland-nesting birds. With thicket now on the right, the trail meanders toward another bridge over the brook. Beyond, the hillside to the left is apparently being allowed to succeed from old field to woodland. Just as you enter the woods, the Homesite Trail comes down the hill from the left. It is now only a short walk through the woods to the junction with the side trail to the parking lot.

5

Conkles Hollow State Nature Preserve

Total distance: 3.5 miles (5.6 km)

Hiking time: 3 hours

Maximum elevation: 970 feet

Vertical rise: 230 feet

Maps: USGS South 7½' Bloomingville; ODNR/DNAP Conkles Hollow State Nature Preserve brochure

When W.J. Conkle carved his name on the face of the sandstone cliff of the hollow that now bears his name, he could not have helped but be struck by the beauty of the place. The year was 1797. The young German immigrant must have been one of the first white men to see the area, and he must have liked what he saw, for he settled there. Conkles of many generations are buried nearby, and many of his descendants still live in the region.

Conkles Hollow truly is one of Ohio's most spectacular natural areas. A north-south-oriented box canyon about 1 mile in length, it was carved into the bedrock by a small tributary of Big Pine Creek. The light gray and buff Black Hand sandstone and conglomerate bedrock was deposited in the region as a delta from no longer extant mountains to the south about 345 million years ago. Ranging from 80 to 250 feet thick, the rock layer is about 200 feet thick in Conkles Hollow. Because the upper portion is structureless and well cemented while the lower portions are cross-bedded and more easily eroded, cliffs with one or more levels of recesses or rock shelters have formed. These features dominate the scenic gorges of the Hocking Hills region and are found to a lesser extent in Licking and Fairfield Counties.

No visit to southeastern Ohio would be complete without a walk along the trails of this very special place. To get a real feel for its grandeur and beauty, you should walk both the rim trail and the gorge trail, a hike of about 3½ miles. Except for the 200-foot climb and descent to and from the rim trail,

The near-vertical cliffs at Cockles Hollow State Nature Preserve add to the area's beauty.

the hike is nearly all on flat, well-defined woodland trail. Even with stops for picture taking, the trip should not take more than 3 hours.

Though short, the Conkles Hollow hike is very special. It is one that should be taken several times during the year to appreciate the ever-changing beauty of the area. Combined with the nearby Grandma Gatewood Trail (Hike 7), it provides a full day of hiking; by itself, it is a good walk for the end of a busy day in the city. The reward of an early-morning springtime walk might be the sound of a drumming ruffed grouse. An early-evening walk on a long summer day may serve up the haunting, flutelike call of the wood thrush or hermit thrush. Not even Michelangelo could match the colors of autumn, and the breathtaking beauty of a new-fallen snow is beyond description.

How to Get There

Conkles Hollow is easily reached from the Columbus area by two routes. From the east side of the city, travel US 33 southeast until 10 miles past Lancaster, where US 33 intersects with OH 374. This scenic route continues only far enough into Hocking County to lead you past all six of the Hocking Hills park and preserve sites. Follow the signs closely, as this is a tortuous route. Drive 13 miles on OH 374 and turn left on Big Pine Road (after passing Cantwell Cliffs and Rock House). There is a church surrounded by a graveyard on the corner. Spend a few moments reading the old headstones before leaving the area. The preserve entrance will appear 0.2 mile down Big Pine Road on your left.

The other route from Columbus is US 23 south to Circleville. From there, travel east to

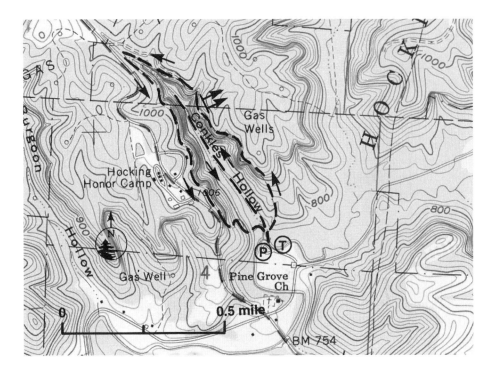

South Bloomingville on OH 56. Turn northeast on OH 664 and continue until it intersects with OH 374. Turn left and drive OH 374 for 1 mile to Big Pine Road, the church, and the preserve. Either way, the drive takes an hour from the I-270 outer belt.

The Trail

Upon entering the preserve, you will be greeted by an uninspiring treeless area where there are picnic tables, latrines, and a pump. Unless those amenities are needed, park at the next lot. There is only one way in and out of the preserve—across Big Pine Creek on a footbridge. A new bridge was being built during the summer of 1997; plans were also set to make as much of the trail into the hollow accessible to the disabled as the terrain would allow. Beyond the bridge, the trail takes a sharp turn to the left.

A gathering place off the right side of the trail about 50 feet beyond the bridge has interpretive signs including a large map of the area and a dispenser where brochures are available. Shortly after passing the assembly area, the trail reaches a set of wooden steps going to the right. Turn onto these stairs to begin walking the east rim trail. (The main trail on which you will return to the parking lot goes directly ahead, then left across a stone arch bridge built by the Civilian Conservation Corps, or CCC, in the 1930s.) After 52 steps, a wide landing is reached where the first of many interpretive signs along the way tells about the rim trail and hillside ecology. In another 37 steps, you come to about 100 yards of steep, log-lined path through an insect- and wind-damaged pine grove. The trail then curves left as it climbs about the same distance through young hemlock and hardwood. A short scramble to the left up a clearly defined trail over bare rock brings you to the rim.

Almost immediately, the trail allows picture-postcard vistas of the valley, many views nicely framed with scraggly pines. Upslope are more Virginia pines, oaks, mountain laurels, greenbriers, huckleberries, and reindeer lichen. Below are the tops of tuliptrees, yellow birches, hemlocks, and maples. At times the trail is on bare bedrock, and often it is close to the cliff edge. Children should be kept close at hand since there are no railings. "Lucky stones"—quartz pebbles that weather their way out of the conglomerate rock—line the low spots on the trail. Two small footbridges span intermittent side streams well back from the gorge. In all but the driest of summers, the sound of cascading water gives away the end of the canyon. As you approach the 95-foot falls, you will see a large wooden deck at the cliff edge that affords a magnificent view. Seventy-five yards beyond, safely upstream from the edge, the stream that creates the fall is spanned by a footbridge, and signs direct you to the west rim return trail and a side trail to a nearby forest service road.

The path on the west rim lies only a short distance from the road and the forest headquarters, but it does not lose its feeling of wildness. Under towering white pines planted in 1931—the legacies of the CCC and the Division of Forestry—you will likely focus on the cliffs across the valley. Canada yew grows above the edge of the cliff in this area. Wind blowing through the pines can magically obscure any intruding man-made noises. The trail takes two sweeping arcs above the rock shelters in the gorge wall. The woods above are dominated by oaks—white, red, chestnut, and scarlet—while below the forest is a blend of hemlock and hardwoods. When it's time to descend, steps in the bedrock, three steeply sloped switchbacks, and a 265-foot wooden staircase bring you to the valley floor only a few feet upstream from the stone arch bridge on the main trail. The trail has come 2½ miles.

A left turn onto the main trail introduces a totally new environment—a deeply shaded, relict boreal forest dominated by hemlock. Although the glacial ice sheets of the Pleistocene period never reached this far (the last one stopped near Haynes, about 6 miles to the west), the colder climate of the times brought boreal forests to the gorges of the area. After the glaciers melted from Ohio, many of these plants continued to grow in the ravines and gorges because of the colder microclimates. Many songbirds breed here, and it is home to many reptiles and amphibians. The northern copperhead is indigenous, but the likelihood of encountering one is very slim. The fern- and moss-covered slump blocks (chunks of bedrock that broke away from a stratum above and rolled down the slope, eventually coming to rest), the patches of Canada yew, the honeycomb-weathered sandstone, the picturesque waterfalls, and the clear-running stream all add to the ambience of the hollow. The log-lined trail crosses several small footbridges and some boardwalk before arriving at the head of the ½-mile-long valley. There, water from the stream above slides over the rock and falls about 50 feet into a plunge pool. After drinking in the beauty of this verdant spot, head back to the parking area via the same valley trail. Note that there are different views to be had when going in the opposite direction. And, of course, remember that all things natural at Conkles Hollow are protected as a preserve, including the critters that creep and crawl and the flowers that bloom—to be admired and enjoyed and perhaps photographed, but to be left for others to enjoy.

In the last couple of decades, a number of notable storms have left their mark on Conkles Hollow, a reminder of the occasional wrath of nature. On July 4, 1982, a small funnel cloud destroyed many of the hemlock in the front part of the valley. That area is now nicely recovered, the young growth providing good bird nesting habitat. In February 1986, a warm period followed by a heavy, wet snow wreaked havoc on the trees in the middle section of the canyon. A 20-inch snowfall on April 4, 1987, left its mark on the entire preserve, and a storm on March 4, 1988, that left the trees ice-glazed for nearly four days took down more than 100 trees on the rim trail. Since the area is a nature preserve, none of these trees was salvaged for timber. Only trees that blocked trails were removed, the rest being allowed to rot slowly to provide homes for creatures large and small, their nutrients eventually returning to the soil. These areas have all recovered nicely, providing good bird nesting habitat in young-growth forest.

6

Flint Ridge State Memorial

Total distance: 1.6 miles (3 km)

Hiking time: 1 hour

Maximum elevation: 1200 feet

Vertical rise: 140 feet

Map: USGS 7½' Glenford

Flint Ridge consists of a chain of long, narrow hills extending more than 20 miles from Zanesville to a few miles east of Newark. An irregular layer of flint varying from a few inches to several feet in thickness underlies the surface of these hills. From this stone, early Native Americans made implements with which to kill and skin game, light fires, and possibly slay enemies. Pioneers also found the stone useful. They produced buhrstones for water-powered mills out of a lower grade of weathered flint from the western portion of the ridge.

Approximately 200 million years ago, this stratum of hard flint began to be uplifted in this region, eventually to be exposed by erosion. In this 5- or 6-square-mile area of what is now east-central Ohio, outcroppings of the colorful rock apparently caught the eye of roving Paleo-Indians 8000 to 10,000 years ago. Until steel replaced stone, Native Americans followed a network of trails from villages and campsites all over the East to reach this flint quarry. Artifacts from Flint Ridge have been discovered on the Atlantic seaboard, in Louisiana, and as far west as Kansas City.

The good-quality flint was the unweathered stone below the surface. The 1- to 10-foot-thick stone was difficult to extract, requiring great physical force. Large hammerstones, granite or quartzite boulders, or mauls are thought to have been used to drive wooden or bone wedges into natural cracks to break the stone loose. Once removed, the flint was reduced to manageable blocks from which blades and points were shipped. Because flint was important to all

Large block of flint along the trail at Flint Ridge State Memorial

tribes, this area was neutral tribal territory.

By the time pioneers began settling Ohio in the late 18th century, the flint pits were abandoned. Steel guns and implements from French and British traders had replaced stone tools. A century later, engineers building the National Road across Licking and Muskingum Counties used discarded flint chips from prehistoric times to form the roadbed for the early highway. Today, the significance of Flint Ridge is largely historical rather than economic. Flint is Ohio's official gemstone, and some lapidaries polish it for use in jewelry.

In 1933 the Ohio Historical Society established Flint Ridge State Memorial to preserve this area of outcrops and flint pits. In 1968 a museum was built over a large pit where model Indians now demonstrate quarrying and chipping. The 525-acre tract includes a system of trails that pass old flint pits, perhaps traveling the same routes as did prehistoric visitors. Here you walk where Native Americans once walked and worked in a time when obtaining food, clothing, and shelter depended on one's personal skills, the abilities of friends, and the natural resources at hand. Visitors are requested to refrain from removing pieces of flint or other natural objects from the area.

Because the area has been protected for more than 60 years, the hillsides here are covered with mature forest. The museum is open 9:30–5 Wednesday through Saturday; noon–5 on Sunday between Memorial Day and Labor Day; and 9:30–5 on Saturday and noon–5 on Sunday during the fall. The grounds are open every day of the year from dawn to dusk. A special feature of the memorial is a ¼-mile paved interpretive

Flint Ridge State Memorial

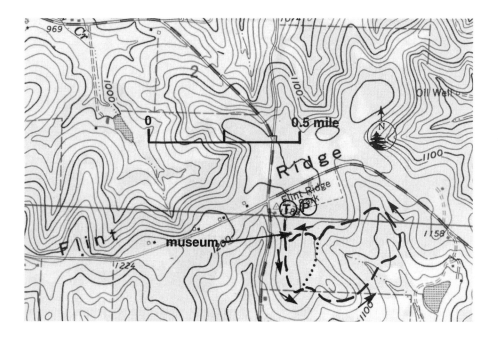

trail for the disabled with a guide rope and signs in both printed text and Braille. There are picnic facilities near the parking lot.

How to Get There

To reach Flint Ridge State Memorial, travel 45 miles east of Columbus on I-70 to exit 141. Travel 4 miles north on County Road 668, passing through the US 40 community of Brownsville, to the entrance to the memorial on the right.

The Trail

The trail begins at the museum. Alongside the walk from the parking lot to the museum, you will see large chunks of flint-bearing rock that came from the excavation for the building. A bulletin board at the plaza alongside the museum displays a map of the trails. Step over the wall of the plaza to a short stretch of blacktopped trail to begin hiking the trails. Most of the flint pits are located in the area near where you begin hiking. Imagine the sounds of hammering on a summer afternoon as Native Americans scrambled to get arrow points ready for fall hunting. Stay to the right, passing up both a closed "Wagon Road Alternate" and a connecting trail to the left. The trail you are following is now known as the Quarry Trail. When I hiked it in the fall of 1996, the old signs were still in place, but new ones were on hand for installation. The Quarry Trail now arcs left, passing the other end of the connector to the museum, and heads north. Follow this path until you reach a trail to the right labeled LOWER TRAIL or CREEK TRAIL. Turn there and follow the trail as it passes over a visible terrace that indicates the presence of the flint bedrock. The lowest branches of the tall beech, white oak, and sugar maple are far from the ground, a pattern typical of trees grown in a forest environment. This form contrasts with that of open-grown specimens, whose fuller profiles are more often used to illustrate books about trees. There is very little understory or shrub layer on this hillside. Young oak trees are not shade-tolerant so you do not expect to find them in deep woods, but where are the young, shade-tolerant maple seedlings and saplings? They have probably been eaten by deer, which learn quickly when an area is protected from hunting. In addition to munching maple, they trim trillium and many other species of wildflowers and shrubs.

The trail crosses two small streams before looping back uphill and recrossing one of the streams as it returns to the museum. There is a side trail to the right that takes you uphill about 75 feet to an outcrop of flint. Take it to view the stone close up, then return to the trail to continue the loop. As the trail climbs toward the intersection with the upper trail, it passes through an area of young trees near a "wolf tree" or two that have served as sources for seed. Note the position of the lower branches on these old trees, which stood in the open for most of their lives.

The Creek Trail soon meets the Quarry Trail. A right turn will take you to the picnic area and rest rooms. Continuing straight ahead will lead you past the Creek Trail entrance on the left, then to the cutoff trail to the right that you can follow to return to the museum and parking lot. If the museum is not open, make a point to come back on a day when it is. You might want to combine this hike with one at nearby Blackhand Gorge State Nature Preserve (Hike 2).

➤ Wolf Trees

The term "wolf tree" is applied by many naturalists and foresters to a mature, open-grown tree found among a stand of much younger trees. A tree that has grown most of its life among other trees will generally have its first branches a long way up its trunk. Not so the wolf tree. Usually such a tree has branches low to the ground, indicating it stood by itself during most of its life. Such trees avoided the logger's ax for a number of reasons. Perhaps it was deliberately left along a fencerow or at the edge of a pasture to provide shade for livestock. Maybe the lumberman saw a piece of old fence sticking out of the bark, giving him fear of the wrath of the sawyer if he hauled it to the mill. It may have even been a shade tree near a long-gone homestead, church, or school. And some lumbermen made it a practice to leave a few trees standing to provide seeds for regeneration. Sometimes when you see an even-aged stand of trees all of the same species, you can look uphill or upwind and see that the seeds came from the replanted trees the year after grazing or cultivation stopped, or after most of the standing timber was skidded down the hillside to the lumber truck. Keep your eyes open for wolf trees as you trek the Ohio countryside.

7

Hocking Hills State Park (Grandma Gatewood Trail)

Total distance: 6 or 12 miles (9.9 or 19.2 km)

Hiking time: 3 to 6½ hours

Maximum elevation: 1068 feet

Vertical rise: 308 feet

Maps: USGS 7½' South Bloomingville; ODNR Hocking Hills State Park map; BTA Old Man's Cave Section map

Old Man's Cave, Cedar Falls, and Ash Cave are among the state's best-known natural features. The caves are not actually underground but are recess caves caused by differential weathering of the nearly 250-foot-thick Black Hand sandstone bedrock of Ohio's Hocking Hills region. All three of these features are spectacular and are easily reached on foot. The Grandma Gatewood Trail, a 6-mile section of the Buckeye Trail, goes past all three.

Since this is an end-to-end trail, not a loop, it can be either walked one way with a prearranged pickup or shuttle or walked out and back. The hike is most frequently begun at the Old Man's Cave end, where there are better amenities—both modern and primitive camping facilities, as well as housekeeping cabins.

Many more trails crisscross the state park and forest complex. The state began purchasing land in this area in 1924 under an early state forest law. The scenic areas were transferred to the Division of Parks with the creation of the Department of Natural Resources in 1949. Millions of Ohioans enjoy the area throughout the year.

How to Get There

From Columbus, the Old Man's Cave parking lot is reached either by taking US 33 southeast to Logan and OH 664 south (right), or by traveling US 23 south to Circleville and then heading east (left) on OH 56 to South Bloomingville. From South Bloomingville you take OH 664 north (straight ahead where OH 56 turns right). By either route, the trip takes about 1½

Hikers are dwarfed by Ash Cave.

hours. For one-way hiking, park an extra car or arrange a pickup at the Ash Cave parking lot. To reach it, follow OH 374 east and south from the Old Man's Cave lot to where it ends at OH 56. Turn right onto OH 56. The lot is on the left after less than 0.5 mile.

The Trail

After leaving your car at Old Man's Cave, cross OH 664 to the Grandma Gatewood Trail dedication monument, where this hike begins. The plaque on the stone tells of Emma Gatewood, who was born in 1887, died in 1973, and began hiking after the age of 67. She walked the Oregon Trail once and the Appalachian Trail three times. This section of the Buckeye Trail was a favorite of hers, and it was designated a National Recreation Trail and named in her honor in 1979. It was my privilege to have known her and to have walked this trail with her on several occasions.

Start hiking by crossing the stone arch bridge over the Upper Falls. Turn downstream and take the steps to the valley floor. For the next mile the trail follows The Gulf to the confluence of Old Man's Creek and Queer Creek. Through the Upper Gorge area, the trail goes beneath honeycombed cliffs. It crosses a bridge by the Devil's Bathtub before climbing stairs to the level where Old Man's Cave itself comes into view on the opposite wall. Like the floor of the Upper Gorge, this recess cave was formed when the weak middle zone of the sandstone was eroded by water and wind. Named for a hermit by the name of Richard Roe, a fugitive from West Virginia who lived there after the Civil War, the cave measures 200 feet wide and 50 feet high and is 75 feet deep. Roe is said to have been buried beneath rocks in the cave.

The trail now goes through a tunnel leading to the area above the Lower Falls. To

explore the cave, cross the bridge and climb stairs through another tunnel. Look downstream from the bridge toward the Sphinx Head profile, carved by natural forces, visible on the face of the cliff.

The trail climbs to the cliff base, then descends past the lip of the Lower Falls. It hugs the cliff before descending to the valley floor below the falls. The Lower Falls is the only scenic feature in the Hocking Hills area that is located in the lower zone of the Black Hand sandstone. At the plunge pool level below the 60-foot waterfall, a deep recess cave has been carved in the underlying Cuyahoga shale, a soft stratum named for the spectacular exposures along the Cuyahoga River in the Cleveland area.

The trail now travels downstream on the left bank. In many places it is unstable because of the seepage of water caused by the relatively impervious underlying shale. Large hemlock and yellow birch trees dominate the forest canopy, and Canada yew is seen in patches on the hillside, all relics of an earlier, colder period. A 160-foot hemlock just across the small stone bridge is a state record.

At the confluence of Old Man's Creek with Queer Creek, the trail turns upstream toward Cedar Falls. It follows the left bank, first traveling along the stream, then rising to the base of the sandstone cliffs and returning to the stream several times. An old Native American trail that connected the Kanawha River region of West Virginia with Ohio's Chillicothe area ran through here. Settlers knew it as the "Road to Hell" because prisoners were marched through here during the frontier wars. Huge sycamores line the stream, and groves of tall hemlock give some areas a cathedral-like majesty. For many years the trail went through an area where it followed a narrow ledge between the cliff base and the stream. It could be very dangerous in the winter, when icicles sometimes broke loose from above and fell on the trail, and the footing could be very slick. That section was recently rerouted to make a safer approach to Cedar Falls. Still, if the going looks difficult, cross the stream and travel to Cedar Falls by taking the trail uphill to the parking lot and turning left to reach the stairs that descend to the falls. In good weather, continue up the trail along Queer Creek, cross the bridge, and drink in the beauty of the falls. Now protected by state ownership, the rim of Cedar Falls was once the site of a gristmill.

Take the steps to the picnic area, where there are rest rooms and drinking water. This is a good spot for lunch. During the state's annual Hocking Hills Winter Hike, corn bread and bean soup are served here. To proceed to Ash Cave, follow the blue blazes around the end of the loop road, then turn right up a forest service road. At the first valley to the left, the trail begins a climb through young mixed oak forest to the ridge, the highest point on the hike. With the help of Norville Hall and some Scouts from Troop 417 of Upper Arlington, I laid out and cleared this trail in January 1967.

After crossing Chapel Ridge Road, the trail drops down a valley, eventually to reach the rim of Ash Cave. Stay on the trail, well back from the rim. The trail goes to the left of the lip of the falls, then drops into the cave on wooden stairs. Shaped like a gigantic horseshoe, this recess cave is 700 feet around the curving lip and 90 feet high. It is 100 feet deep from front to back and has acoustical qualities all its own. It received its name from a huge pile of ashes found here by the first settlers. In earlier days, church services were held here using the large slump block in front of the cave as a natural pulpit. From here, the trail goes out the valley floor to the parking area along OH 56. In 1989, this path was paved and new bridges were constructed to make Ash Cave accessible to the handicapped along this ¼-mile-long trail to OH 56. Rest rooms and drinking water are located where the trail reaches the highway, and there is a shelterhouse across the road.

To return to Old Man's Cave on foot, retrace the route. Buckeye Trail blue blazes are visible from both directions along the trail.

➤ Ohio's State Trail

The Buckeye Trail is a long-distance hiking trail built and maintained by volunteers. The germ of the idea for the trail came from the late Merrill C. Gilfillan of Mount Gilead, who wrote an article for the magazine section of the Sunday edition of the Columbus Dispatch *suggesting that Ohio ought to have a hiking trail like the Appalachian Trail connecting Lake Erie and the Ohio River. Out of the article was born the Buckeye Trail Association for the purpose of providing such a trail from Mentor Headlands east of Cleveland to Eden Park in Cincinnati. Now expanded to connect the four corners of the state in a continuous loop, the 1200-plus-mile trail passes through 40 of Ohio's 88 counties; no population center is more than 75 miles from it.*

The association was incorporated in 1959 and began work developing the trail almost immediately. In 1967, the Ohio General Assembly designated the Buckeye Trail Ohio's official hiking trail. The famous septuagenarian and Appalachian Trail–hiker Emma "Grandma" Gatewood of Thurman, Ohio, was among the early volunteers who blazed out the Buckeye Trail in southeastern Ohio's hill country. Wherever possible, the trail keeps to public lands and is off-road. Where there is no other way to make connections, lightly traveled township roads are used, but the work to get the entire trail into the woods and fields or onto abandoned canal towpaths or railroad rights-of-way never ceases. Information about the trail, the trail-building organization, and available section maps and guides can be obtained by writing to the Buckeye Trail Association, PO Box 254, Worthington, OH 43085.

8

Malabar Farm State Park

Total distance: 5 miles (8 km)

Hiking time: 3 hours

Maximum elevation: 1320 feet

Vertical rise: 260 feet

Map: USGS 7½' Lucas;
ODNR Malabar Farm State Park map

Author and screenwriter Louis Bromfield, born in Mansfield, Ohio, established Malabar Farm in Richland County's Pleasant Valley in 1939. He immediately began applying newly developed conservation farming practices to the worn-out land. During the following two decades, Malabar gained a worldwide reputation as a model farm, largely through the books Bromfield wrote about his experiences. In the 32-room "Big House" he built, he entertained his rich and famous Hollywood friends. After his death in 1956, the farm was managed by an organization he helped form, Friends of the Land, and, after it folded, by the Malabar Farm Foundation. In 1972 the foundation transferred ownership to the state of Ohio, to be operated jointly by the Departments of Agriculture and Natural Resources. In 1976 it became Malabar Farm State Park. Although the large number of livestock of the Bromfield era are gone, the buildings and the crop fields have been restored. Tours of the mansion, preserved just as Bromfield left it in 1956, are offered year-round. The original dairy barn, which had been built in 1890 of timbers from an old mill that dated back to 1830, burned to the ground in 1993. It was rebuilt with a barn raising on Labor Day weekend in 1994 with volunteer help from the Timber Framers Guild of North America. People who have read Bromfield's books come to visit from around the world. Tours, special events, and interpretive programs help visitors understand how much Bromfield cared for the land. You may want to take a tour of the home (for which there might be a small fee), grounds, and outbuild-

Thanks to hundreds of volunteers, a new "old barn" now stands where only ashes remained.

ings. A multiple-use trail around the perimeter of the 914-acre park offers a good half day of hiking.

How to Get There

To reach Malabar Farm from central or northeastern Ohio, travel I-71 to US 30, go east 3 miles to OH 603, and turn left (south). Travel 10.5 miles to Pleasant Valley Road on the right. Signs will direct the way west to Bromfield Road and the park entrance. Immediately after turning south into the park, make a right turn into the driveway to the Big House and barnyard complex. Park there. Rest rooms are located in the toolshed.

The Trail

The entrance to the trail is uphill from the entry walk, across a hay field. A sign says TIMBER MANAGEMENT TRAIL. Usually there is a mowed path around the edge of the field. Be aware of the bees moving to and from their hives to the left at the edge of the woods. The alfalfa and red clover in the field are very attractive to butterflies in late summer, when they rebloom following the second hay harvest. Enter the woods on the interpretive trail. Take time to learn the basics of small woodlot management from the signs spaced along both sides of the trail in the maple/oak/walnut woods. Within 100 feet of entering the woods, the trail is joined by an old farm lane turned horse trail coming in from the right. The path climbs the hill past sandstone outcrops on the left before opening onto another meadow. Remains of an early gas well can be seen on the left as you leave the woods. Turn right and follow

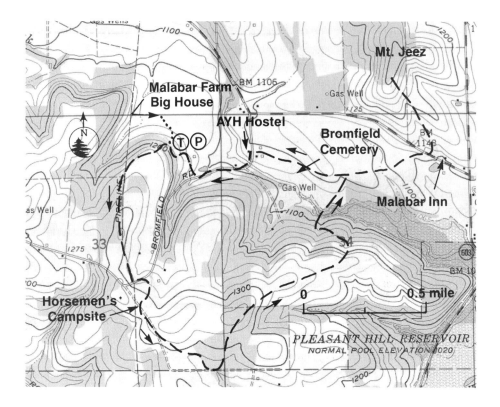

the edge of the meadow, passing an old concrete stock tank, then make a sharp left turn onto a gas-line right-of-way. Sometimes deer can be seen grazing in the meadow downhill in the distance. Follow the right-of-way until it reaches the paved road. Pay no attention to the arrows on posts in this field. This is another good area for summer butterflies since they like to "hilltop" and nectar on the alfalfa and clover. Just before reaching the end of the field, duck right and then left through the woods on the right side of the field. A sign there admonishes cross-country skiers to preserve their skis by removing them before going onto the road. Turn left (downhill) on the road, which at this point changes its name from East Hastings to Bromfield. About 150 yards downhill, a driveway on the right leads you past an old barn complete with a chewing tobacco ad, then uphill into the horsemen's campground. There are toilets located on the right, and behind Campsite 5, drinking water is available from a Baker-type pump. The well is deep, so a strong arm is required to get it flowing.

To get off the pavement and back onto natural turf, continue up the road to the far end of the turnaround, where there is a sign reading PLEASANT VALLEY BRIDLE TRAIL—HORSE AND FOOTPATH ONLY. Avoid the poison ivy as you enter, then turn left. The trail gently rises to cross a gas-line right-of-way, then passes a neatly manicured picnic area. It soon swings right through another overgrown fencerow, then it turns sharply left along the edge of an old field being invaded by trees and shrubs. After 200 yards, it emerges onto a gravel road that is still in use. Turn left. About 100 feet up the road on the right stands a double-trunked American chestnut tree that has somehow avoided the chestnut blight and actually reached nut-bearing age. About 200 feet on down the road another PLEASANT VALLEY BRIDLE TRAIL sign on the left indicates that it's time to reenter the woods. Here is a fine woods, with mature oaks and hickories dominating. After a short climb to the crest of the hill, the trail descends the ridge to the right, then crosses a bromegrass field and an old, tree-lined lane before emerging into a field where hundreds of young sugar maples have been planted. To protect the trees from being browsed by deer, half of them have a short piece of snow fence wrapped around them, and the other half have been planted in pieces of plastic farm tile. The latter do not seem to be surviving well.

At the end of the maple planting, the trail turns left to enter the woods, then turns immediately right on an old lane. Still moving downhill, it eventually enters tall timber, then makes a sharp left turn down a talus slope below outcrops of sandstone. It then turns west along a bench, through a rich mature woods with fern-covered slump blocks. At a 4 x 4 post, it makes a sharp right turn to drop to the stream valley below. An upstream/downstream glance will usually locate a reasonably dry crossing in all but the wettest of seasons. After the crossing you will hike 100 yards or so through riverine forest with aliens such as multiflora rose present. The trail then emerges onto the farm road alongside crop fields.

A turn to the right on the lane leads you to the famous Malabar Inn, which is still serving meals. The 165-year-old structure adjoins a vegetable stand that covers the equally well-known Niman Spring. Most of the water for the farm and garden operation comes from this spring. To the west of the inn parking lot, a trail leads you up the hill that Bromfield dubbed Mt. Jeez, from the words he first uttered upon seeing the view. From the overlook at the top of the meadow, there is a great view of the entire spread. Although the temptation is to descend the hill on the vehicle road and then head for the park entrance via Pleasant Valley Road, the better path is to follow the trail back past the inn to where it emerged from the woods. A quarter mile beyond the trail entrance sign lies the country cemetery where Bromfield, his wife, Mary Appleton, and other family members are buried. Pause and reflect on the words of Bryant on Bromfield's gravestone: TO HIM WHO IN LOVE OF NATURE HOLDS COMMUNION WITH HER VISIBLE FORMS, SHE SPEAKS A VARIOUS LANGUAGE.

Continue on the farm road, past the garden, to a barnyard area where there are rest rooms and drinking water. Out the drive and across the road lies the farmstead where Bromfield lived while the Big House was being built. He did not like the place and referred to it as the "mail-order house." It is now a hostel operated by the Columbus Council of the American Youth Hostels, Inc. Turn left downhill on the road, passing a pond and crossing the bridge. To your right is a good view of the main house and farmyard in the distance. Cows in the foreground complete the rural scene. On your left is the Doris Duke Woods, saved from logging after Bromfield's death by a contribution from the tobacco heiress, which was used to buy back timber rights Bromfield had sold during hard times. The park's sugar camp and buildings used for programs and meetings lie at the end of the road that enters the woods on the left, just beyond the bridge. The unsprayed roadside on the left between there and the Big House drive provides a show of native wildflowers in late summer.

Turn into the driveway on the right and walk by the Big House, then through the barnyard to return to the parking lot. This 5-mile loop is a good hike to combine with the Mohican State Park hike. There is a 15-site primitive campground at Malabar, and more modern facilities are available at nearby Mohican State Park and Pleasant Mill Lake Park.

9

Mohican State Park

Total distance: 3½ miles (5.6 km)

Hiking time: 2 hours

Maximum elevation: 1240 feet

Vertical rise: 265 feet

Map: USGS 7½' Jelloway; ODNR Mohican State Park map

Two waterfalls, tall hemlocks, and the sound of rushing water lie ahead for the hiker visiting Mohican State Park in southwestern Ashland County. Located along the gorge of the Clear Fork of the Mohican River in the center of 60-year-old Mohican Memorial State Forest, the 1294-acre park is best known for river canoeing. Yet it boasts 9 miles of foot trails and 10 miles of bridle trails, and the adjacent state forest has several times that distance in multiple-use trails. The most scenic hiking trail in the park originates in its center at the west side of the south end of the new bridge. The park is an area to avoid on holiday weekends but is beautiful 12 months of the year. Off-season visits reward you with peace and quiet. The Clear Fork has become popular for fly-fishing since the Division of Wildlife began stocking it with golden trout.

How to Get There

The trailhead at Mohican State Park is about a 1½-hour drive from the Columbus, Cleveland, and Akron areas via I-71 and OH 97. Travel east from exit 165 for 18 miles, through Bellville and Butler, to the park and forest entrance located on the left just after you pass the Memorial Shrine on the right. Almost immediately after turning onto the park road, make a left turn to descend to the covered bridge river crossing, a distance of 1.5 miles. Park at the trailhead located on the left side of the road just before the road reaches the covered bridge. During icy or snowy weather conditions, this road is impassable and will likely be closed. If in doubt, call the park office at 419-994-5125.

Modern steel, concrete, and wood covered bridge near the Lyons Falls trailhead

The Trail

Clear Fork Gorge is a special place. The National Natural Landmark monument at the trailhead brings that message home. How did this deep gorge get carved out in this part of Ohio? It was a product of Pleistocene glaciation. The Wisconsinan glacier, the last one to invade Ohio, stopped less than a mile north of this gorge. During the thousands of years when the ice sheet was advancing, then melting, millions of gallons of meltwater rushed through this valley daily on their way to the sea. Since the bedrock was a hard sandstone, the rush of water resulted in this steep-walled gorge. When the glacier melted and the climate warmed, it was still cool enough in this deep, east–west-running gorge for cool-climate plants like hemlock, yellow birch, purple raspberry, and yew to continue to thrive.

Start northwest from the monument and trail entrance sign, following the Lyons Falls Trail. There is no drinking water and no rest rooms along this trail, so go prepared. During the summer of 1988, park personnel spent many hours repairing and replacing the bridges beneath the towering hemlock trees, making the hiking easy. Just short of ½ mile after leaving the road, the trail divides, with a riverside trail continuing straight ahead and a side trail going left to Big Lyons Falls. Follow the latter up the ravine to see the first of the two falls that tumble over the face of the sandstone. Leave Big Lyons Falls on an uphill trail to the right and follow it around the contour to approach Little Lyons Falls from above. Continue on a wide trail, which requires some scrambling over bare rock, to arrive at a level trail that swings right, then left near the rim of the gorge. Momentarily it comes out at the overlook area at the west end of Pleasant Hill Dam.

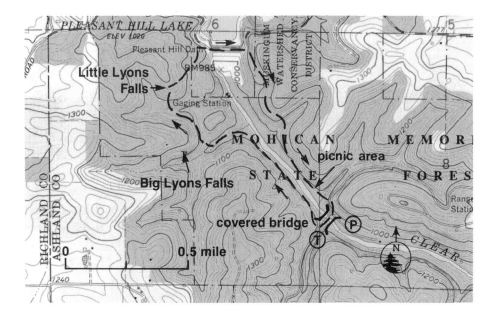

This earthen structure is 775 feet long and 113 feet high. It has a 199-square-mile drainage area. The permanent pool is at an elevation of 1020 feet, and flood stage is at 1065 feet. Like other dams in the Muskingum River Conservancy District system, it has no spillway over the top of the dam. There are steps down the front of the dam for access to tailwater fishing.

To continue a loop hike, cross the dam on the downstream side and, at the east end, turn to the right into the woods where the trail back to the park begins. The trail passes under pines, alongside skunk cabbage, past a patch of cup plant, and past a small cattail marsh before descending to the narrow gorge and the cool shade of more hemlock. After traveling downstream ¾ mile, the trail emerges from the woods near the north end of the covered bridge. Cross the bridge to return to the trailhead parking area.

While in the area, consider hiking the trail at nearby Malabar Farm State Park (Hike 8).

10

Stage's Pond State Nature Preserve

Total distance: 3 miles (4.8 km)

Hiking time: 1 ½ hours

Maximum elevation: 720 feet

Vertical rise: 20 feet

*Maps: USGS 7 ½' Ashville,
ODNR/DNAP Stage's Pond brochure*

As the Wisconsinan glacier melted from what we now know as Pickaway County, an immense chunk of it remained where Stage's Pond is today, probably protected from the melting effect of direct sunlight by a covering of sand and gravel. When the ice buried in the drift finally melted as the result of the ambient temperature, the land dropped, forming a depression in the landscape. Eventually the depression filled with water, creating what geologists call a kettle lake. Though often an outlet to kettle lakes eventually forms (or is created by people trying to drain them), since they develop on gravelly, sandy substrate, many simply rise and fall with the rainfall, draining into the soil to recharge the groundwater of the surrounding area. Like virtually all small bodies of water, kettle lakes eventually close in with vegetation and disappear, the only evidence of their existence being a lacustrine soil in a low spot in the field.

Stage's Pond and the smaller slough pond on the preserve were large enough that they still remain, perhaps 10,000 to 12,000 years after the ice melted from the area. Doubtless mammoth, mastodon, giant beaver, elk, and bison drank from these waters during the intervening millennia. Today, they serve as resting places for thousands of migrating waterfowl each spring and fall and as a year-round home to many nonmigrating species such as kingfishers, great blue herons, and Canada geese. The surrounding marsh, field, and forest provide habitat for many other kinds of wildlife, vertebrate and invertebrate, large and small.

Acquired and developed with help from

➤ Great Blue Herons

The great blue heron (Ardea herodias) *is the largest heron in North America. Though primarily a summer resident in Ohio, a few are seen each winter on open rivers, ponds, and lakes in nearly every county in the state. Most arrive in Ohio from the South in early spring (males arrive first) to mate and raise three or four young in nests built of sticks high in trees in an area where there are other nesting herons of the same species. Such a heron rookery, or "heronry," may have several hundred pairs of birds, although most are in the 10- to 75-pair range.*

Both parents help incubate the eggs, which hatch in 28 days. The parents regurgitate digested or partially digested fish to their young, who remain in the nest until they fledge in July or early August. Tall trees such as sycamore and cottonwood are often used for the 30- to 40-inch-wide nests, and there may be several nests in a single tree. In time, the trees succumb to their heavy dose of excrement and begin to come down. When this happens, returning herons will locate their rookery in a different area nearby. Though great blue herons can be seen along waterways in every county in the state, at present heronries are limited to the northern two-thirds and are most numerous near Lake Erie; they are nearly gone from the southwestern part of the state. It is always a thrill to watch an active heronry, especially in midspring before the trees leaf out, when adults come and go to feed their young.

the Columbus Regional Council of the Garden Club of Ohio and the Pickaway Garden Club, the preserve has been open to the public since 1974. The 3 miles of trail lead through a wide variety of open and woodland habitats, and there is an observation deck from which to view waterfowl during spring and fall migration.

As with any wetland area, take appropriate protective measures against mosquitoes during the warm-weather months.

How to Get There

The entrance to Stage's Pond State Nature Preserve is located on Haggerty Road 1.5 miles east of US 23, not quite 4 miles south of the village of South Bloomfield. A small parking area is provided just inside the entrance, and the trails begin there.

The Trail

Begin walking north on the driveway, then turn where the sign directs you to the trail system. Straight ahead is a trailhead sign with a map of the preserve. Some changes have been made since the map was painted, but it is essentially correct. The trail is of mowed grass in the open and earth in other places, with bridges and short sections of boardwalk as needed. Shortly after entering deep woods, signs at a trail intersection direct you to the Kettle Lake Trail to your left and the Moraine Trail to your right.

Head into the woods on the Moraine Trail. You will soon pass the end of the Multiflora Trail coming in on the left. Continuing ahead, after crossing a bridge you will find yourself among tall oaks and hickories. At the intersection with the White Oak Trail, take the left-hand trail to head clockwise on the woodland loop. This is a good trail for seeing spring wildflowers. It is flat, poorly drained land with vernal ponds that provide

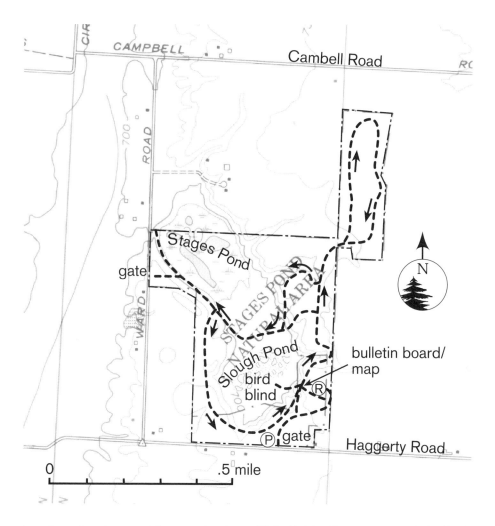

breeding sites for wood frogs and salamanders. There are some really nice white oak trees. Narrow trails used by deer leaving the forest to dine in nearby farm fields can be seen. As I walked the trail on a late-June afternoon, I was watched over by a screaming red-tailed hawk.

After completing the White Oak Trail loop, head south on the Moraine Trail to the entrance of the Multiflora Trail. Follow the latter as it takes you toward the ponds. The trail curves to the left, crosses a small draw on a 12-foot bridge, then meets up with the Kettle Lake Trail headed off to the right. A bench beckons a break, then the trail drops a bit to an area of old field turning into thicket. The rest of the trip will be mostly in this kind of habitat, wonderful for summer wildflowers and butterflies. In the wet area ahead you might hear a common yellowthroat singing its *wichity-wichity-wich* close by, or see a great blue heron take wing. The trail passes through a stand of box elder trees as it approaches Stage's Pond. In 1996, volunteers

---

Stage's Pond State Nature Preserve

New England asters attract a male monarch for a sip of nectar alongside Stage's Pond Trail.

built a new bridge across the flowage in the dip between the two ponds.

If you follow this trail to its end as it skirts along the pond and turns west, you will end up at a gate onto Ward Road. In the past, the only options were to turn left onto the road and follow it and Haggerty Road back to your car or to reverse your course and take the Kettle Lake Trail back to the Moraine Trail and right to the lot. A new mowed trail south from the Kettle Lake Trail inside the west fence, and hence across the southern end of the preserve to the trailhead, was to be completed in the summer of 1997. This is great butterfly country, with an ample supply of milkweed for monarch butterfly larvae and late-summer flowers, such as New England aster, providing nectar to butterflies of many species. Dragonflies abound in the marshy areas near the ponds. It is also good nesting territory for bluebirds in the spring and goldfinches in summer.

Once back at your car or the trailhead, take time to visit the wildlife observation shelter. You may be rewarded with a glimpse of waterfowl on the water or a red fox moving stealthily on the shore. Walking and wildlife watching go hand in hand.

11

Atwood Lake Park (Mingo Trail)

Total distance: 3¾ miles (6 km)

Hiking time: 2½ hours

Maximum elevation: 1125 feet

Vertical rise: 175 feet

*Maps: USGS 7½' Mineral City;
MWCD Atwood Lake brochure*

At 8038 square miles, the watershed of Eastern Ohio's mighty Muskingum River is far and away the area's largest. To protect the towns along the Muskingum River and its many tributaries from suffering a repeat of the devastating flooding that occurred in the first third of the 20th century, the Muskingum Watershed Conservancy District (MWCD) was created in 1933. Independent from state or local government, the conservancy owns and manages 14 major flood-control reservoirs in that giant watershed, 10 with permanent lakes. Over the years the district has established multiple-use recreation facilities at many of the lakes. Such is the case at Atwood Lake, east of the city of New Philadelphia. There the conservancy has built a resort lodge, vacation cabins, campground, nature center, marina, and boat docks as well as provided many fine facilities for walking and hiking.

Atwood Lake was named after the village nearest to the dam at the time of construction, in the tradition of the US Army Corps of Engineers in the era before congressmen began putting their own names on nearly every civil works. Atwood must have disappeared under the lake, because it is nowhere to be found on the modern topographical map of the area.

Though the district owns 3000 acres of land at Atwood, the recreation facilities are concentrated at Atwood Lake Park on the northwest corner of the reservoir.

How to Get There

The area is reached by taking OH 800 and OH 212 northeast from New Philadelphia

The trail at Atwood Lake Park enters the woods a short distance from the parking lot and remains in the forest most of the way.

to New Cumberland, then County Road 93 north and east to the park entrance. There is a small fee for vehicles during the vacation season.

The Trail

Once inside the park, look for a driveway on the left side of the road that leads to parking for the amphitheater. Park there to access the trail system. As you look up the hill toward the woods and the amphitheater, turn to your left, where you will see the trailhead about 100 feet distant. To the right of the trail entrance is a large colored map of the trails; to the left is a sign that gives distances and the times required to walk them.

The trail heads into the woods and starts uphill immediately, swinging first to the right uphill from the amphitheater, then to the left to continue the steep climb through a pine plantation. As the trail nears

the top of this rise, you will see an observation tower. At the time of my visit, it was in disrepair and was closed, surrounded by a chain-link fence. One foot beyond the tower is a sign indicating that the trail goes to the left. Directly ahead is the water reservoir for the park, which explains the wide trail thus far: It acts as a service road, too. The trail follows the contour of the land north from here, still in the woods. It passes the other end of the service road for the reservoir as it continues toward the well-marked intersection with the Cabin Loop and Dogwood Loop Trails. Beyond that intersection, the trail passes under some especially tall white oak trees as it nears the corner of the MWCD property and rises to a high point. In a damp area, the papaw trees had fruit on them when I last passed by. A tiger swallowtail flew by my side as I crossed an open utility line that headed

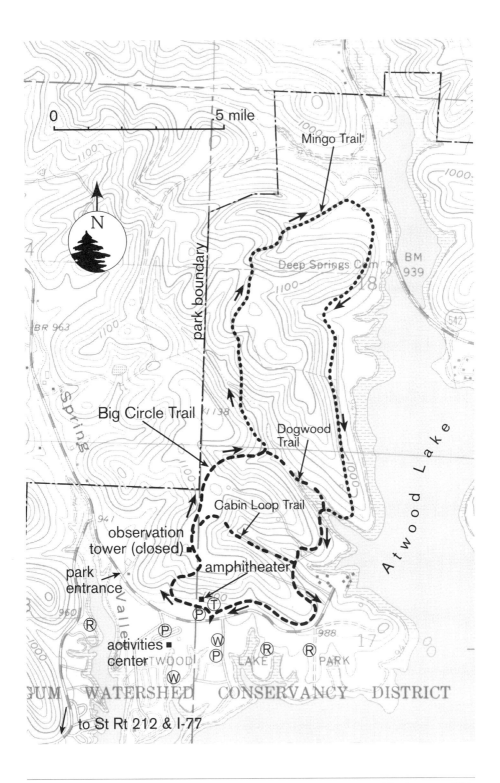

0 _____ 5 mile

Mingo Trail

N

park boundary

Deep Springs Cem

BM 939

BR 963

18

Spring

Big Circle Trail

Dogwood Trail

Atwood Lake

Cabin Loop Trail

observation tower (closed)

amphitheater

park entrance

T

P

activities center

P

W

P

R

R

17

W

UM WATERSHED CONSERVANCY DISTRICT

to St Rt 212 & I-77

down the hill toward the cabin area. The trail next swings to the right, gently easing down a ravine. Passing under tall tuliptrees of the mixed mesophytic woods (and a lot of escaped multiflora rose), the trail enters a pine forest perhaps 25 years old.

After you reach the bottom of the ravine, cross a creek, and begin to climb, you'll reach the next intersection. The Dogwood Trail goes to the right, continuing on down the ravine. The trail to the left, which is the one you want, is now the Mingo Trail. Leaving pines behind, the trail climbs through young hardwood, then past older tuliptrees and a magnificent, tall, wild black cherry. It is headed almost due north now, climbing to reach a long stretch of nearly flat trail past beautiful pines. A sign on a service road that crosses the trail says NO ADMITTANCE. This is the highest point on the trail: 1125 feet.

Beyond the pines, the trail begins its long sweeping curve to the right to turn toward the lake and the return leg. After dropping a bit, the trail makes a hard turn to the right and continues to drop, hanging on the side of the hill below more pines. After crossing a usually dry creek bed, the trail follows the contour of the hill heading south. In the summer, both pale and spotted jewelweed, or touch-me-not, fill the forest floor. Initially the park service road is downhill from the trail, but soon they merge. To the left is an oil pump jack and about 100 feet down the service road there is an intersection where the Dogwood Trail exits hard right (a sign also directs hikers seeking the observation tower to take the hard right).

Follow the trail labeled CABINS straight ahead. This is a narrow footpath through tall pines—and poison ivy. After turning to the right, the trail levels off on the hillside through a patch of ground pine. The trail reaches a service road and follows it a short way to where a sign hidden in the brush directs you to the right for the nature center and to the left for the waterfowl observation area. Go right on the service road, here almost at lake level. About 100 yards down this service road, there is a vertical post labeled TRAIL with an arrow on top of it pointing left. Head for that sign, and soon you will be at the intersection where the Cabin Loop, Dogwood, and Mingo Trails all go right, up the hill toward the defunct observation tower. Another sign directs you straight ahead to the amphitheater—the trail to follow to return to your vehicle. That trail follows the contour of the land as it winds its way around the base of the hill. A well service road crosses it headed uphill. From here it follows an electric service line for a short way, then runs just inside a meadow, a few feet back from the mowed lawn, where the goldenrod greets you in the late summer. From here, your vehicle is in view.

While you are in the area, why not visit some of the other nearby attractions? If you are interested in Ohio history, Zoar Village, Schoenbrunn, and Fort Laurens are not far from here. The New Philadelphia/Tuscarawas County Convention and Visitors Bureau (1-800-BUCKEYE) will be glad to provide brochures and maps.

12

Beaver Creek State Park

Total distance: 5 miles (8 km)

Hiking time: 3 hours

Maximum elevation: 1100 feet

Vertical rise: 140 feet

Maps: USGS 7½' East Liverpool North and West Point; ODNR Beaver Creek State Park map

During the 1820s and 1830s, canal fever swept the Buckeye State, and it didn't miss Columbiana County in eastern Ohio. Finding themselves high and dry halfway between the Ohio River and the new Ohio and Erie Canal, the businessmen of New Lisbon were certain that prosperity would pass them by unless they found a water route to markets in the East. The state legislature did not look favorably upon another public works canal project, so a private stock company, the Sandy and Beaver Canal Company, was formed to construct a 73½-mile canal from Bolivar, on the Ohio and Erie Canal, to Glascow, Pennsylvania, on the Ohio River. Underfunded and undersupported from the start, the canal project ran into one obstacle after another. Construction was started in 1835, but it was 1848 before the first boat, the *Thomas Fleming,* made its way from one end of the canal to the other. Traffic did not commence in earnest until 1851. Canal construction had taken 31 years from the chartering of the company, and the project had required construction of 90 locks, 30 dams, one aqueduct, one large and three small reservoirs, and two tunnels. In 1852 one reservoir gave way, causing the loss of local support, and by 1853 the canal company failed as great chunks of its land were sold to satisfy long overdue judgments. Parts of each end of the canal operated for a few more years, but floods in the early 1860s ruined whatever was left.

Beaver Creek State Park straddles Little Beaver Creek, the route of the eastern division of this ill-fated project. The stream is

Gaston's Mill at the center of Beaver Creek State Park

one of Ohio's most attractive and was the first to be named a State Wild River. It is also a federally designated Scenic River. The nearly intact remains of a number of Sandy and Beaver Canal locks are located within the 3038-acre park. For many years Boy Scout Troop 12 of East Liverpool has maintained the 21-mile Sandy Beaver Trail from Elkton, west of the park, to the Point of Beginning monument on the Ohio River. This hike is along the section known as the Vondergreen Trail as it passes through the state park.

Since this is a linear hike, it is necessary to plan for the return trip. The trail is accessible from two road crossings and at the park campground. With two vehicles, a shuttle can be arranged between any two of these points.

How to Get There

Beaver Creek State Park is located off US 30 about 15 miles east of Lisbon. From US 30, turn north on OH 7. If you wish to hike the entire 5 miles, leave one car at the campground about 3 miles up OH 7. To cut ½ mile off the hike, leave one car at the picnic area across Echo Dell Road from Gaston's Mill in the center of the park. To reach Gaston's Mill, travel 2 miles north from US 30 on OH 7 to Bell School Road and turn right (east).

To reach the parking area at Gaston's Mill, turn left (north) on Echo Dell Road and go about 1.4 miles. To reach the east trailhead, travel east on Bell School Road until you reach Sprucevale Road (County Road 428). Turn left here and travel north to the Sprucevale overlook, where you should stop for a good view of the stream and parklands to the west. Continue on County Road 428 to where the village of Sprucevale once stood along the banks of the river and, after crossing the river, turn left into the park. Leave your car at the picnic area parking lot. From the Columbus area, it is about a 4-hour drive; from Cleveland, 2.

The Trail

Before beginning the hike, walk back to the picnic area entrance on County Road 428 to have a look at the ruins of Hambleton's Mill. Then explore Lock No. 42 (Hambleton's Lock) and the site of Dam No. 13 in the picnic area. A house, said to have been the lockkeeper's, stands next to the lock. The trail is marked with 2- by 6-inch white blazes on trees, posts, and occasionally large rocks. Pick up the trail at the far end of the primitive camping area, upstream from the lock and dam ruins.

Little Beaver Creek lies just south of the farthest advance of the glaciers in this part of Ohio. It is cut deeply into the bedrock, which dates from the Pennsylvanian epoch. Its side ravines contain trees such as hemlock, whose existence in this part of Ohio dates back to the colder era when the continental ice sheet lay only a few miles to the north. The wooded slopes are especially beautiful in the spring, when there is a grand display of wildflowers. A walk along this trail offers a special blend of natural and human history.

About ¾ mile upstream from Sprucevale the trail passes Lock No. 41, Gretchen's Lock, and the site of Dam No. 12. This well-preserved lock lies about 100 feet to the left of the trail. The timbers and planking of the dam can be seen in the stream in times of low water. Gretchen was the daughter of canal engineer E.H. Gill. Her mother died on the trip to America from their home in Europe. Gretchen died of malaria during canal construction, and her casket was entombed in this lock. When Gill left the project after the money ran out, he removed Gretchen's casket and took it with him on his return voyage to Europe. His boat sank, and both he and the casket were lost at sea. The ghost of Gretchen is said to haunt this lock still.

Less than ½ mile beyond Gretchen's Lock is a cliff area where, in the past, the trail was difficult to travel in wet weather. It was very narrow and located on a shale bank. Stairs have now been built around the shale bank, but caution is still in order along this stretch of the trail.

About ¼ mile beyond the shale bank area lie Locks No. 40 and No. 39. The trail goes through Lock No. 40, which is in poor condition. Lock No. 39 is in very good shape and is unusual because of its 140-foot length, its gatework at different levels, and its steps. Shortly beyond the lock near a fork in the trail lies an old foundation, possibly that of the locktender's home. Notice the mason's marks—his "signature" in the form of anchor and cross—on some of the stonework. Be careful to avoid poison ivy and snakes around this and all other stonework.

The trail continues upstream using the left fork. The footpath is blazed with white. A horse trail also traverses this valley; it crosses and on some occasions uses the same path as the hiking trail. The bridle trail is easily discernible by the ruts made by horses' hooves.

Not far upstream stands Vondergreen's Lock, No. 38, and the earth embankment of Dam No. 11. This is a good place to contemplate the skill of the workmen who built this well-preserved lock perhaps 150 years ago. Gill is said to have been a perfectionist, and it shows in the workmanship here. Try to imagine the excitement of the arrival of a canal packet at the lock on its way to Philadelphia with a load of Ohio salt pork.

In the middle of the stream, ½ mile beyond Vondergreen's Lock, sits a massive rock. The cliff face reveals where this tremendous piece of rock came from. What a roar it must have made!

A foundation marking the remains of a home or storage building is seen along the

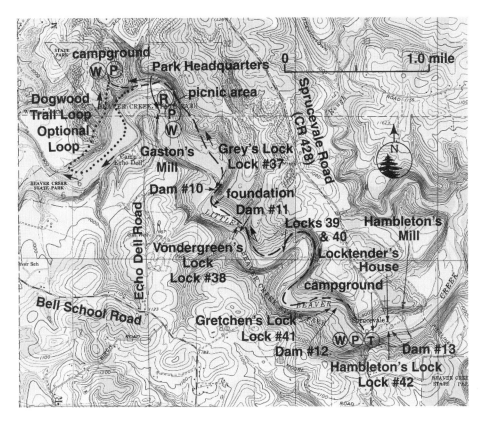

trail about ½ mile farther upstream. The rock in this formation probably originated at the next lock area, having been pirated away after the failure of the canal. Grey's Lock, No. 37, and the site of Dam No. 10 are just beyond. The trail now heads gently upslope, away from the river, to intersect a paved road. Upon reaching Echo Dell Road, turn left and go downhill, then cross the iron bridge to explore restored Gaston's Mill (built in 1837 to take advantage of the canal dam) and the pioneer village. At this point the canal has moved to the south side of the stream, where it will continue for many miles. Lock No. 36, located at the picnic area, is another well-preserved structure. It has been rebuilt with new wooden gates and lining to help visitors visualize its

original appearance. Rest rooms and drinking water are available at this area and the park office is only a short distance up the road beyond Gaston's Mill.

To continue hiking to the campground, recross the iron bridge and turn upstream (left) through another picnic area. The trail begins climbing the hillside beyond the last picnic site. The camping area is uphill about ¼ mile to the northwest. Signs along the trail can direct you to the Dogwood Trail loop through the old strip mine area, to add 1½ miles to your 5-mile hike.

Little Beaver Creek offers good fishing and canoeing. The camping area is primitive, with few modern conveniences, but the rewards of the more than 15 miles of trails in the park are worth the trouble.

13

Brecksville Reservation Metropark (Deer Lick Cave Trail)

Total distance: 4 miles (6.4 km)

Hiking time: 2½ hours

Maximum elevation: 855 feet

Vertical rise: 20 feet

*Maps: USGS 7½' Northfield;
USGS 7½' Broadview Heights;
CMPD Brecksville Reservation map*

With 3392 acres, Brecksville Reservation is the largest jewel in the Cleveland Metroparks' Emerald Necklace. The wooded reservation is cut by seven distinct gorges. It has a spectacular native tallgrass prairie planting. Its nature center is probably the oldest structure built for that purpose in any park system, having been constructed by the Work Projects Administration (WPA) in 1939. For the hiker, it has an extensive system of well-labeled trails, including a section of the Buckeye Trail (BT).

How to Get There

To reach Brecksville Reservation, take I-77 or I-271 to OH 82. The entrance to the park is just east of the intersection of OH 82 and OH 21, to the south off OH 82. The park is open every day of the year during daylight hours.

The Trail

The trailhead is located at the main parking lot at a three-sided kiosk with a map and seasonal information. From the kiosk, follow the walkway to the nature center. Facing the building, go to the left on the trail marked with red blazes—the Deer Lick Cave Trail. Pass the amphitheater and head down a slope into mixed mesophytic woodland. After crossing a bridge over a ravine, take the stairs to the left. Turn right at the top of the stairs and for 200 feet skirt the edge of a pine planting. Cross a paved driveway and pass through a wooded picnic area. Look far ahead for the blazes on the trees. After a right turn, the trail joins the bridle path to go downhill. A footbridge complements a horse

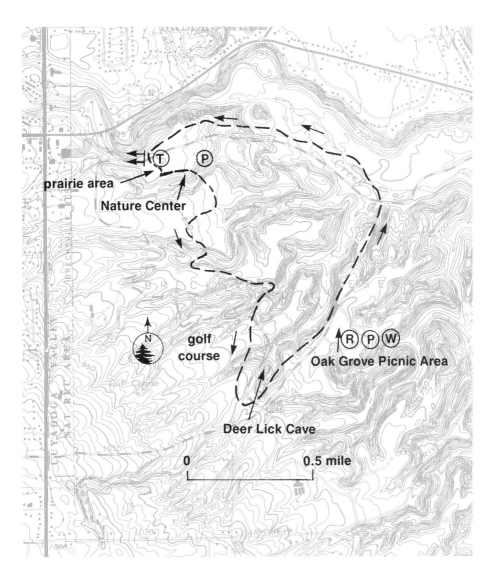

prairie area

Nature Center

golf course

N

Deer Lick Cave

Oak Grove Picnic Area

0   0.5 mile

ford. The trail then swings right past a huge white oak tree to another bridge/ford, after which it travels along the edge of the woods.

Where the trail splits, take the right fork downhill through an area of tall, forest-grown trees. When you see a ford ahead, take the trail to the right across a wide bridge, then go up the left-hand valley on the left bank. There is an excellent example of exposed shale at the bridge.

After crossing the road, the trail reenters the woods about 200 feet to the left (east), near the end of an old red pine planting. A red blaze is located about 150 feet into the woods on the trail. Here is also a Scotch pine planting that is being invaded by deciduous trees.

As the trail swings left, the golf course greens are visible to the right through the trees. It is interesting to note the different diameters of the pine trees, which were all planted on the same day. Those whose crowns get full sunlight are much bigger.

The trail now goes downhill to cross a stream on another wide bridge. Bedrock is exposed in the streambed, but there are also many granite boulders, erratics carried to the area by the glaciers. At this point the BT joins the red trail from the right as the red trail turns east toward a road crossing. Just beyond the road, another set of blue blazes indicates that the BT goes right. Actually, this is a side trail for horseback riders, a bypass of the foot trails in the park for BT travelers on horses, that leads to the metropark's stable across the road.

The trail turns left and crosses the park road about 50 feet north of Valley Parkway. Seventy-five feet into the woods after the road crossing, the BT and Deer Lick Cave Trail turn left. A sign warns that horses are not allowed on the trail. The blazed trails lead down a set of stone steps past Deer Lick Cave, for which the red-blazed trail is named. Two footbridges lead you past the lovely sandstone ledges and shelter caves. As the trail returns to the upland, an interpretive sign tells of the geologic history of the caves. A short way beyond is a kiosk telling the story of Ohio's BT. According to the signs, the trail from here travels 441 miles to Cincinnati through western Ohio, 552 miles to Cincinnati through eastern Ohio, and 65 miles to Mentor Headlands, its northern terminus.

This is about the halfway point on the hike. Water and rest rooms are available at the Oak Grove Picnic Area to the east, across Valley Parkway.

The Deer Lick Cave and Buckeye Trails continue along the west side of the parkway for a short way, then the BT exits to the right across the road on a bridle trail. Your trail now descends to a new footbridge on 23

wooden steps that have been around for a while. The BT returns from the right rear to join the Deer Lick Cave Trail on an old road along the rim of the ravine, before they rise to a ridge, a high point of the walk. Young hemlocks grow on the hillside to the right, and at first beech trees are seen on the left on the north-northwest-facing slope, then on both sides mixed in with young hemlocks.

The trail descends to the road on what looks like an old logging skid. Cross the road to travel the green-blazed Chippewa Gorge Trail. Enter the green trail off the blacktop just before you see an exercise station on the all-purpose trail that parallels the edge of Chippewa Creek Drive. The green trail leads through a young riverine forest to a suspension bridge designed and built by the 26th Engineering Company of the Ohio National Guard of Brecksville in April 1981.

The trail follows the edge of an old channel before crossing another footbridge. There are lots of wild black cherry trees, a big barberry patch, and a good understory of spicebush. The presence of basswood on the slope below a shale bank indicates the presence of limestone. The trail follows the Chippewa Creek valley upstream halfway between the slope to the left and the creek. Cinnamon fern and the presence of hemlock tell of a cooler microclimate as the trail approaches the cascades area of the stream. On top of sandstone now, the trail passes some huge red and white oak trees. A number of side trails enter from the left. There are huge sandstone slump blocks below the cliffs. An old WPA-era shelterhouse overlooks the stream valley.

Where the trail reaches the scenic overlook, take the white trail to the left along the road, then, after about 150 feet, cross the road at a spruce planting to reach the Harriet Keeler Memorial Area. Turn left about 100 feet into the woods to get to the memorial stone. On a glacial erratic in a grove of hemlock, a plaque reads HARRIET L. KEELER, 1846–1921, TEACHER-AUTHOR-CITIZEN. SHE LIVETH AS DO THE CONTINUING GENERATIONS OF THE WOODS SHE LOVED. There is a bas-relief profile and oak leaves. Beyond to the east is a Metropolitan Park Wildflower Area. A sign admonishes visitors: ENJOY THE BEAUTY OF THE BLOSSOMS. TAKE ONLY PHOTOS AND MEMORIES. LEAVE ONLY FOOT PRINTS. Here is the splendid prairie planting that was developed under the direction of former senior park naturalist Karl Smith. An elevated deck with signs illustrating 31 prairie species stands at the east end of the planting. According to the sign, the Emerald Necklace Garden Club of Brecksville provided initial funding and continues to support this project and these exhibits.

The trail just beyond the platform leads to the nature center, where the trail began. Be sure to visit the center and learn more about this fine metropark from the exhibits and staff.

14

Cuyahoga Valley National Recreation Area

Total distance: 9½ miles (15.3 km)

Hiking time: 5½ hours

Maximum elevation: 850 feet

Vertical rise: 200 feet

Maps: USGS 7½' Northfield; BTA Akron Section map

Just as the Cuyahoga National Recreation Area is a study in contrasts, so, too, is this 9½-mile trail. For 6½ miles it traverses high hills and stands witness to tall timber and deep ravines. For the other 3 miles it travels open fields, roads, and a very level canal towpath.

The Cuyahoga Valley National Recreation Area was created in 1974 as an urban park of the National Park System (NPS). It preserves 33,000 acres of pastoral valley along 22 miles of the Cuyahoga River between Cleveland and Akron. It is a diverse area, with some places of pristine beauty, while others have been badly despoiled by the hand of man. Preserving the artifacts of civilization is as important to this park as preserving natural things; thus company towns and canal locks receive attention along with mature woods and endangered species.

Before the NPS came to the valley, both public and private agencies in Cuyahoga and Summit Counties protected many of the valley's special areas through the establishment of parks, preserves, and camps. Most of these have remained under the jurisdiction of the agencies that originally developed them, although the NPS works closely with them. The Buckeye Trail (BT) runs through the park on its way between Cincinnati and Mentor Headlands. Section by section, this trail is gradually being relocated off roads that were used on a temporary basis and onto true trails in woods and fields. Between Boston and Jaite, the BT is totally off-road, traveling on the high land on the west side of the valley. Combining it with a section of

Restored Jaite Mill company houses are now part of the National Park Service's park headquarters complex.

the Miami and Erie Canal Towpath Trail that has been restored and maintained by the NPS makes a challenging and interesting loop day walk.

Jaite, where one of several trailheads is located at a small parking lot east of NPS headquarters, was once a company town for the Jaite Mill located east of the river, adjacent to the canal. The town buildings have been renovated for offices and living quarters for park personnel, and the town now looks much like it must have during its heyday. Though it is probable that the sprawling Jaite paper mill will eventually be demolished, other properties of historic interest along the canal within the park have been restored or are being preserved for future restoration. Only minimal restoration work has been done on the aging locks, but trees and vines have been removed to keep their roots from doing further damage to the old stone structures. A Canal Visitor Center has

been open for several years in a canal-era building at Lock No. 38, 7 miles north of Jaite at Hillside Road and the canal. The 1836 Boston Store located along this hike in Boston was opened in 1996, with exhibits on the craft of canalboat building.

There are minimal facilities of any sort along this hiking route, and there are few places along this trail where you can obtain soft drinks or snacks, so be sure to carry ample drinking water and whatever food and other supplies are needed.

How to Get There

To reach the Jaite trailhead, take US 271 to OH 82 (exit 19), turn west on OH 82, and travel 4.5 miles to Riverview Road. Turn left (south) to go 3 miles to the intersection of Riverview and Vaughn Roads, where the park headquarters complex is located at the former community of Jaite. Turn east onto Vaughn Road. One trailhead is at the parking lot on the left (north) side of Vaughn Road, just beyond a railroad crossing about 200 yards after the turn. Alternative parking is located at Red Lock about 0.25 mile east of Jaite, east of the Cuyahoga River on the north side of the road. Since the Red Lock lot is heavily used by bicyclists on weekends, the Jaite lot may be a good choice. Access to the trail is easy from either: Cross Jaite Road and pick up the trail.

The Trail

From either trailhead parking lot, cross Vaughn Road and follow the blue blazes on posts to where the trail turns south beneath the power line. After a few hundred yards, you will reach a T in the trail. The outgoing trail turns west across the railroad tracks and comes out onto Riverview Road where it intersects with Snow Road. Cross Riverview and head up the left side of Snow Road; after about 100 feet, watch out for the place where the trail enters the woods to the left. Upon leaving the road, the trail immediately begins climbing a steep hill to a long northeast–southwest-aligned ridge. Over the next mile, as it climbs the ridge, the trail will gain more than 200 feet in elevation. Using a combination of old lanes and a newly created trail, it travels through mixed mesophytic forest of varying age and past occasional pine plantings. Eventually the trail makes an S-curve before crossing Columbia Road.

After crossing Columbia, the trail heads northeast parallel to the road for several hundred yards beneath a stand of magnificent old white oaks. It then drops into a ravine, where hemlocks grow in the cool environment along a beautiful shale-bottomed stream. An occasional glacial erratic on the upland is a reminder that, unlike the hills of southern Ohio, these have seen glaciation as recently as 10,000 years ago; yet the ravines

cutting through the Mississippian-aged bedrock where hemlocks grow are reminiscent of Hocking County.

The trail begins to climb once more, crossing ridges and more ravines on its way toward Blue Hen Falls. Here the stream cascades over sandstone bedrock as it cuts its way to the Cuyahoga valley to the east. The trail crosses the creek on a bridge just upstream from the falls, then turns upslope to emerge at a parking lot and Boston Mills Road.

The trail crosses the road and heads east to pass in front of the National Guard establishment. Passing between more Guard buildings, it turns south to drop rapidly into a highly eroded valley close to I-271. It then climbs a set of steps to the top of the ridge, which it follows east as it descends to the intersection of Boston Mills and Riverview Roads. Cross Riverview and the Cuyahoga River on Boston Mills and head into Boston. Just beyond an abandoned service station garage with a Pure Oil/Union 76 sign is the Boston Store, which has fine exhibits on the building of canal boats. Behind it is the trailhead area.

Across the road from the store, begin hiking north on the Ohio and Erie Towpath Trail as it heads toward Boston Lock (No. 32). A short way up the trail, on the left (west) side of the canal, is the Boston Mills Cemetery. From this point back to the trailhead, the hike is level walking along the long-abandoned but now restored towpath. Be alert, because bicyclers as well as joggers and walkers now use the trail. Lock No. 33, which the trail passes just north of the cemetery, has not been rebuilt, but trees along its banks have been removed. Because there are no plans to water this part of the canal, it is unlikely that it will ever be rebuilt. As the trail reaches the Jaite Mill area, it moves to the left toward the hillside

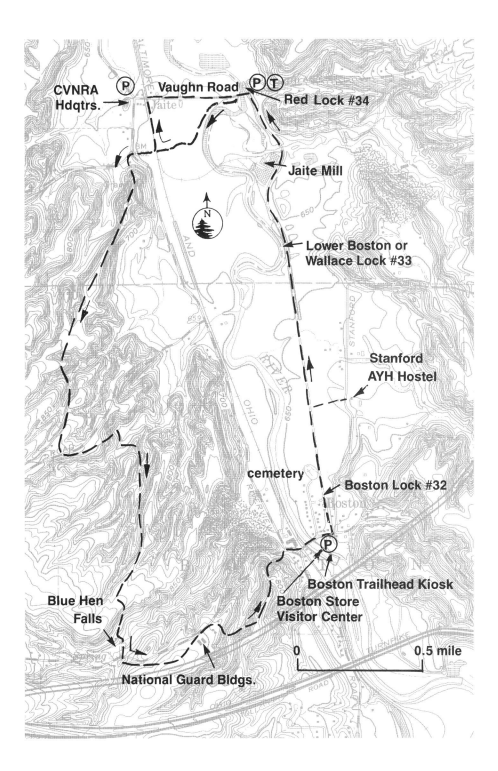

CVNRA Hdqtrs.

Vaughn Road

Red Lock #34

Jaite Mill

N

Lower Boston or Wallace Lock #33

Stanford AYH Hostel

cemetery

Boston Lock #32

Boston Trailhead Kiosk

Boston Store Visitor Center

Blue Hen Falls

National Guard Bldgs.

0   0.5 mile

as a section of the canal carries water into the mill where it once was used in the milling process. The trail continues on the towpath as it approaches Highland Road.

On the north side of Highland Road lies the Red Lock Trailhead, an access point for people walking or riding the trail. The towpath trail continues another 8¾ miles to the north to Rockside Road. To complete this hike, turn left (west) along the south side of Highland Road (Vaughn Road on the Cuyahoga County side of the river) and cross the Cuyahoga River. Just beyond the bridge, a connecting trail to the Buckeye Trail drops off the left side of the road, then turns right to parallel the river before swinging toward the west. At a trail intersection beneath the power line, turn right to head north to the parking lot.

There are many other fine facilities to be found in this park. A special treat is an excursion trip on the Cuyahoga Valley Scenic Railroad that travels between Akron and Rockside Road. Write or call the park for details of this and the many other public programs they offer.

15

Eagle Creek State Nature Preserve

Total distance: 4¾ miles (7.5 km)

Hiking time: 3 hours

Maximum elevation: 960 feet

Vertical rise: 20 feet

Maps: USGS 7½' Garrettsville; ODNR Eagle Creek State Nature Preserve brochure

Skunk cabbage is among the first flowers to bloom.

A walk along the trail of Eagle Creek State Nature Preserve, a 442-acre area northeast of Garrettsville in Portage County, can truly be a "walk with the wildlings." In addition to being one of the largest intact tracts of mature woodland in this area, it is home to many birds, mammals, reptiles, and amphibians infrequently seen in more intensely developed parks. Beaver, fox, white-tailed deer, raccoon, and skunk live here. Hundreds of Canada geese use the larger ponds as rest stops during migration, and the woods are full of songbirds during spring. Two species listed as rare and endangered in Ohio, the spotted turtle and the four-toed salamander, are known to live here.

There are more than 100 species of woody plants on the preserve, including many less common trees such as cucumber magnolia and yellow birch. The rich beech/maple forests on the north-facing slopes contain abundant spring wildflowers. The white oak forest communities, more common on the drier, south-facing slopes, have a sparser but equally interesting show of spring flowers. Over 70 species of wildflowers have been observed blooming in the preserve during May. Pin oaks are found in the swamp forest, and buttonbush swamps, small bogs, and marshlands dot the area.

Located on the eastern edge of an isolated area of terminal moraine, the preserve is mostly underlain by sandy glacial outwash. Eagle Creek meanders in a southern direction through the middle of the preserve in multiple channels, and the manipulation by beavers of water levels for their own

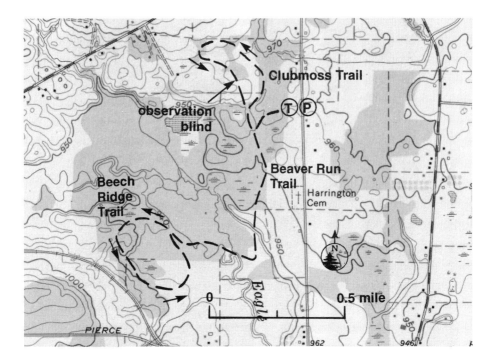

purposes has created more bottomland ponds.

A well-planned and -maintained trail system allows the visitor to walk through the woods and fields past beaver ponds and beautiful wildflowers. Rather than a fast-paced, recreational walk, this hike is better suited to a quiet stroll through nature's realm. The collection of any natural material is, of course, prohibited here, as are dogs, picnicking, alcoholic beverages, and camping. Bring water and other needed supplies since nothing is available at the preserve.

This preserve, with its easily hiked trails, is one of those special places that can be visited throughout the seasons. It is open from dawn to dusk year-round.

How to Get There

Garrettsville, near which the preserve is located, is about equidistant from Akron, Youngstown, and Cleveland on OH 82. The preserve entrance is on Hopkins Road, which runs north and south about 2 miles east of Garrettsville. To reach it, travel OH 82 or OH 88 to Garrettsville, then take Center Road 3 miles northeast to Hopkins Road. Make a hard right turn onto Hopkins Road and go less than 1 mile to the entrance on the right, just north of Harrington Cemetery. The preserve is within an hour's drive of the Akron, Canton, Cleveland, and Youngstown areas.

The Trail

Shortly after leaving the parking lot, the trail enters the woods. A small buttonbush swamp is to your left. At the T in the trail, go north (right) on the 1 ½-mile Clubmoss Loop Trail. After passing a sphagnum bog on the left, the trail divides to make its loop. Turn right. This trail passes another bog and a skunk cabbage patch, then goes through an old field area and young woods before turning south and east alongside a large beaver pond. An observation blind beckons you to spend a few minutes scanning the area with binoculars in search of wildlife. Since the blind faces southwest, great photographs can be taken shortly after sunrise, or—for spectacular, backlit pictures—just before sundown.

Now traveling south, the trail completes its loop. Continuing beyond the side trail to the parking lot, the Beaver Run Trail stays on the high ground overlooking the East Branch of Eagle Creek and many small beaver ponds and dams. A half mile after passing the trail to the parking lot, the Beaver Run Trail drops down the slope to cross both branches of the creek. A trail up the slope beyond the second bridge is the connection with the ¾-mile Beech Ridge Loop Trail. Walk it in a counterclockwise direction. Tall beech trees provide shade for the vernal flora of the forest floor. The trail circles but does not pass through a wetland. In this corner of the preserve, former agricultural fields are being allowed to return to woodland.

After completing the Beech Ridge Loop, return to the parking lot via the Beaver Run Trail.

16

Fernwood State Forest

Total distance: 4 miles (6.6 km)

Hiking time: 2½ hours

Maximum elevation: 1120 feet

Vertical rise: 220 feet

Maps: USGS 7½' Steubenville West (OH and WV); ODNR Fernwood State Forest map

At 2107 acres, Fernwood is one of Ohio's smaller state forests. Located in the coal belt of southern Jefferson County, it did not get its name from its plant life but from a nearby community that no longer exists. Unlike the large state forests of the southern part of the state that were acquired primarily to ensure a continued source of timber, Fernwood was purchased mostly for its recreational potential. So-called "pre-law" land, it was strip-mined by earlier methods that left standing highwalls with ponds at their bases.

The forest is in three units. The central section, which is also the largest, has a small picnic ground known as the Little Round Area and a well-developed and -maintained foot trail. There are three parking lots here, including one at an overlook where there is a good view of the Cross Creek valley.

The western unit, which is the smallest, has a camping area known as Hidden Hollow, an area designated for handheld trap shooting, a rifle and pistol range, and a short nature trail known as Hidden Hollow Trail.

The third area, to the south, has not been developed and is accessible by road at only one corner. All three areas are open for public hunting. Deer, turkey, squirrel, and ruffed grouse are the most frequently sought-after game.

How to Get There

To reach Fernwood from the Columbus area, take I-70 east to I-77. Turn north on I-77 and travel to OH 22, where you turn right (east) to Wintersville. From northeastern Ohio, travel I-77 south to US 250, where

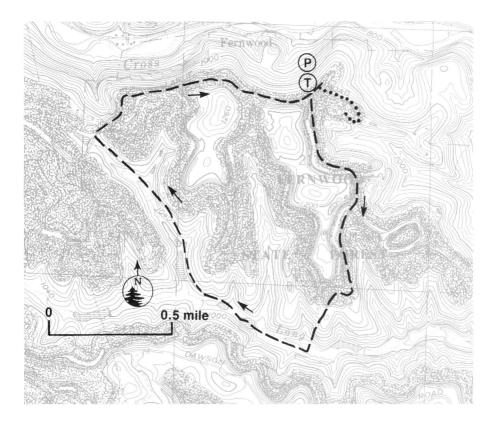

you turn east to Cadiz. There go left on OH 22 and continue to Bantam Ridge Road. Take Bantam Ridge Road right (south) 3 miles to County Road 26, turn right, cross a railroad, and go over Cross Creek. Go up a hill to Township Road 181, where you make a left turn and immediately arrive at the forest service center. There is no office maintained there, and no fee for camping. A patrolling ranger will write you a permit. The area is remote, with very few visitors during most of the year. The trailhead for the foot trail is at the second parking area, about 0.7 mile east of the service center.

The Trail

The trail starts south from the parking area, rising at first but then dropping to follow the contour of the land. Beaver ponds lie between the trail and the base of the highwall. The timber is regrowth oak/hickory with black locust. After ½ mile, a spur goes to the left. The main trail continues straight ahead, eventually dropping to Long Run. There was formerly a side trail to the left across a small footbridge that leads to several small ponds about ½ mile downstream, but it is no longer maintained. If you can get through, these ponds are worth exploring for views of wildlife. I carried a pack rod and reel with me and spent some time fishing, but had little success. The loop hiking trail makes a right turn upstream past several beaver ponds.

After another ½ mile, the trail turns north and passes the right side of a small, man-

Dead trees in a beaver pond at Fernwood State Forest

made lake. It does not cross the dam but continues up the right side of the valley, passing more beaver ponds before ascending to the township road just west of the service center.

To complete the loop requires that you hike ¾ mile out the road to the parking lot and trailhead. A walk along the nature trail at the Hidden Hollow campsite would be a worthwhile venture while in the area. It is located on the north side of County Road 26, about 3 miles west of the service center.

17

Findley State Park

Total distance: 3 miles (4.8 km)

Hiking time: 2½ hours

Maximum elevation: 915 feet

Vertical rise: 35 feet

Maps: USGS 7½' Sullivan; USGS 7½' Wellington; ODNR Findley State Park map; BTA Norwalk Section map

Findley State Park's origin as a state forest is evident from the moment you enter the area. Row after row of tall pine trees greet you. These trees were probably planted in open fields shortly after the area was purchased. Named for the late Judge Guy Findley, an early advocate of protection for the area, the original 890-acre tract was transferred to the Division of Parks and Recreation shortly after its creation in 1949. An additional 107 acres have been added since that time. Virtually all of the park's nearly 10 miles of trails, which include about 1⅓ miles of the Buckeye Trail, are within woods. The park includes a modern 275-site campground, several picnic areas, and a 93-acre lake with a public beach and boat ramps.

How to Get There

The park entrance is off OH 58, not quite 2 miles south of Wellington in Lorain County. For this hike, turn right just after entering the park and drive down Park Road No. 3 for about 0.5 mile. Park at the Picnic Pines parking lot on the left. The Buckeye Trail enters the park directly west of here and heads south. Take the south trail through the pine groves along the lakeshore. Watch for poison ivy under the pines. These pines, like those planted elsewhere around Ohio, are being invaded by hardwoods that will eventually reclaim the area.

Findley Lake is well stocked with fish, and only electric motors are permitted. It is a good place for some lake canoeing, perhaps "plugging" the shores for bass or using catalpa worms, red worms, or crickets for

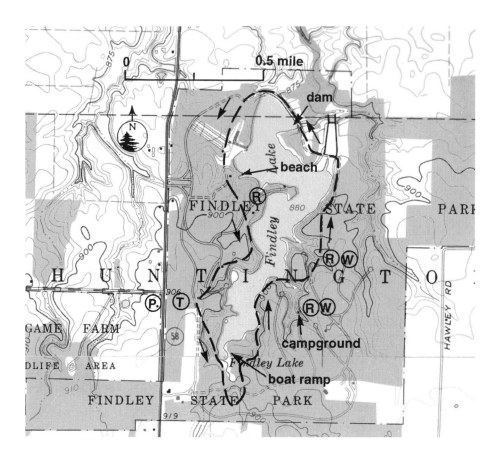

bluegill. It is a pleasant park for an outing within an hour's drive of Cleveland, Akron, or Mansfield.

The Trail

As the trail leaves the pines and approaches Wellington Creek, the woods turn to maple/ash swamp forest, with a small grove of papaws. This bottomland can be wet. The main stream is spanned by a footbridge. Beyond the bridge, the Buckeye Trail goes straight ahead to pass the park office and exit the park to the east. To get to the Lake Trail, make an immediate left and follow the Creekbank Trail north to the boat ramp road. Turn right up the road,

passing a material yard on the left, just beyond which the trail enters the young mixed-hardwood forest on the left. It then returns to the lakeshore, which it follows for ⅛ mile.

By making a sharp turn to the right, the path skirts campsites on the turnaround at the end of the camp road. Heading east, it reaches another camp road between sites 84 and 85. There are latrines and drinking water close by. The trail does not cross the road directly but exits the campground between sites 87 and 88, which are to the left. Please respect the privacy of campers while traveling through this campground.

For the next ½ mile the trail, now called

the Spillway Trail, follows a wide service road. When it arrives at the emergency spillway, the trail turns left (northwest) across the grassy area. Then it climbs the other side of the spillway and enters a narrow strip of woods before coming back into the open to cross the dam. Leaving the west end of the dam on a service road, the trail reenters the woods to the left. It is now the Larch Trail. Follow the trail southwest into the woods, passing the end of the beach and the marina parking lot, where water and rest rooms are again available.

Cross the edge of the beach next to the woods and enter the path where a vertical sign says LARCH TRAIL. Take this trail, an old road, to where it comes out on a road to a lakeshore picnic area. The trail is difficult to find across the road. It enters the young hardwood forest about 100 yards to the right of where it emerged. After about ⅛ mile of walking and a swing to the west, the trail reaches another picnic area among a nice grove of oak trees. At the far (south) end of the parking lot, the trail enters the woods, crosses a bridge, and makes the short connection to the Picnic Pines parking area where it began.

18

Hell Hollow Wilderness Area

Total distance: 2½ miles (4 km)

Hiking time: 1½ hours

Maximum elevation: 1020 feet

Vertical rise: 155 feet

Maps: USGS 7½' Thompson and Painesville

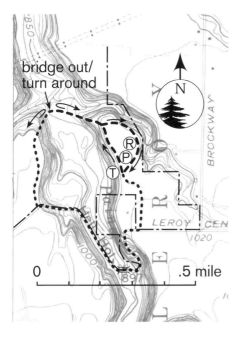

How the shouts and curses of the coach drivers and wagon masters must have echoed in Hell Hollow when they urged their horses or oxen to pull just a bit harder. It's bad enough that even the present-day county engineer seems to have given up on keeping a road across Paine Creek in the spot traditionally known as Hell Hollow. It is a 150-foot-deep gorge through which Paine Creek flows on its way north to join the Grand River, which then empties into Lake Erie at Fairport Harbor. In the hollow, the low steel-truss bridge across the creek (which, from the looks of its abutments, replaced a covered wooden bridge, which replaced a fording place) carries only foot traffic now. These days the land is part of the Hell Hollow Wilderness Area of the Lake County Metro Parks system, a lesser-known, natural recreation area with a minimum of development. With high shale banks along the creek, a mixture of hardwoods and evergreens, and a quietness uncommon in busy northeastern Ohio, it is well worth exploring on foot.

How to Get There

To reach the entrance, travel east from Cleveland on I-90 to exit 212, OH 528. Turn south on OH 528, traveling about 2½ miles to Ford Road. Turn right (west) and go about 4 miles to Trask Road. Turn left (south) on Trask Road and when, in about 1½ miles, it angles left, go straight ahead on Brockway Road. When, in just over a mile, Brockway makes a T with Leroy Center Road, turn right and go a few hundred yards to the park entrance on the right.

There are rest rooms and picnic facilities at the parking lot.

The Trail

Cross the mowed picnic area to the far right corner. The cliff above the creek is beyond a rail fence. The trail exits right and runs parallel to the stream about 25 feet from the edge of the cliff for several hundred yards. Before the trail reaches the top of a staircase, it is joined by a side trail coming in from the right. This is the alternate trail back to the picnic area. Before starting down the stairs, pause to enjoy the great view of the valley. If you walk this trail in the autumn, as I did, the colors of the aspens and red maples across the way and the tulip poplars overhead will be worth the trip. Two hundred thirty-five steps carry you down the shale cliff to streamside, where you will be in a lovely hemlock grove; another short staircase will take you to the water's edge.

Though the trail continues on the other side of Paine Creek, at present there is no bridge here. While it may be tempting to do, wading across the creek at any time except when it is nearly dried up is risky business. I believe the best way to reach the other side of the creek is to backtrack on the trail. Turn around and climb the stairs to the gorge rim, then take the alternate trail back to the parking lot through the hardwood forest and spruce stand. The view going that way will not be the same as the one you had coming out, and except for the huffing and puffing, you will enjoy it just as much.

From the picnic area, now walk out the entrance drive to Leroy Center Road and turn right to follow the old road downhill to the bridge. The shale bank with fine-grained siltstone intrusions alongside the road, and visible alongside the stream from the bridge below, is Chagrin shale, the oldest exposed rock in Lake County. At some places in the county, the Chagrin shale is 750 feet thick. Like the Ohio black shale in central Ohio, it dates from the Upper Devonian age, about 360 million years ago. Seeing its texture makes it easy to understand why the road along here is difficult to maintain. At the bridge, look for the builder's nameplate and date of construction and examine the unmortared blocks of sandstone of the foundation, likely left from its wooden predecessor. Note that it sits high off the floor of the floodplain, with the roadbed coming back on the floodplain off the ends of the bridge. This was common early bridge-building practice. In times of flood, the water could easily flow past the bridge. Bringing the level of the road even with the bridge would have made a dam across the valley, with a major washout apt to occur with each high-water event.

Take a picture or two upstream or down, then begin the gentle climb up the road to the west side of the stream. Not far up the road, the trail exits right over the bank of the road and into the woods. Following an old work road, sandbars, and floodway, the trail eventually carries you to the point opposite the east bank staircase.

The walk back though the floodplain forest to the old road and then across the bridge usually grows quiet as hikers concentrate their energy on the climb. If you walk with your head down, you may see quartz pebbles on the road surface. The bank-run gravel that was used must have come from a place where the pebbles eroded out of Sharon conglomerate on a nearby hillside. At the top of the hill, follow the road back to the parking lots, walking on the left side facing what little traffic there might be. The Hell Hollow Wilderness Area is a small but beautiful refuge in a crowded corner of Ohio.

19

Hinckley Reservation Metropark (Buckeye Trail)

Total distance: 6 miles (9.6 km)

Hiking time: 3½ hours

Maximum elevation: 1290 feet

Vertical rise: 368 feet

Maps: USGS 7½' West Richfield; BTA Medina Section map

Like the swallows returning to Capistrano in California, the turkey vultures return to Hinckley, Ohio, right on schedule each spring. On the first Sunday after March 15, the return of the buzzards is celebrated in this metropark and in the nearby community of Hinckley. The timely arrival of the large black scavengers is usually reported on the wire service news. People come from far and wide to see the birds ride the thermals as they pass over the high ridge that runs through the park.

The land for this southern anchor of Cleveland's Emerald Necklace park district was purchased in 1925, and in 1926, 90-acre Hinckley Lake was built by damming the East Branch of the Rocky River. Hinckley is the only reservation in the Cleveland Metroparks System located entirely outside Cuyahoga County.

How to Get There

Located about 30 miles from downtown Cleveland in Medina County, 2288-acre Hinckley Reservation is reached from north or south by traveling I-71 to the OH 303 exit (Center Road). Head east 4.5 miles to OH 606 (Hinckley Hills Road). Turn right (south) and drive 0.5 mile to Bellus Road. Turn left (east), go 0.25 mile, and enter the park to the right on West Drive. After about 1 mile on West Drive, you reach a road labeled BOAT HOUSE and JOHNSON'S PICNIC AREA. Enter to the left and drive past the boathouse to the far end of the driveway and the picnic area parking lot. Here is the location of the trailhead.

Though located within 50 miles of sev-

Hikers explore rocks at Whipps Ledges.

eral million people, Hinckley offers good hiking in a natural setting. By virtue of being in park district ownership for over 60 years, those areas that were young secondary succession woods at the time of purchase are now mature forests. As an island of green in an increasingly urban area, it is a haven for wildlife.

The Trail

The Buckeye Trail (BT) passes through the park and alongside this picnic area. The 6-mile loop hike described here includes that trail and a part of the park's bridle trail system. It is a favorite "Short Hike on the Buckeye Trail" for members of the Buckeye Trail Association and other hiking groups in this part of the state.

Start hiking by crossing the wooden bridge to the blacktopped All-Purpose Trail. At the far end of the bridge, make a hard left onto a dirt trail at the base of the hill. There is a BT blue blaze about 100 feet down the trail, the first of many along this hike. For the next ¾ mile, the trail follows the Hinckley Lake shoreline, sometimes close to the water but more often upslope 25 to 50 feet. When the trail intersects with the All-Purpose Trail along State Road, turn left, cross the stream on the foot/bicycle bridge, and go to the second drive crossing the blacktopped trail. At this point, turn right to cross the road and enter the Whipps Ledges Picnic Area drive. Fifty feet up the road, turn right through a hole in the dirt piles that block entry into an old park road. Follow the old road past a trail leading to the left, clear to the loop at the road's end. Here, take a blazed trail to the left up the hillside until you come out behind the picnic area rest rooms. Water is available from a Baker pump across the parking area. The shelterhouse just up the hill was built by the Works Progress Administration in 1938.

Take the trail to the right, up steps through a beech forest toward the Mississippian-aged, Sharon conglomerate cliffs known as Whipps Ledges. At the base of the rock wall, the blazes lead you to the left, along the base of the cliffs, and eventually up to the rim. Whipps Ledges are 350 feet above the elevation of Hinckley Lake. The trail does not turn right at the first turn as it reaches the rim, but goes ahead another 75 feet before making a right turn into the oak/hickory forest of the upland. Still climbing, the trail soon reaches a group camping area in a meadow beyond the edge of the woods, where, with ranger permission, Scout units are allowed to camp. Climbing on the cliffs of Whipps Ledges also requires permission from the rangers.

At the woods' edge, the trail turns right. After passing behind the rest rooms, it leaves the woods, traveling along the edge of the adjacent meadow. After about 1000 feet the trail turns right. In another 1000 feet it turns left, tracing the edge of a young woods on the left and a meadow on the right. Moving downslope, you then turn right beside the beech/maple woods. One thousand feet later, you enter the woods to the left on a service road and hook counterclockwise and downhill to Parker Road, coming out just opposite the park service center driveway.

To continue on the loop hike, turn right and travel the edge of the blacktop for about 1 mile. Notice the nautical artifacts in the first farmyard on the right—a large old anchor and a capstan. Just beyond the vineyard next door stands an old chicken brooder house, a relic of earlier days when poultry was raised in the area. At the first turn in the road, a chain-link fence marks the border of the Taki Nature Research Area within Hinckley Reservation. This area protects the watershed of Hinckley Lake. It was at one time the location of YMCA Camp Craig. Wild turkeys were released here in 1987 and 1988; they have survived well and are occasionally seen throughout the park. There is also a great blue heron rookery within the boundaries of the research area.

Scotch pine and Norway spruce stand on the right side of the road inside the fence. The view to the left is across open meadow and the valley of the East Branch of the Rocky River. The road now passes between woods on both sides before making a sharp left turn beside a gate to the research area on the right. It is now called Harter Road. After dropping to cross the stream, the road begins climbing, with pine plantations and hardwoods along both sides. It passes the entrance to Camp Bradlo on the left. Notice the large number of glacial erratics along the edge of the woods to the left, indicating that this area was once cleared and cultivated.

As the road approaches a farmstead and the edge of the park district land, take the bridle trail that enters the woods on the right side. (The pedestrian route of the BT continues straight ahead on the road.) A blacked-out message on a tree at the right of the bridle trail entrance indicates that this is the Buckeye Trail horseman's bypass. (The BT over Whipps Ledges is a footpath only.) For the next 1½ miles, the bridle trail travels nearly due west just inside the park boundary. The woods are mostly oak/hickory, but there are many small stands of white pine and one large area of beech/maple. Sometimes the tops of the sycamores along the river downhill to the right are visible, and the ravines running up to the trail from the right are covered with the blend of hardwoods referred to by botanists as a mixed mesophytic woods.

After traveling gently up and down, crossing a number of streams, and passing a cattail marsh or two, the trail reaches a barrier of posts beyond which there is a

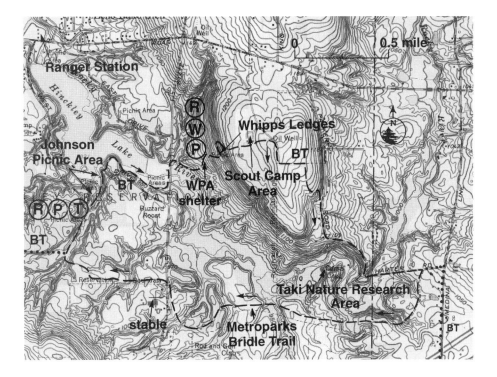

natural-material dump area. A bridle trail goes left. Don't take it: It goes to the private stable a short distance beyond. Another track leads straight west, past the trash to State Road. Don't take it either: It's the service road for trucks using the dump area. Rather, turn right along a trail that parallels the road. This track shortly emerges at the edge of the road, crossing it to reenter more park district land.

Still heading west, the trail passes between evergreens as another wild trail comes through the fence from the adjacent stable area. Skirting the right side of a large meadow area, the trail makes a right turn at the far end of the field, then a left turn into the woods. The T junction is with a trail to the right that goes to a private camp building area. The bridle trail goes left again,

staying on high ground above the heads of the ravines that run to the lake. One-half mile after the road crossing, passing oak/hickory woods and pine plantings along the way, you drop steeply into the head of a ravine, where you turn right toward the lake. After 100 yards, the Buckeye Trail footpath comes in from the left. Do not take it, but follow the trail down the ravine to the horseman's staging area on the opposite side of West Drive from Johnson's Picnic Area. There are three or four shallow stream crossings on this last ¼ mile of the hike.

To return to the trailhead, cross the road, then walk the blacktopped All-Purpose Trail to the wooden bridge, where a left turn completes the loop hike. There are picnic facilities and rest rooms at this area, and water is available at the boathouse.

20

Quail Hollow State Park

Total distance: 5⅓ miles (8.5 km)

Hiking time: 3½ hours

Maximum elevation: 1200 feet

Vertical rise: 60 feet

Maps: USGS 7½' Hartville; ODNR Quail Hollow State Park map

It was June 12, 1811, when Conrad Brumbaugh filed his claim at the state land office in Steubenville for part of the land now known as Quail Hollow State Park. Twice more over the next four years he made the trip to the Ohio River town to register additional land, paying $1.25 per acre and eventually acquiring a large holding in the area of Hartville. The Brumbaugh family grew and prospered, and the log house that was built shortly after settlement became only one of many buildings on the homestead. The family continued to live on the land until the death of Conrad's son, Lewis, in 1901. The story of the Brumbaugh family is revealed on the tombstones of the family cemetery, which lies in the park close to where the family home once stood.

Early in 1900, Harry Bartlett Stewart Sr. began acquiring Brumbaugh and other lands, finally accumulating a total of 720 acres. At first the Stewarts used an old brick and wood structure built in 1838 as a summer home and weekend retreat. In 1914, they began planning an addition to their house that would turn it into a large structure reminiscent of the Greek Revival style popular in the Western Reserve area of Ohio at the time. The house was carefully designed to fit the needs of the family, and the finest material, much of it from the area, was used in the construction. The home was beautifully landscaped, and additional buildings, such as servants' quarters, were constructed close by. H. Bart Stewart Jr. and his wife, Catherine, moved into the 40-room manor in 1937, raising a family there. Stewart, who was chairman of the board and

Natural History Education Center at Quail Hollow State Park

chief executive officer of the Akron, Canton, and Youngstown Railroad, continued to own the land until 1975. That year, he donated half the estate's value to the state of Ohio, and the United States Department of the Interior matched the gift with a $1.7 million grant from the Land and Water Conservation Fund. At that point the state land became Quail Hollow State Park, dedicated to nature study and appreciation. The name was chosen because bobwhite quail were commonly seen in the area. The manor is now called the Natural History Study Center. Over 10 miles of hiking, skiing, bridle, and nature trails have been established. The center, which houses exhibits and holds special programs and workshops, is open 1–4 on weekends. Of course, any trek that passes swamp forest and marshland is in mosquito country during the warm season, so preparation for insect pests is a must.

How to Get There

To reach Quail Hollow from Akron, take OH 43 from I-76 4 miles south to Hartville. From the center of Hartville, take Congress Lake Road less than 1 mile to the entrance to the park. From Canton, take US 62 east of OH 43, then travel 11 miles north to Congress Lake Road in the center of Hartville.

The Trail

Enter the trail system from the northwest corner of the main parking lot, going uphill past picnic tables to an old road heading directly north. At first, woodland occurs only on the right, but very soon there are trees on both sides, with swampland beginning on the right. After about 2000 feet, the trail makes a 90-degree right turn to avoid a large beaver pond in the woods ahead. It soon turns north again, with white pine and Norway spruce on the right and deciduous

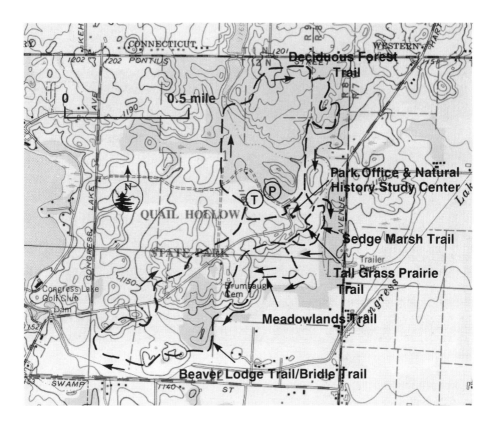

forest on the left. Making a curve to the right, it runs parallel to Pontius Street, the northern boundary of the park. An animal track demonstration area is found along the trail, which then detours around the right side of a small beaver pond. The path continues another 800 feet to the east and then turns abruptly south.

After going a short distance, you reach an intersection where you go left. This is the Deciduous Forest Trail. It winds through a mature woods, passing a water-filled depression on the right and traveling along a hillside before heading north to return to the main hiking path.

Turning to the left onto the main trail, head south once more. The trail travels about 1200 feet between hardwood and softwood forest, passing an entrance to the Woodland Swamp Trail on the right, before breaking out into an old field. Now following a mowed path, you veer slightly to the left, sharply left, then right as you enter the Sedge Marsh Trail. This winding trail goes through open marsh, then through swamp forest, before rejoining the main hiking path. Again, continue on the main path by turning left. A sign at this junction indicates the entry to the Meadowland Trail loop. Moving clockwise on the Meadowland Trail will take you through more pine plantation, then through a wooded fencerow, before looping through meadow back to the main trail. At the far end of the loop are two trails leading left that connect the Meadowland Trail with the bridle trail system to the west.

To take a shorter 4-mile hike, do not take either of the trails to the left, but continue on the Meadowland Trail to complete the loop. Then follow the main hiking trail northeast, past the entrance to the Sedge Marsh Trail on the right, to enter the Tall Grass Prairie Trail to the left. After exiting this trail through the planted prairie, make the short walk across the mowed lawn and past the gardens to the Natural History Education Center in the distance. From there, it is just over ½ mile to the parking lot via the entry walk.

To complete the 5⅓-mile hike, take the first trail to the left off the Meadowlands Trail to connect with the bridle trail. Followed to the left (clockwise), the bridle trail travels through woodland and thicket, skirting the south boundary of the park. Heading west for a little less than ½ mile, it passes another beaver pond to the right, then swings to the east. There, a trail to the left (north) brings you out onto the park entry driveway. Shortly after crossing the driveway, the trail reaches a T. Turning right on the trail takes you past an ash grove, past more white pine, and across the old north–south road before reaching the parking lot driveway just south of the lot.

21

Tappan Lake Park

Total distance: 9 miles (14.5 km)

Hiking time: 5½ hours

Maximum elevation: 1210 feet

Vertical rise: 310 feet

Maps: USGS 7½' Deersville; MWCD Tappan Lake Park trail map

The watershed of the Muskingum River, which runs to the mighty Ohio, covers one-fifth of the state. The people living along that river and its many tributaries suffered many decades of seasonal floods that destroyed their homes, farms, and businesses. In 1933, the Muskingum Watershed Conservancy District (MWCD) was organized to provide flood control, conservation, and recreation in that eastern Ohio area. By 1938, 14 reservoirs were established, and permanent lakes were being retained behind 10 of the dams. The other four dams would be closed only at times of high water. Since 1939, the Army Corps of Engineers has been responsible for flood-control operations, but the MWCD is totally in charge of conservation and recreation throughout the district's 16,000 acres of water and 38,000 acres of land. At five of the reservoirs, the conservancy district operates parks. These are not state parks, but they fill the function of state parks in their respective areas, providing campgrounds, lodges and cabins, interpretive programs, picnic areas, beaches, marinas, and miles of hiking trails.

Tappan Reservoir is a 2350-acre impoundment of Little Stillwater Creek in western Harrison County. The district owns 5000 acres of land surrounding the lake, including the fully developed Tappan Lake Park on its southwestern side. Food, water, and rest rooms are available in the camping area but nowhere along the trail. This area makes for a good weekend family outing that meets the interests of everyone. The campground includes facilities for many recreational activities such as basketball

The author pauses along the trail at Tappan Lake Park.

and horseshoes, and the lake allows for water sports.

Tappan Lake Park has six hiking trails, five of which originate at and return to the campground. Three of these are combined for this hike. The Deer Trail is 4 miles long, the Pine Trail is 2 miles long, and the Fox Trail traverses 6 miles. Since they overlap in some places, a combination of the three trails makes a 9-mile trek. Although directional signs on the trail are the reverse of the way described here, I prefer walking this direction because parking is available at the campground marina where the Deer Trail comes out, but not in Campground 4, where the Fox Trail starts. Two additional trails, the Cabin Beach Trail and a nature trail, are located elsewhere in the park area. A new trail, the Turkey Ridge Trail, is accessed outside the park entrance. It links the park to the Tappan Wetlands and Nature Study Area.

How to Get There

The park is easily reached from the northeastern Ohio metropolitan area by traveling I-77 south, then US 250 east. It can be reached from central Ohio by traveling east on I-70 to I-77, then north to OH 36 (Newcomerstown exit), then east to US 250. To get to the park from US 250, travel south on County Road 55 near the eastern end of the lake. Turn right (west) on County Road 2. The park is 3.5 miles from US 250 on the right. During the summer vacation season there is a charge for admission to the park. If you tell the person at the camp check-in station that you want to take a day hike on the trail, you will be admitted without paying a camping fee.

After passing the check-in station, turn left into the campground, then take the first road to the right. At the next road to the left, turn left to drive beyond the campsites to the campground marina parking area.

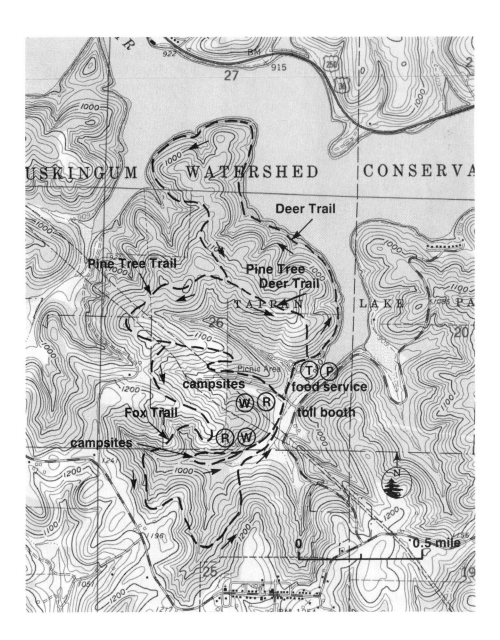

The Trail

Walk straight ahead on the left side of the embayment past the amphitheater to begin the Deer Trail. After it enters the woods, the trail stays at about the same elevation, 100 feet back from the shoreline, for a little over 2 miles. This part of the trail is a section of the Buckeye Trail that passes through the park. Secondary succession oak/hickory forest covers the hillside above the trail, while rows of 30- to 40-year-old white pine fill the hillside below it clear to the shoreline.

Now and then there is an old "wolf tree" with a large bole and low-growing branches alongside the trail.

When you approach the upper end of another large embayment, turn to the left on what must have been a township road. After climbing for about ½ mile, the trail reaches a pine-covered ridge, where it travels about 100 feet below the summit. It arcs gently to the left at that level for several hundred feet, then climbs steeply to the right to meet the Pine/Fox/Deer Trail coming up the valley from the campground.

Your trail now turns to the right into another white pine plantation. Pine Trail is certainly a good name for this trail, which runs from Campground 1 to 3, because the ridge here is planted with white pines nearly all of the way. The Fox/Pine Trail travels either on or just off this ridge for less than ½ mile, where it meets the Fox Trail coming in from the right.

At this point the trail is close enough to the lake that the noise of boats can be heard. Take the Fox Trail downhill alongside a white pine planting, crossing a pipeline and passing through more pines. The trail goes straight, crosses another utility right-of-way, then goes uphill to the left with white pines on the right. After making the ridge, the path makes a sharp curve to the left downhill past poor second-growth hardwood. Returning to white pines, the trail goes along the hillside close enough to Campground 4 that campers can be heard.

The pines disappear as you veer left. A couple of handsome old oaks stand along the right side of the trail. Climbing again, the path turns left as it hits the ridgetop, where there is an old, spreading white oak and more pines. The trail takes a steep drop into the pines. The road at the end of Campground 4 is visible downhill to the left. The trail goes right through medium-aged hardwood, down to a fill crossing over a culvert. From there, it climbs steeply to a junction with a trail coming in from the right. Go left, climbing gently, dip, and then rise again. This time, turn to the right at another trail junction. The path climbs gently through more pines at the top of the ridge, after which it quickly begins to drop. Making a hard right, it continues to drop, levels off, rises, then levels off again among some old wolf oak trees. It then crosses a culvert, turns uphill, and finally descends among sandstone slump blocks and large beech and tuliptrees on its way to Campground 4. There it drops behind a culvert, passing the Red Fox trailhead sign and Campsite 526 on the left.

When you arrive at the campground road, turn right to leave Campground 4. Then turn left, walking past the trailer dumping station and the activity center to return to the camp marina parking lot at the far end of Campground 1.

22

Cooper Hollow Wildlife Area

Total distance: 9 miles (14.4 km)

Hiking time: 5 hours

Maximum elevation: 875 feet

Vertical rise: 186 feet

*Maps: USGS 7½' Oak Hill;
USGS 7½' Rio Grande; ODNR Cooper
Hollow Wildlife Area map*

The gentle grade, sweeping curves, narrow cuts, and strange name (CH&D) of the road leading to the Cooper Hollow Wildlife Area give away its past as a railroad right-of-way. A hundred years ago, this eastern branch of the Cincinnati, Hamilton & Dayton Railroad wound its way through the hill country, serving the early industry of the area. Among these businesses was Ohio's once thriving charcoal iron industry. The Madison Furnace, located on the state wildlife area, was one of the most unique. Rather than being entirely made of cut stone blocks, it was partly carved out of solid sandstone. A mile north on the CH&D, now nearly lost among the vegetation, sat Limestone Furnace. Madison operated from 1854 to 1902, but Limestone was only in blast from 1855 to 1860. Both furnaces were the victims of exhausted supplies of iron ore and wood for charcoal and of newer processes and richer ores from other regions of the country. Not only are the railroads and iron industry gone now, but the subsistence farms of the 19th and first half of the 20th centuries have almost completely disappeared as well. The hilly country of this part of Jackson County is now either being stripped for coal or largely left as old fields and forest, good country for hiking.

Remember, this is a wildlife area, paid for by hunting license and sporting goods tax monies, so it is managed for hunting and fishing as well as biological diversity. Avoid the area on weekdays during deer and turkey seasons, and at least wear a blaze orange cap or vest during squirrel season.

The lower half of the Madison Furnace was carved from solid sandstone.

The Division of Wildlife owns and/or manages hundreds of thousands of acres of land for wildlife throughout the state, but not many of them have good, interconnecting foot trail systems. Parking lots and trails on most have been designed to provide the best access for hunters, but in recent years the division has begun constructing some observation towers and blinds. Most are good places for short exploratory walks and a number are especially good for watching wildlife. These are described in the *Ohio Wildlife Viewing Guide,* which can be purchased from the ODNR publications office. A free brochure listing all areas and maps of individual areas can be obtained from the same source. (See the introduction to this book for ordering information.)

How to Get There

Cooper Hollow Wildlife Area is reached from the southern edge of Jackson, the county seat, via OH 32 east to US 35 south. Travel 5.5 miles on US 35 south to the OH 327 exit. The road to the right here, traveling south, is County Road 2, or CH&D Road. Take that road to the wildlife area entrance, a distance of 3.5 miles. The drive is on the right. Park at the pull-off just beyond the furnace, or 0.3 mile up the hill at the headquarters.

The Trail

Start hiking by walking back out the drive, past the furnace, to CH&D Road. Turn right, then immediately left onto Vega Road. At ½ mile on the right, follow a recently reopened stone drive uphill to the Madison Cemetery. The tombstones tell the tale of infant mortality, epidemics, and industrial accidents. From the cemetery, head north beneath tall oaks and hickories on a long-abandoned ridge road. After a few hundred feet the trail swings northeast, where it joins another old

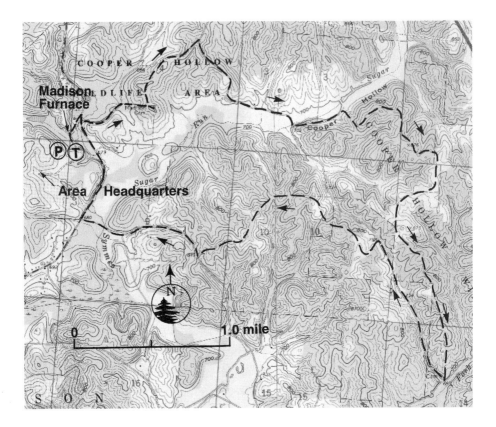

township road to go due east to Cooper Hollow Road. Turn right on this lightly traveled gravel road, walking about 1 mile and crossing a small creek. You will pass a parking lot on the left before crossing the Sugar Run bridge. A short distance beyond this small creek, there is a gated gravel road to the left (formerly ODNR Road 4). Follow it several hundred yards to where there was once an active parking lot. In the late summer, as you walk this road, look to the bottomland beyond the creek, where (if the beavers have not flooded it) there may be a gorgeous display of summer wildflowers, including cardinal lobelia.

Hike beyond the old parking lot for 100 yards to where there is an opening that leads to the left toward a wetland. In the late summer, there is a large stand of joe-pye weed here. Now turn right and bushwhack up the hill past a pine planting to intersect another abandoned road, now a forest trail. Turn left and follow this lane through forest and field for better than 2 miles until it comes to another parking lot and a pond. Turn left on the trail below the earthen dam. Walk the wide, grassy lane that heads south on a ridge paralleling Cooper Hollow Road for 1 mile. At Moriah Road, turn right, then immediately right again, and head back up the hill on Cooper Hollow Road. At the top of the rise, a road on the right leads to the pond and parking lot you passed 2 miles back. Directly opposite this road is a dirt track that heads up the hill through the woods. Take the latter, winding through the woods to the edge of a hayfield. The trail you want to take exits this hayfield catty-cornered from where you enter. To reach it, turn right just as you reach the field and walk two sides of the field until you locate the entrance of the trail into the woods. From experience, I know that missing this turn can lead to becoming hopelessly lost (or, at least, temporarily misplaced).

After entering the woods, for the next 3 miles the trail follows ridge and saddle for some of the most delightful hiking anywhere. Old "wolf trees" (which grow in the open, producing large, low-growing branches) and patches of honeysuckle give away the locations of pioneer homesteads. The wolf trees will not yield even one 8-foot saw log, so they are often left standing by foresters as sources of seeds for natural regeneration.

At one point the trail uses a deeply cut old road that has seen many a wagon pass its way. A gate at the end of the trail prevents off-road vehicles from entering the area from the parking lot.

Now turn right onto Joe Evans Road and follow it about 1 mile, first downhill, then across Symmes Creek to CH&D Road. Turn right, and another mile of road walking, this time heading north, will lead you back to the area entrance and the trailhead. Before leaving Cooper Hollow Wildlife Area, take time to explore the beaver ponds behind the furnace and pull-off. If you sit quietly, particularly in the evening, you might see beavers repairing their dam or storing vegetation for the cold season ahead; in the spring there is a quite a cacophony of amphibian calls.

23

Marie J. Desonier State Nature Preserve

Total distance: 2½ miles (4 km)

Hiking time: 2 hours

Maximum elevation: 920 feet

Vertical rise: 220 feet

Maps: USGS 7½' Alfred and Coolville

In midsummer, great spangled fritillaries are attracted to the butterfly weed in the high meadow.

A walk on a woodland trail sometimes brings totally unexpected pleasures. Who would think that a 490-acre forested tract close to the Ohio River in Athens County would include an isolated high meadow full of butterfly weed and busily nectaring butterflies, "wildflowers of the air"? But that is the case at Marie J. Desonier State Nature Preserve. Three hundred and one acres of this remote preserve were given in 1975 by Henry I. Stein in memory of his sister, Marie J. Desonier. The remaining 189 acres were purchased by the Department of Natural Resources with federal dollars that were a match for the value of the gift. No money came out of Ohio taxpayers' pockets. The nature preserve's remoteness has kept visitors away, but not scientists. Two Athens-area entomologists have caught, identified, cataloged, and published on the butterflies of Desonier preserve.

To explore the trails of Desonier on your own requires no permit. The preserve is open during daylight hours every day of the year. As in all nature preserves, pets are not permitted.

This is a trail of the Appalachian oak country of eastern Ohio. I do not remember seeing a single evergreen on the entire trail, and the high meadow, probably created by a farmer to grow hay for livestock in an earlier time, is on its way to becoming hardwood forest. In time it will be a marvelous unfragmented tract of old-age forest where the neotropical songbirds that spend their summer in Ohio can breed. The flash of red, yellow, orange, brown, black, and blue butterfly wings in the fields will be replaced by

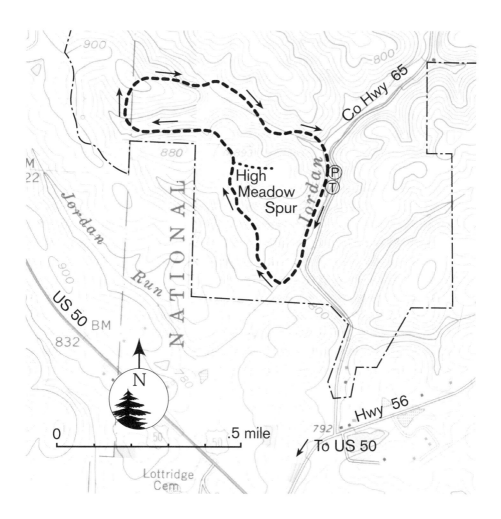

the sights and sounds of beautiful birds such as the scarlet tanager. Nothing stays the same.

How to Get There

Reach the preserve by traveling east from Athens on US 50 approximately 23 miles to County Road 65 (near where US 50 turns to four lanes). This road goes left (north) and is easy to miss. After 0.3 mile, turn left on Deep Hollow Road (County Road 65). The preserve entrance sign can be seen on the right side of the road less than 0.5 mile

away, and the entrance is about the same distance beyond on the left. Park in front of the gate, taking care not to block it in case emergency vehicles need to get in.

The Trail

The trail begins at the south corner of the lower lot (the left when you are facing it). A short way from the parking lot is a borrow pit on the right side of the trail where gravel was taken for the parking lot. It is now well hidden by vegetation. The trail follows Jordan Run, crossing the main and side branches of the stream on plank bridges as the need arises. Walking in late June, I was serenaded by singing northern yellowthroats; the damp air was full of damselflies and dragonflies; and bergamot, milkweed, tall boneset, mountain mint, Queen Anne's lace, joe-pye weed, and other flowers of summer wafted their aroma into the air to attract nectaring butterflies. A large patch of the amber-colored, twinning, chlorophyll-less common dodder spread itself over a group of milkweed plants. The hum of female mosquitoes looking for a blood meal was not far off in this creek-bottom environment, but that is the trade-off we make in order to enjoy the flora and fauna of wetlands. A school of minnows swimming in the stream below is not an unusual sight along this trail.

After ¼ mile of streamside travel, the trail crosses Jordan Run and heads uphill into a relatively young mixed oak woodland. With sandy soil underfoot and an occasional chunk of sandstone alongside, the trail winds its way up the slope through woods and openings, from time to time overlapping an old farm lane. After ¼ mile it reaches a T, where a sign directs you right to the High Meadow spur or left to the Oak Ridge Trail. The distance given on the sign is from an earlier time when the trail system was more extensive. Pay no attention to it. After a rest on the bench provided, take the spur to the right and you will be rewarded shortly with sunshine and wildflowers if you are a summer hiker. The trail at one time circumnavigated what was then a large meadow, but it now extends only to the middle of the meadow. The late-June flight period of this single-brooded great spangled fritillary seems guaranteed to provide you a glimpse of this orange and brown beauty on the scads of butterfly weeds that grace this meadow. No longer being mowed, this old field opening is slowly closing in and will someday be hardly distinguishable from the rest of the woods.

Returning up the trail to the intersection, take the Oak Ridge Trail as it moves around the hillside among the ferns, crosses small streams, and eventually climbs almost straight up it to come close to the high point in the preserve. The trail begins to reverse itself and head in an easterly direction. Sandstone cliffs appear upslope and the vegetation becomes more lush. The trail eventually drops steeply off the hillside toward a tributary of Jordan Run. Beech trees join the mixed mesophytic forest. Crossing and recrossing the stream, the trail passes many mounds of soft, gray-green pincushion moss and large patches of Christmas fern as it swings slightly up and down the toe of the hillside. It was in this valley that a ruffed grouse and I surprised each other. The trail utilizes more plank bridges to stay out of the streambed as it winds its way toward the parking lot. The flowers of summer once again line the trail as the canopy opens up.

24

Dysart Woods Outdoor Laboratory

Total distance: 2 miles (3.2 km)

Hiking time: 1½ hours

Maximum elevation: 1340 feet

Vertical rise: 180 feet

Maps: USGS 7½' Armstrongs Mills and Hunter, Ohio University Dysart Woods Laboratory brochure

A walk through Dysart Woods is a walk among the giants; there is no other way to describe it. The largest number of 36-foot-and-higher trees that I know of in Ohio are along the trails of this preserve. Acquired by Ohio University over 30 years ago with the assistance of The Nature Conservancy, it was one of the first natural areas in the state to be designated a National Natural Landmark by the federal government. Ohio University, whose Belmont campus is less than 12 miles to the north, uses the woods as an outdoor laboratory, with busloads of students and their teachers frequently visiting the area. There are no facilities at the area but it is open to the public. Note that smoking is not permitted while in the preserve. Picnicking and camping facilities are available at Barkcamp State Park just a few miles to the north.

How to Get There

Finding Dysart Woods is not difficult. Travel east of Cambridge on US 70 to exit 208, OH 149. Take this road south 3.5 miles into Belmont. There, take OH 147 out of the southeast corner of the community and travel 5 miles until you see the Dysart Woods sign on the right side of the road. Turn right onto Township Road 234, then right again immediately onto Township Road 194 (Ault Dysart Road). The preserve headquarters is at the farmhouse on the right (east) side of the road. A brochure that includes a map is usually available from a self-dispensing box there. The trailhead is at a grassy area labeled DYSART WOODS PARKING on the left side of the road about 0.75 mile beyond the house.

The author "takes the measure" on a sizable tuliptree along the trail at Dysart Woods.

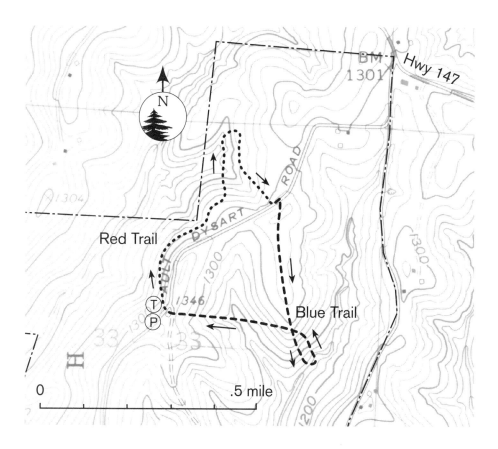

The Trail

There are two connected trails: the Red Trail on the west side of the road and the Blue Trail to the east. Their routes are marked with posts and/or blazes of the appropriate color. I prefer to begin to the west, crossing the gravel road to enter the woods past a red blaze, and then traveling downhill. You are soon struck by the size of the trees around you, including tall, forest-grown beeches and maples. The plaintive call of a wood peewee greeted me as I walked this way on a hot July afternoon. This is a dirt trail, with an occasional water bar to reduce erosion. The relatively wide track the trail starts on soon leaves to the left, and the red-post-marked trail becomes a narrow footpath and continues to wind around the hillside.

As the larger trees give way to much younger ones, you can look through the woods to the left to a large hillside pasture beyond the boundary fence. A well-kept barn stands out on the horizon uphill from the fence. As a red-tailed hawk screamed overhead, a female black rat snake appeared on the path in front of me. It was docile, as are most of its species, and it allowed me to lift it off the trail with my walking staff.

Beyond the opening in the young trees that affords a view of the farm, the trail enters a growth of much larger trees while moving gently downslope toward a small

➤ Storm Damage and Renewal

Severe storms can strike Ohio at any time of the year. They are viewed with alarm by the public because of their potential damage to life and property. To the naturalist, they are considered an important element of the eco-system. Prairie fires set by lightning strikes from autumn storms contribute in many ways to the health and vigor of the prairie grasses and forbs. Heavy winter snowstorms effectively prune or even bring down dead, dying, or weak trees, allowing stronger, healthier trees to take their place in the canopy and creating openings where creatures that need brushy habitat can live. Springtime tornadoes or heavy wind- and rainstorms like-wise bring trees crashing down, allowing more light to reach the forest floor, thus creating new habitat. Untold numbers of species of invertebrates and vertebrates make their homes in, around, and under downed tree trunks and branches, and cavity-nesting creatures soon go to work on the dead snags left standing by such weather events.

ravine. There the trail turns left before hitting the bottom of the ravine, where it turns right. Stay left at a split in the trail, following the red posts. Here the large trees stand about 15 feet apart with small sugar maples in the understory and spicebush in the shrub layer. Beechdrops can be seen beneath a large beech tree that appears to guard the approach to a very narrow footbridge across a seasonal stream. Beyond the bridge, the trail turns upstream and winds its way up the hill, then turns right around the hillside

to pass giant white oak trees, as well as a beautiful, straight, wild black cherry, and finally arrives at the fallen giant of the forest—a huge tuliptree that succumbed to a windstorm in the summer of 1995. Somewhere in my files is a slide of me standing in front of this tree in 1972. That was the first of many visits I made to Dysart Woods, and the tuliptree was magnificent to behold. I had to use binoculars to see the leaves on its lower limbs to identify its species. Even in death and returning to the earth, it is an impressive specimen.

The trail continues to make its way though the open forest of huge white oak and tuliptrees as it drops downslope to the creek. Down the valley, at a fork in the stream, the trail crosses the streambed on another picturesque but rather insubstantial 2-foot-wide bridge with a single handrail. There is a nice small photogenic waterfall downstream from the bridge. Fifty feet beyond is another footbridge that looks even less durable. The trail winds and dips, but mostly climbs as it makes its way toward the township road. As the trail makes an oblique approach to the road, multiflora rose begins to appear in the understory. At the road, a sign suggests crossing over to take the Blue Trail, the entrance to which is about 60 feet up the road to the left.

The Blue Trail begins between a poison ivy–covered black walnut tree and a hawthorn tree, then heads on a wide, grassy trail toward the woods. The grass runs out as the trail enters a young wood of maple, ash, tuliptree, and other hardwoods. Soon the trail reaches an area of open forest with good-sized trees. A wood thrush broke out in song as I passed through here in the summer of 1996. At a trail junction you have the option of exploring more deep woods by taking a short loop trail to the left, or continuing straight to the parking lot on this trail. Take the loop trail, of course. A less traveled trail, it winds among large beech and maple trees where spicebush makes up the shrub layer. It looks as if it would be a great spring wildflower trail. At a large blank sign, intended to tell you that this is as far as you can travel up this valley, turn right and hang onto the side of the hill as the trail returns to where it began.

Turning downhill and then downstream, the trail soon reaches a bridge over a small stream. At the far end of the bridge there are steps poorly carved into the hillside, and there was once a handrail here to help the hiker up a short steep place. Once over this hurdle, the trail climbs steeply up a ridge between two streams. The trees along here are of incredible dimensions. At the top of the slope, the trail turns left to follow a fairly level terrace for about 100 feet before breaking through the edge of the woods onto the parking lot.

This extra-special woodland is a place to cherish, as are your memories of a walk along its trails. It strikes me as a place to return to—at different seasons of the year and at different times of the day. It's a place to share with the other living creatures whose presence makes it so very special.

25

Lake Katharine State Nature Preserve

Total distance: 4½ miles (7.2 km)

Hiking time: 3 hours

Maximum elevation: 800 feet

Vertical rise: 170 feet

Maps: USGS 7½' Jackson; ODNR Lake Katharine State Nature Preserve map

More species of plants have been recorded from Jackson County than any other in Ohio. This fact could be attributed to the late Circleville farmer and botanist Floyd Bartley, who spent decades collecting in the area. In addition, this area served as a refugium for plants from the Teays River Basin during glaciation. Because of its deep, cool ravines, it retained relict communities of boreal plants after the last glacier melted. Bigleaf magnolia, a tree of the southern highlands whose northern limit is only a few miles to the north, is found on the preserve. The rare round-leaf catchfly grows on the slopes below the sandstone cliffs of the preserve, and the small, thorny tree known as Hercules'-club can be found in the mixed mesophytic woods that dominate the area.

Though unusual plants and spectacular cliffs reaching as high as 150 feet in places are the main features of Lake Katharine Preserve, wildlife also abounds. Deer and wild turkey are seen often, and bobcats have been reported from the area in years past. Needless to say, the spring wildflowers are spectacular, and for many years the Division of Natural Areas and Preserves has conducted a wildflower workshop here at the peak of the wildflower season. Information on this and other programs is available on the bulletin board in front of the lodge or from the division office in Columbus.

There are no facilities for picnicking or camping at Lake Katharine, but both are available at Lake Alma State Park about 12 miles to the north off OH 93, just above Wellston. For the person interested in in-

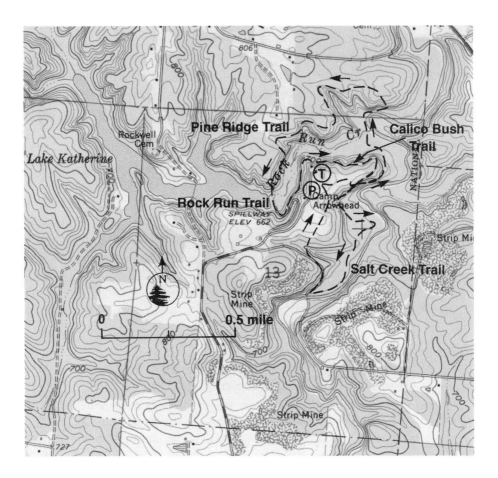

dustrial archaeology, there are a number of old charcoal-fired iron furnaces located in the area around Jackson. A map giving their locations is available from the Ohio Historical Society in Columbus.

Lake Katharine offers good fishing for bass and panfish, but fishing is on a written-reservation basis only. Restricted to five boats per day, with no motors of any sort allowed, fishing is permitted Monday through Friday between April 1 and October 31. To obtain a permit, call 614-286-2487 during normal working hours on the last Friday of the month before the month for which fishing permission is desired. To reach the lake, you must haul your boat down a 110-yard slope, which, of course, you must clamber back up to leave.

How to Get There

The preserve can be reached from Chillicothe by traveling US 35 to Jackson. Turn right (east) onto County Road 84, following it 3 miles into Jackson to State Street. Follow State Street out of town (it becomes County Road 76) for about 2 miles, then turn right onto County Road 60. After traveling a little over I mile, this road ends at the location of old Camp Arrowhead, where the preserve office and trailheads are located. It

This blockhouse at Lake Katharine remains from Camp Arrowhead days.

takes about 2 hours to reach the preserve from the Columbus area.

From the Cincinnati area, travel OH 32 to the OH 93 exit on the south side of Jackson. Turn left and take OH 93 north past downtown Jackson to State Street, where it makes a right turn. Instead of turning right, turn left there, and follow the directions above.

The Trail

At the right end of the parking lot, three trails head toward the woods' edge: the Calico Bush Trail, the Pine Ridge Trail, and the Salt Creek Trail. This hike uses all three in a figure-8 manner. You will travel the top loop in a counterclockwise direction, and the lower loop clockwise.

About 200 feet from the parking lot, the combined trail passes through a stand of young tuliptrees, then encounters Virginia pines before entering mature oak woods.

The trail turns right when the old road it has been following continues straight. Rock outcroppings begin to appear on the right, with hemlock and mountain laurel making an appearance. Fifty feet beyond a sign for Salt Creek Trail there is another sign that points to the right for the Pine Ridge Trail and to the left for the Calico Bush Trail. (After hiking the Pine Ridge Trail, you will come back to this point from the left on the Calico Bush Trail. You then go back up the combined trails to leave to the left [south] on the Salt Creek Trail.)

Going right, the Pine Ridge Trail heads down an old logging skid, with cliffs on the left. At the bottom of the slope the trail turns left, then right, then crosses bottomland before crossing a bridge across Rock Run close to where it empties into Salt Lick Creek. The latter gently curves to the right. Cliffs appear on the left, with tall hemlock at their base, and tuliptree, bigleaf magnolia, and wahoo on the talus slope. The cliffs end, then reappear. The trail heads up the valley. There is a good spicebush understory in this area. Large slump blocks of the Sharon conglomerate, the exposed rock of the preserve, lie between the trail and the overhanging cliff. A small arrow indicates a turn from the old road uphill to the left. In wintertime you can see US 35 traffic and a farmstead from here. The trail climbs, using multiple switchbacks, reaching the Virginia pine–covered summit shortly. It then winds its way through young hardwood, with an occasional young white pine and ground pine on the forest floor.

The trail drops to hardwood-covered hillside above Rock Run Creek and follows the hillside just above the steep, hemlock-covered slope. It then climbs back to the pine-topped ridge, from which it likely got its name. There is an interesting invasion of young hemlock under the pines in this area. The trail can be particularly handsome given a light snowfall. Two short boardwalks cross a wet area above the cliffs. Here the forest contains a lot of red oak, white oak, and chestnut oak with an occasional scarlet oak. The trail leaves the ridge, dropping into the hemlock-filled valley to a small footbridge below a rock face. Moving alongside the cliff, it drops to the bridge over the Lake Katharine spillway, then emerges from the woods to cross the lake's earthen dam.

Beyond the dam, the path enters a hemlock woods, heading uphill past a cliffside on the right that shows evidence of having once been quarried. Bore holes for blasting charges are visible. About two-thirds of the way up the slope, a sign indicates that the Pine Ridge Trail leaves the roadway and turns left. Take the five wooden steps to the left and follow a lovely trail through young hemlock below low cliffs. After 100 feet, a sign indicates that the Pine Ridge Trail goes

upslope to the right toward the road, that the parking lot is straight ahead, and that the Calico Bush Trail goes to the left.

To continue the hike, follow the Calico Bush Trail as it travels among the calico bush and hemlock just downslope from rock outcroppings. Here you can easily see the layers of quartz pebbles in the Sharon conglomerate. Shortly the trail meets the Pine Ridge Trail, completing a loop. After a right turn, in 50 feet the combined trails split, with the Salt Creek Trail going to the left down the hillside and the trail to the right taking you back to the parking lot.

If you want to go farther, take the Salt Creek Trail to the left. The trail follows the old road downhill, then turns right up a set of wooden steps between a cliff and a slump block. There are lots of pebbles in the rock wall here. The trail descends to the valley floor and continues beneath the base of the 75-foot-tall cliffs along the stream edge. It then goes up another set of steps to travel along the middle level of the conglomerate. Where the cliff meets the stream, the trail climbs nearly to the clifftop via the stairs, then returns via more steps to the valley floor. The sheer cliff face demonstrates centuries of erosion as the stream cut deeper into the valley. At a boardwalk beneath a cliff overhang, the layer of quartz pebbles in the conglomerate lies about 6 feet above the ground. There are ant lion holes in the dry sand below the overhang. This is a good place to observe vertical fractures and horizontal bedding in the rock, a quartz pebble lens, and honeycomb erosion.

A sign points left to the long loop and straight ahead to the short loop. Go left, where you cross a wet area on several hundred feet of boardwalk, passing beneath umbrella magnolia, sweet gum, red oak, black oak, spicebush, and hemlock. Reaching a nearly pure stand of hemlock, the trail

The common name "catchfly" is used for two of the most attractive wildflowers of the state: one a plant of the woods, the other of the prairies, although the two are closely related. There are only five native wildflowers that are scarlet in color: Oswego tea (Monarda didyma), a mint; cardinalflower (Lobelia cardinalis), of the bellflower family; and three members of the pink family, fire-pink (Silene virginica), round-leafed catchfly (S. rotundifolia), and royal catchfly (S. regio). The name catchfly is used for a number of other members of the genus Silene, including some from Europe. Where did that strange name come from? All three of these bright-red-flowered Silenes of our Ohio flora have what could best be described as sticky stems. They have a viscid sap that exudes from the stem. If you touch them, they feel tacky, but it does not come off on your skin. Most botanists believe that this sap prevents crawling insects from stealing the nectar without pollinating the flower.

The Latin name is also derived from this sticky characteristic. Most sources say it comes from the Greek word sialon, which means "saliva." Another opinion is that it is named for Silenus, who was Bacchus's foster father in Greek mythology and was said to have been found with sticky beer all over his face. Believe what you wish, but do gently touch the stem of the next fire-pink or round-leafed catchfly you come across on a southeastern Ohio hillside, or the next royal catchfly you encounter in a prairie preserve in Madison County. Don't pick it, though. Let it live in your memory, not die in your hand.

goes up and then back down the slope, with the cliffs above disappearing and reappearing. It bears left to cross a Little Salt Creek tributary on a bridge, then swings right to follow once again the right bank of Little Salt Creek. Cliffs and hemlock are visible across the stream, and magnolia along the trail. Passing through a hemlock stand on an old sandbar, the trail moves at floodplain level through sycamores, cottonwoods, and willows before passing more magnolia. As the stream moves back toward the cliff face on the right, an arrow on a post indicates that the trail goes right up an old road. After a steady climb of several hundred yards through hardwood forest, the trail turns right to cross streams on bridges at the heads of ravines. It then follows the hillside to the left, rising and falling as it crosses more small streams that parallel the hemlock/hardwood ecotone. Moving back into hemlock and then uphill to hardwood, the trail continues to climb, passing an especially handsome shagbark hickory. A left turn and a gentle curve left take you to just inside the edge of the woods. In a few hundred feet, the trail emerges from the woods just below a blockhouse that was part of the old camp. It then passes through a pine planting and meadow to return to the trailhead and parking lot.

26

Scioto Trail State Park and Forest

Total distance: 4½ miles (7.24 km)

Hiking time: 3 hours

Maximum elevation: 1100 feet

Vertical rise: 271 feet

Maps: USGS 7½' Waverly North; ODNR Scioto Trail State Park map; ODNR Scioto State Forest map

The Scioto Trail was the main route taken by Native Americans to travel between the neutral hunting grounds in Kentucky and the fishing grounds of Sandusky Bay and Lake Erie. The trail ran from the present-day Portsmouth up the Scioto and Olentangy River valleys and down the valley of the Sandusky River to the marshes at the head of Sandusky Bay. It was probably the most traveled trail of Native American days. The route was nearly level across the state, except in Pike County, where a narrowing of the valley necessitated going over the hills, and in Ross County, where it left the Scioto valley to head north, only to return via Indian Creek to the same valley east of Chillicothe.

Today, US 23 follows the route of the Scioto Trail (or Warriors' Path) from its southern terminus to Upper Sandusky. The 9616-acre state forest and park complex that lies in the triangle between the highway and the Scioto River near the Ross Pike county line keeps alive the name of the famous Native American and frontier footpath and wagon road.

Because of the large acreage uninterrupted by roads, the Scioto Trail is an excellent place to see and hear woodland birds during their spring breeding season. Wild turkey and ruffed grouse are common, and the camper will often go to sleep with whippoorwills calling nearby. Deer, squirrel, raccoon, and other native mammals abound.

Scioto Trail State Park has 55 campsites, 20 with electricity. There are several more miles of hiking trails and 17 miles of bridle trails in the park/forest complex. Fishing in Caldwell Lake is allowed, but no motors other than electric trolling motors are permitted.

The outdoor drama *Tecumseh!,* written by Allan W. Eckert, author of *The Frontiersmen,* is presented from late June through early September at the Sugarloaf Mountain Amphitheater just north of Chillicothe. There is an admission fee.

The Hopewell Culture National Historic Park on OH 104 northwest of Chillicothe contains a prehistoric Hopewell Indian complex of 23 mounds as well as a museum and visitors center. Adena, the estate of Ohio's first governor, Thomas Worthington, is located in Chillicothe and is operated as a state memorial by the Ohio Historical Society.

How to Get There

The entrance to Scioto Trail State Park and Forest is along US 23, where the old trail crosses the divide between the south-flowing Crooked Creek watershed and the north-flowing Indian Run. OH 372 (Stoney Creek Road) goes east into the state-owned land. Fifty-seven miles from Colum-bus, the trailhead is about an hour's drive from the city's south outerbelt.

The Trail

The trail leaves the south side of Park Road No. 3, Lake Road, just west of the parking area at the upper end of Lake Caldwell. It enters the woods and immediately climbs steeply. After leveling off, the path curves to the right around the hillside where, having traveled ¼ mile, it joins a trail coming in from the right from the campground. From that point the trail climbs to a ridge, which it follows nearly due west for more than 1 mile. A sign at a side trail to the right identifies the DeBord Loop, a short trail to a scenic viewpoint named for former park manager Leonard DeBord. Following it will bring you back to the main trail, which continues west along the more than 1000-foot-high ridge. After gently rising and falling several times, the trail intersects Park Road No. 3. Turning left against traffic on this sparsely traveled, one-way road, the trail passes a radio tower

A replica of the first Presbyterian church in the Northwest Territory is located near the trailhead.

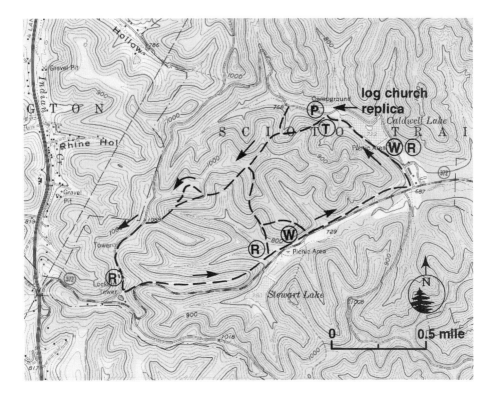

on the right and, after ½ mile of road travel, reaches the fire lookout tower. Staffed only during periods of high fire risk, the tower allows for a good view and photographs of the surrounding countryside, even if the tower room is closed. In the autumn, the kaleidoscope of color is especially nice.

The trail leaves the road on a utility right-of-way, which exits to the left about 150 feet before you reach the fire tower. After a gentle ¾-mile descent down a hill used for sledding in the wintertime, the trail reaches a pine grove and a parking lot used for a walk-in camping area located about ½ mile from the road above Stewart Lake.

The main trail continues along the right-of-way, passing the park pump house, where drinking water is available at a hydrant. Paralleling Park Road No. 1, the trail passes a stand of hemlock, then hugs the hillside at an elevation of about 750 feet. It drops to cross the stream that flows out of Caldwell Lake. Beyond the stream, which is fordable most of the year, the trail turns left. It goes upstream past a picnic area (where there are public toilets) to arrive shortly at the Caldwell Lake dam. Following the left side of the lake, it passes the park water plant before returning to the point of origin.

27

Shawnee State Forest (Backpack Trail)

Total distance: 6¾ to 36 miles (10.8 to 62 km)

Hiking time: 1 to 7 days

Maximum elevation: 1280 feet

Vertical rise: 682 feet

Maps: USGS 7½' Buena Vista; USGS 7½' Otway; USGS 7½' Pond Run; USGS 7½' West Portsmouth; USGS 7½' Friendship; ODNR Shawnee State Forest and Backpack Trail map

The hills of Shawnee State Forest, in the rugged Appalachian Plateau country of western Scioto County, have been called Ohio's Little Smokies. From the highest points in the forest, you see ridge after ridge rolling away to the horizon in a gentle blue haze. The color comes from the moisture in the air, generated by the thousands of acres of forest.

At 59,603 acres, Shawnee State Forest is Ohio's largest public landholding. Lying as it does just north of the Ohio River, to which all streams in the southern two-thirds of the state flow, it also has the greatest relief of any state forest. The area was hunting ground for the Shawnee Indians, one of the last tribes to occupy Ohio as the frontier was being pushed back. Having migrated from the south into the Ohio valley, the Shawnees called themselves the Shaawanwaaki, literally "the Southerners." The Shawnees established a major village, known as Lower Town, near the confluence of the Scioto and Ohio Rivers. As pressure from white settlers mounted, they moved northward up the Scioto valley and then northwest into the valleys of the Little Miami, Mad, and Great Miami Rivers. Eventually they were defeated and driven from the state.

Prior to pioneer settlement, a mixed oak forest covered these ridges. The valleys and coves were mixed mesophytic forest, with good stands of beech on some of the gentler slopes. Game, including deer, black bear, wolf, beaver, and river otter, was abundant. Bird life was plentiful. These resources housed, heated, fed, and clothed the settlers trying to make it in the wilderness. By

Shoes in hand, the author wades a stream on Shawnee State Forest Backpack Trail.

the early part of the 20th century, the virgin timber was exhausted and the big-game animals gone. The land was too rugged to provide a living from farming, so many descendants of the early settlers abandoned the land for homes and factories in the big cities. The production of moonshine was one of the last profitable enterprises of the area, and the federal "revenuers" did not take kindly to that activity. Shawnee State Forest was established in 1922 with the purchase of 5000 acres of land that had been cut over for timber and ravaged by fire. During the same year, acquisition was begun for the Theodore Roosevelt Game Preserve. These were the first of many purchases made to assemble the large state forest and park complex of today.

In 1973, a 22¾-mile-loop foot trail lying north of OH 125 was constructed. A year later, nearly 40 more miles of foot trails were opened south of the highway, completing what is called the Shawnee Backpack Trail. The 29-mile south loop of the backpack trail is described here, but you can easily add the Shawnee Wilderness Area side trail to make a 36-mile, 6-night trek.

Designated camping areas complete with outhouses lie along the trail, and all but one have fresh drinking water available nearby. All water supply sites are along forest service roads, where Division of Forestry tank trucks can reach them. They consist of buried tanks with a spring-loaded, frost-free hydrant located about 25 feet downhill. The Division of Forestry may not service water tanks in the winter due to bad road conditions. If in doubt, inquire at the Forest Headquarters before starting out on the trail.

A word of warning: This is copperhead and timber rattlesnake country. It is unlikely that either will be encountered, but you should be mindful that these creatures share the forest. Be especially careful when

Shawnee State Forest (Backpack Trail)

stepping over logs and through deadfalls and brush. It is also wise to use caution when scrambling over rocks. Vigilance is the best snakebite prevention. Do not kill any living thing along the trail, including poisonous or nonpoisonous snakes. Given some space, they will always move out of your way. Ticks and deerflies can also be a nuisance at certain times of the year, so be prepared to deal with these pests.

Shawnee State Forest is one of Ohio's most precious resources. It is home to many species of amphibians, reptiles, and mammals, and, because of the vast tracts of forest, to a great many species of birds. In recent years a black bear was seen in a remote part of the forest, and deer and wild turkey are seen frequently. Many rare or endangered species of plants live on the ridges and hillsides and in the ravines of the forest, protected so that future generations of Ohioans may know their natural heritage. It is a special privilege to be able to hike in this vast preserve where, except for the passing of an occasional airplane, the only sounds are those of the natural world. In a state as densely populated as Ohio, its citizens are indeed fortunate that such an area was set aside so long ago.

How to Get There
Shawnee State Forest and Park are easily reached from the central Ohio area by going south on US 23 to Portsmouth. There, travel west on US 52 and OH 125. The distance from Columbus is 120 miles, requiring about 2½ hours traveling time.

From Cincinnati, the trip takes 2 hours and is a little over 90 miles via OH 125. There is a large state park sign on the north side of OH 125 about midway into the state forest. The turn leads to the resort lodge, park office, housekeeping cabins, and the Turkey Creek Lake beach. You also turn

here to reach the Shawnee Backpack trailhead. Immediately after the turn onto the park road, a driveway to the right leads to the trailhead parking lot. A sign along the right side of the lot says SHAWNEE FOREST BACKPACK TRAIL PARKING. A sign on a wooden kiosk says SHAWNEE BACKPACK TRAIL INFORMATION. PLEASE REGISTER. One box on the front of the kiosk holds maps, and another contains self-registration cards. It is important that every hiker register. Registration cards are checked daily, and if you do not return to your vehicle close to the time and date indicated on the registration card, rangers begin a search. The map includes a list of trail tips, backpack trail rules, and a list of emergency telephone numbers.

Alternate Routes
The Shawnee Backpack Trail is divided into loops and segments that, combined with sections of the forest road system, can provide a great variety of hikes lasting from 1 to 9 days. With the usual precautions, day-hikers can park cars along the roads with a reasonable expectation that they will not be bothered. Overnight hikers should leave their vehicles on patrolled lots and inform park or forest personnel of their plans.

There are a number of places where the backpack trail can be combined with sections of the gravel forest roads for nice day hikes. I strongly recommend combining the 4½-mile S-N-T section of the trail with a 1⅓-mile walk along the road from Point T to Point S. The scenery and serenity along this section, which is in the Shawnee Wilderness Area, are hard to beat. With two vehicles, one parked at Point S and one at Point T, you can avoid the road.

Point J is a good point of origin for another backpack trail and forest roads. You can park your vehicle on the lighted lot in front of the log cabin at the Vern Riffe Civilian Conservation Corps (CCC) camp and walk up the road to begin hiking the back-pack trail at Point J. A 14¾-mile loop, with the possibility of overnighting at Camp 5 and/or Camp 6, can be obtained by hiking the J-K-L-M-N-O segments of the trail (see Days 3–5) and returning to the CCC camp via Forest Roads 2 and 1. Replacing the N-O segment with the N-S-T-P Shawnee Wilderness Area side trail and returning to Point J via the P-O segment of the main trail and Forest Roads 2 and 1 makes a 23-mile loop with three camps available along the way.

Walking the north loop, segments A-B-C-D-E-F-G-H-A, provides a 22¾-mile trip, which can be done in 3 or 4 days. There are three overnight campsites along the way. This loop contains the most rugged terrain on the backpack trail.

The Trail

Day 1: Trailhead to Camp 3
Distance: 4½ miles (6.4 km)
The trail begins with 13 log steps on the north side of OH 125, across the road and slightly to the left of the trailhead shelter. This is the starting point for hiking the entire trail, the north loop only, or the south loop only, and is shown as Point A on the map. At the edge of the woods are two signs, the first of many to be encountered at road crossings along the trail. The one on the left says SHAWNEE BACKPACK TRAIL SEG. A.B. To walk the entire trail or the north loop, turn left here. The turn to the right, following the sign that says SHAWNEE BACKPACK TRAIL SEG. A.H., will start you on the south loop, the route described here. The main trail is blazed with orange paint, and white paint is used to blaze the side trails. The orange blazes are well spaced, with one almost always in sight. If you do not see blazes after a few minutes, backtrack and see if you missed a turn. The

white blazes on side trails are sometimes a bit more sparse.

Having left Point A with a right turn, you cross over three washes and a 5-acre area that was burned over by a human-caused fire in 1981. The trail parallels OH 125 on the end of a ridge, then drops into Williamson Hollow. Heading upstream, you cross two small streams before climbing the next ridge. The trail drops partway down the other side of the ridge and travels along the hillside above Long Hollow, headed downstream. After dropping to cross the stream, you will see a "wild" trail, which goes to the Roosevelt Lake campground. The main trail climbs and heads downstream. The path nears the phone-line right-of-way and turns left to follow this clearing near OH 125. Climbing again, it traverses the heads of two small ravines before cresting the ridge. It switches back to the left as it descends the ridge. The trail travels along a side ravine until it crosses the small creek and heads downstream, where it crosses the main stream of Upper Shaw Hollow. After climbing over the end of a ridge, the trail meets an old road climbing in from the right. Together, they head up Lower Shaw Hollow and cross the streambed. After crossing the creek, the trail leaves the old road and begins climbing to a rock-strewn side wash. A quarter mile later, you reach Point H, 4⅔ miles from Point A. A sign at Point H directs you to Camp 3. The campsite is located on a wooded point about 200 feet above Turkey Creek, so it is wise to pick up water before heading up the side trail.

Day 2: Camp 3 to Camp 4
Distance: 5½ miles (8.8 km)
Head south from Point H past the sign pointing to the water supply. Just beyond, the trail enters an open field, which it crosses to the left, heading for the water

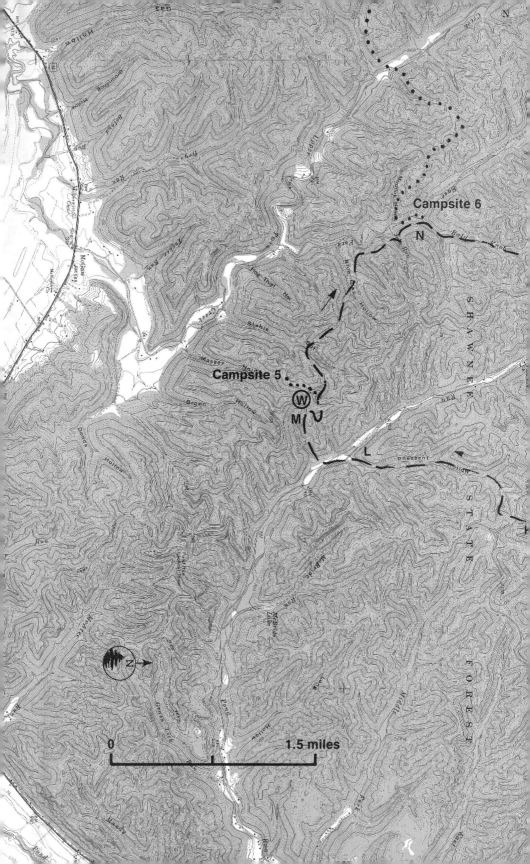

Campsite 6

Campsite 5

N

0   1.5 miles

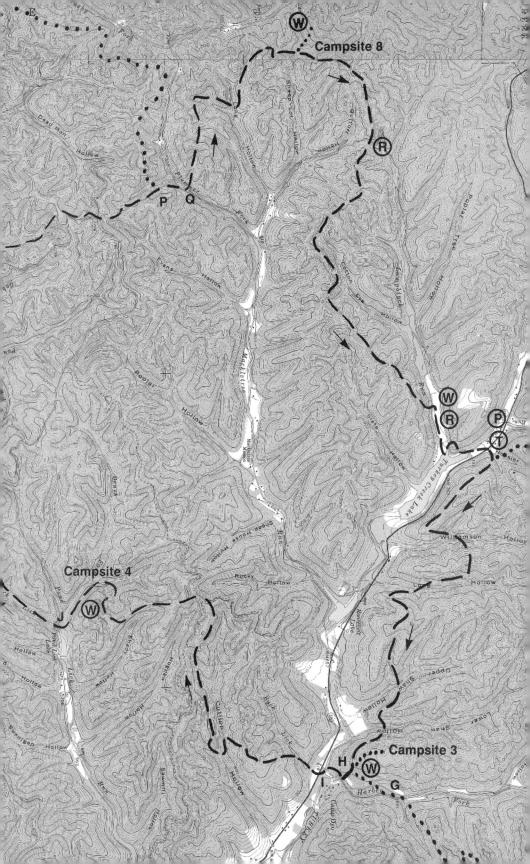

Campsite 8

Campsite 4

Campsite 3

supply road. The orange-blazed trail turns right onto Forest Road 1, where it almost immediately crosses Turkey Creek. It then crosses OH 125, on which it turns left. About 25 feet beyond a group of mailboxes, the trail leaves the highway through an opening in the rose hedge. After crossing an open field, the trail passes through another rose hedge and into the woods. Beyond an abandoned road crossing, it skirts the left end of a small pond that has a rock cliff hanging above it and hemlock trees overhead.

After the pond, the trail climbs to the right to get above the cliff, then heads left uphill. Soon it is paralleling the beautiful Buck Lick Gorge below it on the left. The trail drops into the sandstone gorge, where it crosses the stream and heads briefly up the gorge. It then angles up the left slope, headed for the corner of state property. (State forest boundaries are blazed with yellow paint.) It follows an old wagon trail shortly, but it soon exits to the left and, after crossing the heads of several ravines, begins a slow descent into Cutlipp Hollow, once again on state land. This valley abounds in wildflowers in the spring.

When the trail reaches the creek, it turns left, downstream, to the first side stream on the right. It climbs rather steeply beside this stream to a knob at 950 feet. Turning left at the knob, it continues a gentler but steady climb up the ridge and the left flank of Cutlipp Hollow. There it passes through a magnificent stand of large oak trees with many wildflowers, including the rare spotted mandarin, scattered on the forest floor. Passing to the right of an 1160-foot knob, the trail joins the fire access road utilized by the Pond Lick Bridle Trail and reaches a saddle on the ridge. The bridle trail and hiking trail separate and rejoin twice, with the Back-

pack Trail taking the higher ground to the right and the road to the left. The downhill slope to the left is covered with an even-aged stand of mixed oaks and hickories, the result of a clear-cut operation made 20 or so years ago. Quite a bit of mountain laurel grows here, even under the secondary-growth forest.

Where the road goes to the left, the trail turns right over a high knob that is more than 600 feet above the benchmark at the entrance to Cutlipp Hollow. Beyond that high point, the trail rejoins the road, and Mackletree Bridle Trail comes in from the right. Your route once more drops off the ridge to the right of the bridle trail, then comes back up to the ridge to cross the bridle trail and leave it for good. The Back-pack Trail swings left to follow a ridge and cross over or pass around knobs to the south for about ¾ mile. The trees are large here and the forest rather open. Greenbrier once again can be an annoyance along the trail. When the ridge ends, the trail drops from 1160 feet to 760 feet, the elevation of Camp 4, in ½ mile.

Where the trail reaches the valley bottom, there is a T. Camp 4 is across the creek to the right. In contrast to previous camps, there is no long side trail to this one. Apparently because of its closeness to the road, the campground appears to be heavily used. The sound of the nearby rippling water is conducive to a good night's sleep.

The water supply is beyond the camp along the main trail. This water tank is the most recently installed on the trail, replacing a former water source at the nearby CCC camp that was frequently vandalized. The new tank is slightly up the left flank of the valley and may be partially obscured by wildflowers in the late summer, but it can be found by looking for the access road.

Day 3: Camp 4 to Camp 5
Distance: 5 miles (7.8 km)

The trail leaves Camp 4 by heading downstream out of the valley and past the water supply. Following a logging road, the trail heads toward Pond Lick. A cable blocks vehicular access to the valley. The trail leaves the road to the right to cross Pond Lick just upstream from Pond Lick Lake. This crossing requires removing shoes and socks and walking across. After the crossing, the trail goes to the paved road. This is Point J, the distance from Point I at the OH 125 crossing being 5¼ miles. The Vern Riffe CCC camp is located a few hundred yards down the valley beyond Pond Lick Lake.

Leaving Point J, the trail goes to the right, up the paved Pond Lick Road, for about 15 feet before turning left to enter the mouth of the Rock Lick Creek valley. This is a damp section of trail. A half mile from Pond Lick Road, the trail passes a hillside on the left that was recently clear-cut. After traveling below the timber harvest area for ⅓ mile, the trail climbs and turns left onto a ridge where you can get a different view of the regenerating forest. The trail then crosses Forest Road 2, the Panorama Road, about ¼ mile from its intersection with the McBride Road, Forest Road 13. This is point K, almost 2 miles beyond Point J.

After crossing the road, the trail reenters the woods, travels a ridge for a short distance, then descends into Pheasant Hollow. How this hollow got its name is a puzzle, because this is not pheasant country. These big alien game birds do not survive in the hill country of southern Ohio, even if stocked there. Perhaps the native ruffed grouse was mistaken for pheasant. The trail reaches Pond Run Road, Forest Road 1, after 1½ miles of travel along a stream, which it crosses frequently. This is Point L, an easy 1¾-mile trek from the last checkpoint.

The trail now follows the road to the left to just before the bridge that crosses the branch coming out of Pheasant Hollow. There it turns right across a meadow to the riverine forest along Pond Run, where a stream crossing is required. This can be difficult, if not impossible, if the water is high. After the crossing the trail turns left, following a terrace above the stream. It swings right into the mouth of one ravine, crosses a small stream, then comes back out to the terrace. It heads downstream before entering another ravine to begin a climb to Forest Road 5, the Panorama Loop Road. This valley is very narrow and rocky and is filled with ferns and wildflowers. At the head of the valley, the trail ascends via four switchbacks to a ridge that carries it out to Forest Road 5. A tenth of a mile after the trail turns right onto the road, a white-blazed side trail leads out a ridge to the left to Camp 5, less than ½ mile away. This is Point M, only 1⅛ miles beyond Pond Lick Road, but the rigor of the walk might make it seem farther. The water supply is just off the gravel road to the left of the white-blazed trail. Since Camp 6 is only 2 miles away, many hikers skip this campsite to reduce their time on the trail by a day. The decision to do this requires careful thought, for the next 2 miles of trail are difficult and Camp 6 is the only site with no supply of fresh drinking water.

Day 4: Camp 5 to Camp 6
Distance: 2 miles (3.2 km)

Though only 2 miles long, the next section of trail may take as much as 2 hours to cover. Along this section of trail are a number of signs, erected by a local Sierra Club group, that interpret some of the natural features of the area. The RIVER OTTER sign at Camp 6 is perhaps wishful thinking, but if there are any wild populations of this beautiful mammal left in southern Ohio, this spot might be a likely place for them.

Leaving Point M, the trail drops off Forest Road 5 to the left just before the gravel road begins to make a curve to the right. It may be hard to see this exit when the tall summer wildflowers are at their peak. The trail heads west down a ridge, then drops off steeply to the left into a small ravine. It then turns right to descend 200 feet into Stable Gut Hollow. After crossing a stream, the trail begins a 400-foot climb. Quite steep at first, the trail uses three switchbacks to gain elevation with less slope. After crossing a 1060-foot saddle in the ridge, the trail turns left to descend on an angle into Blue Clay Hollow. Be careful not to slip, as I managed to do, on the steep sections of this trail. Eventually it uses a couple of switchbacks to slow the rate of descent.

The trail crosses the stream close to the mouth of the hollow, then heads up the valley of the East Fork of Upper Twin Creek, which is still out of sight off to the left. One side stream crossing goes over a sandstone ledge with a lovely low waterfall just to the left of the trail. In the springtime, treasures such as pink lady's slipper, showy orchis, and whorled pagonia can be seen along this section. Soon after passing through this picturesque area, the trail turns left downslope to come closer to the East Fork, then turns right up the valley on an old road. The deep cut that this old track has made into the earth indicates that it has seen much use over many decades. On the rainy day that I hiked here, the trail was more of a stream. After following this track for a short distance, the trail exits left and drops close to the stream. Still on the right bank of the East Fork, the trail skirts the left edge of an open brushy area, then returns to the old track to enter a stand of hemlock.

At the edge of this evergreen grove, a side trail goes left down to the stream. This is the side trail to the Shawnee Wilderness Area and one possible route to Camp 6. The orange-blazed main trail goes straight ahead under the hemlocks, where it shortly reaches Point N near the confluence of the East Fork and Bald Knob Run. In a hemlock grove across the East Fork, which at this point is cutting its way through sandstone bedrock, is Camp 6. This is the most remote of all the sites, and one you will not soon forget. Reaching the campsite from Point N requires a short ford, but it is well worth it. The outhouses are on the camp side of the East Fork, downstream about 100 feet.

Day 5: Camp 6 to Camp 8
Distance: 5½ miles (9 km)
A 10½-mile white-blazed side trail (N-S-T-P), about half of which is located in the Shawnee Wilderness Area, leaves from Camp 6. For those choosing to take this trail, a campsite is situated about 6½ miles down it.

The orange-blazed main trail from Camp 6 leaves the site from the opposite side of the East Fork. You can either ford the stream at the campsite or go downstream beyond the outhouses to the trail fork to cross and come back the other side. The trail follows the valley of Bald Knob Run, the right fork of the stream, for its entire length. Eventually the trail arcs up the slope around the head of the valley, making one switchback. It comes out on the ridge just short of Forest Road 5, the famous Panorama Loop that tourists drive while admiring the fall leaf coloration. There it turns left and stays just below and several hundred feet to the left of the road until it reaches Point O, 2½ miles from Camp 6. Although the trail climbs nearly 500 feet between Point N and Point O, it does so gradually.

The trail crosses the road directly. It starts down the center of a sloping ridge, then drops steeply off to the left before swinging around to the right in a more gradual drop, headed for the upper end of a small hollow. After crossing several side streams, it crosses the main stream to the left just before its junction with the Shawnee Wilderness Trail, Point P.

From Point P, the trail goes on out a hollow, through a small, weedy area, and then intersects Plummer Fork Road. This is Point Q, 1 mile beyond Point P.

The trail turns right for 50 feet of road travel before entering the woods to the left, just opposite a parking spot used by hunters and mushroomers. Twenty-five feet after leaving the road, the trail crosses Plummer's Fork, then turns left to begin a gradual 320-foot ascent to the ridgetop. After dropping in and out of one saddle, the trail enters a second saddle, from which it descends to the right into a small ravine that empties into yet another hollow, called Long Hollow. (Perhaps an early inhabitant's name was Long, for this hollow certainly is not long.) Turning to the left, upstream, the trail crosses the main stream once and a small side stream twice. It then enters a headwater ravine to climb rather easily to the ridge. The trail follows the ridge to the left and then swings to the right, passing a grassy area on the left. The path continues on the ridgetop until it drops into a saddle that was once crossed by a wagon trail.

The white-blazed side trail to Camp 8 goes to the left down the old wagon road. Descending the hill, the trail to the campground leaves the track to the right. At first glance the area around Camp 8 appears to have been recently timbered, but a closer inspection reveals the charred remains of a devastating, 500-acre arson fire that occurred in April 1981. What looks like logging was actually a salvage cut designed to recoup as much of the loss as possible by taking out the large trees killed by the fire. This cutting also helped prevent an infestation of forest insects and disease in the area, since injured trees are highly susceptible to such pests.

The water supply for this camp is 10 minutes away. Instead of turning right off the old road to Camp 8, follow the track downhill to where it makes a T with a logging road. Turn left and follow the logging road toward the paved road. The tank is on the hillside to the left of the logging road and can be spotted by the muddy track that swings up over it for refilling. The campground, or what is left of it since the fire, is on a gentle slope in a rather sparse stand of hardwoods. Two latrines are located around the hillside beyond the old road. Although it is about 5¾ miles from the Camp 8 side trail to the trailhead parking lot at Point A, the easy walk takes no more than 3½ hours. With a sufficient number of remaining daylight hours, you can bypass Camp 8 and reduce the length of your trip by a day.

Day 6: Camp 8 to Trailhead
Distance: 6½ miles (10.5 km)
The main trail back to Point A is an easy one. It continues out the ridge for a little less than 1 mile, then leaves the right side of the ridge to drop to Point R at Forest Road 16. The openness of the forest along the ridge reveals more about the 1981 fire. Just before the trail reaches the gravel road, it passes a short auto lane littered with the trash of modern American civilization, the only really unsightly spot along the entire trail. The trek from Point Q at Plummer's Fork to Point R has totaled 3¾ miles.

The last leg of the Shawnee Backpack Trail covers a distance of 4¾ miles. From Point R, it climbs immediately to a ridge,

➤ Minimum-Impact Camping

Campsite etiquette has changed quite dramatically in the 50 years that I have been hiking the trails of the Buckeye State. Gone are the days of treated-cotton canvas army surplus pup tents with hastily dug trenches around them to carry away the runoff. So too is the practice of doing your business over a fallen log in the woods, leaving toilet tissue to "weather" away. Big, roaring evening fires just for the sake of the ambience are also taboo.

Backpackers are expected to practice extremely low-impact camping. That means no damage to trees, and minimal damage to the ground cover; no open fires for cooking, and fires for warmth only in emergencies. Plan to carry out all empty food containers. Bury human waste sufficiently deep that animals won't unearth it, and many yards away from the trail and any water source. Use little or no soap for washing up, and dig a hole in which to dispose of your gray water. Don't forget to fill it in before you leave. Respect the desire for space and privacy of other campers. If others are nearby, keep your noise level reasonable at all hours. When you pack up your tent, return the leaf litter in the footprint of the tent to as near like you found it as possible. Leave your campsite in a natural-looking condition.

---

which it then more or less follows for 2½ miles. The drop to the Lampblack Run valley and the end of the hike begins when the trail hits an old wagon trail, which it follows for a short spell before dropping off to the left to begin its descent. Sometimes following a rock-strewn wash, and several times using switchbacks, the trail soon reaches a hillside terrace that it travels for a short distance. It then uses two more switchbacks to drop to the valley floor opposite the park service center. Blazes seem to end as a paved road near the beach comes into view. A wooden bridge to the left leads across an embayment of Turkey Creek Lake, beyond which a smaller bridge crosses another stream. A concrete staircase then leads up to the lodge driveway. Following the blacktopped road to the right, across Turkey Creek and to the parking lot, completes the trail.

28

Tar Hollow State Park and Forest

Total distance: 12 miles (19.3 km)

Hiking time: 7 hours

Maximum elevation: 1200 feet

Vertical rise: 498 feet

Maps: USGS 7½' Hallsville; USGS 7½' Laurelville; USGS 7½' Londonderry; USGS 7½' Ratcliffburg; BSA Troop 104, Dayton, Logan Trail map; ODNR Tar Hollow State Forest map

Tar Hollow State Park and Forest lie just east of where the glaciers ended, close to the intersection of Ross, Hocking, and Vinton Counties. When the area is approached from Circleville, the unglaciated hill country can be seen from the high hills 5 miles east of that city. The country is rugged, with little mineral wealth. Its major asset at the time of settlement was the trees that covered the steep hillsides and narrow valleys. Now dominated by several species of oak, the forest once contained the native American chestnut and, on some of the ridges, pitch pine. When cleared, the rocky hillsides of the area could barely grow enough crops for a family to eke out a living; so, in addition to cutting the virgin hardwood for lumber, the settlers distilled pine tar from the pitch pine.

Pine tar was commonplace on the shelves of many 19th-century households. It was blended with grain alcohol and used as an expectorant or, in its viscous form, as an antiseptic salve. It also served as a sticky lubricant for the wooden gears and axles of early implements. With the advent of petroleum distillates, pine tar fell into disuse. What probably was never a very lucrative enterprise died out, leaving only another place-name derived from its long-gone economic activity—in this case, Tar Hollow.

Tar Hollow is a special place for wildlife. Turkey, deer, squirrel, ruffed grouse, pileated woodpeckers, and many species of woodland songbirds abound. Since all but the park area is open to public hunting, it is a good idea to avoid the area during the week of deer gun season in the fall and the short turkey season in the spring. The wildflowers are beautiful during the last week of April and the first two weeks of May, and dozens of species of mushrooms can be seen throughout the warm months. Tar Hollow should be visited often, for despite its size and nearness to the well-known Hocking Hills parks, it is not very heavily used. It deserves to be better known, for its excellent Logan Trail if for no other reason.

The hiking trail system at Tar Hollow owes its existence to neither the Civilian Conservation Corps nor the state. The present-day Logan Trail, with its north and south loops originating out of the park area, was developed by Boy Scout Troop 195 of Columbus and is currently maintained by Troop 104 of Dayton. Named for the famous Mingo Indian chief, the trail was originally opened in 1958, using park and forest roads. It was not popular with Scout units, however, who felt that in a state forest hiking should be on woodland trails. Completely shut down and carefully rerouted off roads and into the woods, the trail was reopened in 1965. I walked the trail with my Scout troop shortly after its reopening. Like most Scout trails, an award is available to Scouts and Scouters who complete the hike. Unit leaders can get more information about the trail from Roy Case, Logan Trail Treasurer, 643 Weyant Avenue, Columbus, OH 43213. The hike described here utilizes only part of the 21-mile Logan Trail. To walk the entire trail requires 14 or 15 hours of daylight.

The Logan Trail is well marked. There are directional and checkpoint number signs on 4 x 4 posts at road crossings and other appropriate points along the trail. In some places, red metal arrows are nailed to trees. The trail is blazed with red paint, but because it is designed to be walked in only one direction, it is blazed only in the direction of the numbered checkpoints. If you do not see a blaze after 100 feet or so, retrace your steps, as you probably missed a turn. Although road crossings are minimal on this neatly laid-out trail, the few that do remain allow you to walk shorter loop hikes utilizing the forest roads. The trail has been divided into named segments between numbered checkpoints, which are, for the most part, at road crossings.

There is no potable water along the route, so you must either carry a supply for the full trip or cache some water at one or more of the checkpoints. Camping is not allowed along the trail. A primitive, pack-in camping area known as Camp N.A. Dulen, located about midway on a 2-mile side loop off the south loop, is available for Scout units. Troops or posts planning to camp there must inform the park ranger in advance. There is a drive-in campground in the park for use by the general public and backpackers are permitted to camp at the fire tower area. At the latter site, a small fee can be paid at a self-registration-system kiosk.

How to Get There

Tar Hollow is reached from the Columbus area by traveling south on US 23 to Circleville. From Circleville, go east 28 miles on OH 56 to OH 180, where you turn right (south). Travel 0.7 mile to Adelphi, then turn left (south) onto OH 327, which you travel 7.5 miles to the park entrance. The trip takes about 1½ hours. From Cincinnati, take either US 50 or I-71 and US 35 to Chillicothe, then continue on US 50 east 12 miles to OH 327 at Londonderry. Take OH 327 left (north) 9 miles to the park entrance. From the Dayton area, use US 35 to reach Chillicothe and the route described for Cincinnati travelers. The parking lot for the trailhead is located about 1.2 miles inside the park, below the dam at Pine Lake.

The Trail

The north loop trail leaves the parking lot on a gravel service road opposite the dam. The trailhead sign, which has been there for many years, was missing when I last inspected this area, but the red blazes on the trees to the right side of the trail indicated the correct route. Just before the trail reaches a small creek, there is supposed to be a Checkpoint 1 sign pointing left to the beginning of the Hocking Segment. It was missing in the winter of 1996–97, the victim of vandalism or the construction that was going on at the time. The trail goes to the left before the service road reaches the creek crossing. Take this trail along the streambank uphill to the park entrance road. There is no checkpoint sign here, but there is a large paint blaze on a tree across the road indicating the continuation of the trail. After crossing the road the trail climbs sharply, making a left turn through the pines. Beyond them, the trail enters deciduous forest as it drops to a creek crossing. It then turns right up a ravine, climbing smartly up the left slope. This climb of over 300 feet in just over ½ mile is the only such climb on the north loop.

After following the ridge for a short distance, the trail turns left to descend on the spine of a side ridge. A red arrow points right as the trail drops off the ridge and into a hollow, where it makes a T junction with another trail. Your red-blazed trail turns right, then left across a stream. It goes left again as it begins climbing the hillside. Partway up the slope, it levels off to follow the hillside above the group camping area driveway. At a fork in the trail it goes right, still in the woods above the campground. There are a number of "wild" trails in this area, so it is necessary to keep red blazes in view. At another T, this one with a trail coming in from the campground, turn right. Eventually the trail drops to the valley to cross a small stream. The number on the tree here identifies Checkpoint 2, almost 2½ miles from the start of the trail.

The 1¾-mile Ross Segment begins by climbing out of the streambed. The trail leads up the slope a short distance before turning to the left to round the end of a ridge. There are more wild trails here, used by hikers starting from the campground. Shortly thereafter the trail drops to the bottomland, goes straight across the streambed, and then heads uphill. It eventually levels off, turns left, and then curves to the right around the end of a ridge. It drops into a small ravine to cross a side stream, then crosses another stream after 125 feet. At yet another T, the trail turns right to start a moderate climb up the valley to a crossing with the blacktopped North Ridge Road. The trail reenters the woods across the road, slightly to the left. A red arrow can be located on a tree alongside the road, and the post announcing Checkpoint 3, where the trail turns to the right, is about 30 feet off the road.

Going north, the trail occasionally uses an old wagon road as it passes through a brushy area and then to the right of a small pond. Reentering the oak/hickory woods, the trail leaves the old road and turns left to begin dropping into a hollow. Now headed in a westerly direction, it moves back and forth across the streambed and up and down the valley wall, then passes near an old dump and a rotting slab pile. Moving down the hollow, the trail hugs the left slope as it approaches Swamp Hill Road. Instead of dropping to the road as it draws near, the trail swings left around the hillside parallel with the road for several hundred yards before turning toward it. This approach detours around a private inholding at the mouth of the valley and keeps the trail on state-owned land. Just across the road is Checkpoint 4, the end of the 2-mile Sawmill Segment.

After reentering the woods the trail crosses a stream, then turns right, angling up the slope on what may have been a logging skid. At an easily missed left turn, you begin the steepest climb of the trail. Fortunately you climb only a short distance, and at the top there is a nice grassy spot under oaks that begs to be used for a respite. For the next mile the trail follows the ridge in heavy forest. Turning left onto an old wagon road, it shortly reaches Checkpoint 5, where a sign on the right indicates a turn to the right off the old road. Here ends the appropriately named 1½-mile Lookout Segment.

The trail follows the ridge for another ½ mile before beginning a steep descent into Slickaway Hollow. There are no switchbacks, and the trail is badly eroded and quite rocky in places. At the bottom, the trail crosses the hollow and turns to the left to begin a mile-long climb back to the ridge. The trail crosses the stream several times and, at times, follows an old road that once came all the way up the valley. Toward the head of the ravine the trail follows a fork to the left, hugging the right slope as it makes a gentle climb. Just before reaching the ridgetop and the edge of the woods, the trail hits a T. A sign identifies Checkpoint 6 and the junction of the north loop, which goes to the left, and the south loop, which goes to the right. The sign also points to the right to Camp Dulen for Scouts, who are now about 5 miles away from their overnight spot. The Slickaway Hollow segment has covered 2⅓ miles.

At this point you have traveled a total of 10 miles. Another 2 miles of easy hiking will complete the north loop. Proceed via a left turn at the T. The trail climbs a few feet and emerges from the woods onto a logging road, which takes you to the left. Shortly up the logging road, your red-blazed trail exits to the right. It goes down and around the head of a ravine, then up and over a knob. After you cross a stream, you climb steeply and then more gently to the Brush Ridge fire tower. The trail emerges onto Forest Road 3, South Ridge Road, directly west of the tower. This is the end of the ½-mile Firetower Segment. The "official" trail through the woods can be bypassed for a slightly longer but less rugged route by continuing on the logging road until you reach pavement, where you turn right to the fire tower.

Checkpoint 10, the beginning of the Pine Lake Segment, is identified by a red-topped 4 x 4, but this sign is also subject to frequent vandalism and is not always there. Normally it is to the left of the fire tower across the gravel loop driveway. There is also a forestry sign there identifying the trail as the Brush Ridge Trail, 1½ miles long, which the Logan Trail uses to complete the loop.

Here the Logan Trail comes close to the Buckeye Trail (BT), which passes through this area both on and off the road. The entrance to a short, white-blazed connecting trail is marked by a round post near where the fire tower loop drive meets the paved road just south of the tower. About 100 feet beyond the post, a T is formed where the blue-blazed BT goes both right and left. In some places in the state forest, the BT utilizes the same trail as the Logan Trail.

The Brush Ridge Trail is easy and well defined. It is probably the most used trail in the park/forest, since many day-hikers travel it between Pine Lake and the fire tower. After rounding the head of a ravine, the trail rises gently to head out to a ridge. After ¼ mile, there is a fork. The left branch goes to a group camping facility in the valley below. The Logan Trail continues on the right fork, where it rises gently to and over an 1100-foot knob before starting its descent to the lake. Near the bottom it crosses a power-line right-of-way. Beyond the Brush Ridge Trail sign pointing back the way you came, the trail continues along the hillside past another sign that announces the end of the trail and the location of the trailhead. Yet another sign points back up the trail to the BT, 1½ miles away. The trail comes out at dam level and follows the spillway downhill, which it then crosses on a bridge. The trail ends on the mowed lawn of the earthen dam within sight of the Pine Lake parking lot, where there are rest rooms and a shelterhouse.

29

Wayne National Forest (Archers Fork Trail)

Total distance: 9½ miles (15.2 km)

Hiking time: 6 hours as a day hike or 2 days as a backpack trip

Maximum elevation: 1125 feet

Vertical rise: 375 feet

Maps: USGS 7½' Rinard Mills, OH and Raven Rock, WVA; USFS Wayne National Forest hiking and backpacking trails map

On a warm spring morning, I made the 175-mile drive from my home in the Columbus area to eastern Washington County to walk my last unwalked section of the Archers Fork Trail. The hike could not have been nicer. Though the trees were still bare, spring peepers were calling, mourning cloak butterflies (which overwinter as adults) were on the wing, and a dozen wild turkeys crossed the trail about 75 feet in front of me. I saw not another soul the entire time I was in the forest. It was a wonderful wilderness retreat for me. I returned to Columbus late in the evening, buoyant after my walk on this forest path. As in other Wayne National Forest areas, had I chosen to do so I could have camped overnight along the trail.

The Archers Fork Trail is a loop trail in an Appalachian oak forest area of southeastern Ohio. Along the route is a beautiful natural rock arch, many rock shelters, early oil-pumping rigs, and lots of tall timber. The North Country Trail (NCT) uses part of the Archers Fork Trail as it crosses the state; there are connecting trails to the Ohio View Trail to the east and the Covered Bridge Trail to the west should you want to make an extended backpacking trek.

How to Get There

To reach an Archers Fork trailhead (there are two other parking sites), travel east from Cambridge on I-70 to exit 202 (OH 800). Turn south on OH 800 and follow it through Barnesville and Woodsfield to its intersection with OH 26. Go south on OH 26 to its intersection with OH 260. Turn east and drive approximately 4 miles to Hohman

The Archers Fork Trail crosses this large natural arch not far from the trailhead.

Ridge Road (Township Road 34). The road goes to the right just as OH 260 turns sharply left, so it is easy to miss. Turn right (south) and follow this gravel road 1.3 miles until you see a NORTH COUNTRY TRAIL PARKING sign on the left side of the road. Enter here and drive past the front of St. Patrick's Cemetery to the parking area. A sign directs you down the abandoned road to where you pick up the Archers Fork and North Country Trail. If you started in the Columbus area, you will have driven about 165 miles.

The Trail

You pick up the trail just a few hundred feet due south from the parking lot. Blue diamonds with arrows on them indicate you are headed toward the NCT. The combined NCT/Archers Fork Trail will come in from the left and continue straight ahead and will be blazed with two different signs: a white diamond with a blue disk for the Archers Fork Trail, and a solid blue diamond for the NCT.

Archers Fork is the name of the principal stream that drains this area through its two tributaries, Irish Run and Jackson Run. Archers Fork drains into the Little Muskingum River and thence to the Ohio. It is also the name of a small community downstream, a little over a mile from where the trail crosses the stream.

The bedrock nearest the surface in this part of Ohio is Permian, the youngest in the state, thought to date from 280 million years ago. As you walk the rutty old road toward the trail, the fine Permian sandstone is visible underfoot and the cliffs and rock shelters of the area are of Permian sandstone. The presence of oil in the deeper bedrock of the area is indicated by the number of wells you will pass along these trails, including one to the right as you walk toward the juncture of the trails.

Turn left at a sign that points left and says HIKER on a tree on the left side of the old road. Just down the trail is the corner where the combined trails go both east and south. There is a sizable cave (really a rock shelter) located near here. To visit it, walk east across the dip in the trail and scramble down the slope of the east side of the ravine. The cave is virtually under the trail you just traveled.

You can, of course, travel either direction on the Archers Fork loop trail. Since the day I was walking was "cloudy-bright," a good day for taking photographs without hard shadows, I wanted to get to the natural bridge, so I began walking south, counterclockwise on the loop. The trail travels at a fairly constant elevation on the hillside above the ravine for ¾ mile before rising to the right, then turning left to where a sign says BRIDGE. There is an open area along the trail just prior to the bridge that would make a good campsite. The natural bridge or arch is up against the hillside, and it takes a bit of scrambling to get into position to take a picture. (Though the forest service map calls it a natural bridge, most geologists save that term for a feature that water flows under, or has in the past. The preferred term for a structure such as this one is an arch.) This one has been called by two names: Archers Fork Natural Bridge and Independence Arch. Take your choice. When the forest service map was created, the authors knew of only four natural bridges in Ohio. Since then, Tim Snyder of the Ohio Division of Natural Areas and Preserves has scoured the countryside for such features. He now has a list of 63 confirmed locations of arches and natural bridges, and he is still looking.

The forest is not what is called old growth, the area having been logged many times since settlement. Nevertheless, it has gone half a century or more since its last clear-cut, and it provides a nice environment for walking. Beyond the arch, the trail turns west and rises more than 100 feet before crossing a hilltop, making a downhill arc to the right, and then crossing the ridge to begin its descent to Archers Fork. Over the next ½ mile the trail makes a 300-foot descent on trail that angles gently down the hillside. After crossing a small side stream, the trail stays above the valley floor on the right side of Archers Fork for another ¼ mile before crossing an old farm lane, then dropping to the floodplain. The March 1, 1997, storm flooded this bottomland and the trail, but it should be repaired by now. There is a trail junction here where a connecting spur goes to the right toward the Covered Bridge Trail along the Little Muskingum River.

Following this hike requires fording the stream (the roads of the area do that, too) before coming off the floodplain to cross Township Road 14 and head on a right oblique up the hillside. The rise over the next ⅓ mile is from the 740-foot elevation of the road to 1100 feet. An uninterrupted climb of short steps with a slow pace brings you alongside a small old hilltop field. From there, the trail heads southeast to drop into a saddle; then rises again to the same elevation; then turns east, following a winding ridge for ½ mile before passing another 1100-foot knob. This is the country of ancient oil well rigs and pipelines. Lots of Ohio crude oil from this Washington County well field helped fuel an oil-hungry nation before low prices for Middle East oil made further development here uneconomical. Oil did not gush from Ohio wells as it did from wells in the American Southwest or the Middle East. Some oil is still pumped from the area, but not as much as before.

After about a mile of ridgetop travel on

Gas Well

900

1020

13

1013

BM
1075

1000

Cem

1086

P

1017

T

cave

1100

900

900

natural bridge

800

BM
773

18

900

1000

Archers Fork

1000

1000

17

900

747

774

connector to
Covered Bridge Trail

800

JEEP
TRAIL

1118

800

17

110

Fork

741

stream crossing

North Country Trail

P

connector to Ohio View Trail

Bell

N

P 803

Jackson Run

Gas Well

Gas Well

Bell Cem

North Country Trail

0   5 mile

➤ The Wayne National Forest

The Wayne National Forest has its roots in the Weeks Law of 1911, which allowed the federal government, with the concurrence of state legislatures, to purchase land to create national forests. Ohio approved such action in November 1934, and between 1935 and 1942 approximately 77,000 acres were acquired in the five purchase units in southeastern Ohio. During the 1930s the Civilian Conservation Corps planted trees, halted erosion, and built much of the infrastructure of what, in 1951, was to officially become the Wayne National Forest. In 1983 it was targeted for disposal, but strong public reaction saved it. In the late 1980s and early 1990s, the Wayne (as it is generally referred to) received strong support from Congress and Ohio's citizens.

Though scaled back in the number of purchase units, the forest has worked hard to reduce the checkerboard pattern of ownership. On October 1, 1996, it comprised 227,054 acres. There has been a steady increase in the number and mileage of high-quality hiking trails in the Wayne during the past decade, to the benefit of those of us who enjoy the deep woods of southeastern Ohio's hill country.

an old well service road, the trail reaches a junction where the NCT goes straight ahead and the Archers Fork Trail heads through a gap between two hills to the left. Follow the white diamonds with blue dots as the trail arcs right and begins its slow descent toward the 800-foot elevation of the valley of Jackson Run. Once in the valley, the trail stays a couple of hundred feet back from the road, crossing first one stream, then another. It is at this second side stream's valley that a gas well road connects the trail to a forest service parking lot along Township Road 14. This is a grassy parking area cut in among young trees and, unlike the other two parking lots, has no sign. If you want to make an overnight trip using camping gear that you do not want to carry, it would be an adequate place for such a venture. During hunting seasons, especially those for turkey and deer, there will likely be hunters in pickup truck campers parked here.

Beyond this access point the trail headed northeast makes a steep climb, gaining 300 feet in ½ mile. After reaching the 1100-foot level it hangs on the hillside to drop gently, then more steeply, to the upper reaches of Jackson Run. Another connector trail exits the loop, headed right (east) to carry you to the Ohio View Trail. From here it is a short climb to reach a nearly flat section of trail and the crossing of TR 14.

The third forest service parking area that serves the trail is but a couple of hundred feet up the road to the right (east). If you have a vehicle there, head right on the road. If not, continue on the Archers Fork Trail by climbing the steps across the road and following the trail through the woods. It soon joins a wide old service road to head northwest, rising and falling along a ridge for less than ½ mile. The trail crosses gas lines that may confuse you—watch for the blazes. This is where I saw the 12 wild turkeys I mentioned above. Just beyond a point where the trail stays on high ground and the road (or gas line) that the trail was following falls off the left side, the old road then turns left and the trail goes straight ahead for a very short distance. Where the gas line/road heads steeply downhill ahead, the trail ducks through a hole in the woods to the left to stay on high ground. This is an easy turn to miss. Watch for the blazes. The trail then begins to drop off the point of the ridge, soon catching an old logging skid to head down a valley to Irish Run. There are very picturesque small rock shelters above the trail here, and there is a wonderful carpet of moss underfoot. One of these rock shelters would surely protect a lone hiker from a sudden thundershower and might even provide cover for a night's sleep.

The trail reaches the road and although the NCT map makes it appear to go directly across the road, it does not. Turn right and go the length of a football field, then look for a road dropping off the left side of the road. On the floodplain next to the creek there is a sign marking another juncture with the NCT, which goes to the right back up onto the road to head northeast, then north, eventually crossing OH 260 a couple of miles to the east of Hohman Ridge Road. The Archers Fork Trail, combined once again with the NCT, heads across the creek. Be prepared to wade.

The trail is now about a mile from closing the loop. After crossing the creek, it heads to a rise about 150 feet up the hill, curving left as it does so to follow the hillside, then dropping gently down to cross Township Road 40. There are wonderful tall trees up this valley, and the forest service has considered designating it a Special Interest Area. Across the road, the trail drops down to cross a small unnamed headwater creek of Irish Run, again by fording. Heading up a small ravine, it curves right, then left to head due west toward the cave and the service road to the parking lot at St. Patrick's Cemetery. May the luck of the Irish travel with you on the trail and your years of hiking be many.

30

Wayne National Forest (Lamping Homestead Trail)

Total distance: 3¼ miles (5.2 km)

Hiking time: 2½ hours

Maximum elevation: 1000 feet

Vertical rise: 240 feet

Maps: USGS 7½' Graysville and Rinard Mills, USFS Wayne National Forest hiking and backpacking trails map

It is hard to say why the Lamping family chose to settle in the valley between Pleasant and Haney Ridges near the Clear Fork of the Little Muskingum River, but they did. As far as we know, they were the first to put down roots and build a cabin on the land this trail traverses. The land had been part of the first seven ranges surveyed in 1786 in what was to become Ohio in 1803. Though initially part of Washington County, in 1813 it became part of Monroe County. There was a land office to file patents on unclaimed land as close as Marietta. During those first two decades of the 19th century a steady flow of Americans headed to Ohio, Indiana, and Illinois. In 1816, on just one turnpike in Pennsylvania, 16,000 wagons rolled past a tollbooth as they made their way west carrying families eager to carve new homes from the wilderness. Even so, by 1840 there were only 533 people living in Washington Township, where the Lampings had settled.

No one seems to know where the Lampings came from—or, for that matter, where they went when they left here—but they did not stay long. We will never know why they left, but perhaps the graves in the Lamping Cemetery, located on a knoll alongside this trail a couple of hundred yards from the house, may provide a clue. At least two young Lamping children are buried there, victims of who knows what sort of malady. In moving on, the Lampings would not be the first family, nor the last, to uproot themselves to leave behind the site of sad times. In any case, the house and barn of what more than 100 years ago had

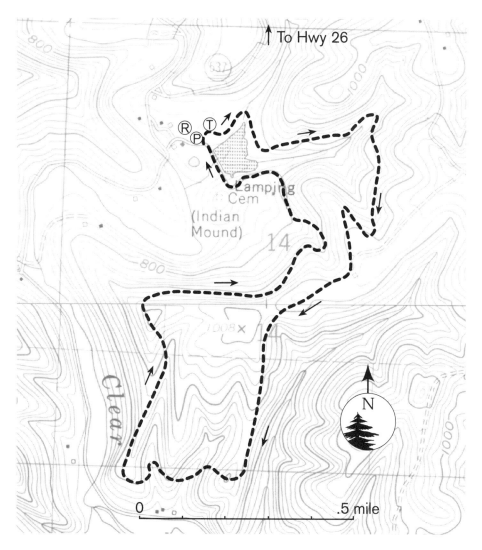

been the Lamping homestead were removed when the forest service acquired the land in 1971. Over the next two years, the Youth Conservation Corps aided the forest service in developing the Lamping Homestead Recreation Area on the shore of a new lake.

How to Get There

The Lamping Homestead Recreation Area can be reached by driving east from Cambridge on I-70 to exit 202 (OH 800), then turning south on OH 800 to take it through Barnesville and Woodsfield to its intersection with OH 26. Follow OH 26 south; 1 mile beyond Graysville, turn west on winding OH 537 and follow it about 1.5 miles to Township Road 307. Turn left onto this gravel road, then almost immediately turn left again into the parking lot. There are picnic shelters and rest rooms overlooking Kenton Lake.

Wayne National Forest (Lamping Homestead Trail)

The Trail

The Lamping Homestead Trail is well marked with white diamond-shaped plastic blazes nailed on trees and fence posts. It is a loop trail and the blazes for outbound and inbound routes are visible from the lawn between the dry hydrant and the lake. Before I began hiking on a warm August day, I took my camera and a 100 mm macro lens and walked alongside the expansive patches of joe-pye weed, milkweed, and ironweed, taking pictures of tiger swallowtails, red-spotted purples, and other scale-winged beauties sucking up nectar with their proboscides.

Head left of the lake through the pines that shade picnickers to begin walking. There is a white diamond with a hiker on it and another white diamond with an arrow pointing the direction to walk to gain the trail. At the far end of the picnic area the trail passes more pines, these planted too close together for good growth. The trail turns left to cross a bridge over one of the tributaries of the stream that was dammed to create the lake. Beyond the bridge it follows around the lake past more pines, then makes a left oblique to rise up the hillside and head up the other headwater valley. Leaving pines behind, the trail hangs on the side of the hill as it enters a stand of young trees and follows the creek upstream. After ½ mile or so of travel, the trail has crossed from the Lamping Homestead Lake watershed into a steep-sloped valley with drainage directly into the Clear Fork of the Little Muskingum River. It is now heading around the hillside in a clockwise direction, beginning to drop slowly. There are signs of good spring flora through here. The trail passes another pine planting, then follows a natural terrace. Curving around the hill, the trail rises again and becomes grass surfaced out in

The graves of Lamping children overlook the Lamping Homestead.

the open. Through the trees ahead, the Clear Fork is visible.

The trail now maintains its elevation for a while as it works its way in and out of small ravines. After crossing a gas line and gaining a bit of elevation, it passes through nice Appalachian oak woods. Soon it begins climbing north-northeast, at first on a hillside, then up a small valley. It continues to gain altitude and reaches the 1000-foot point as it turns right (east) to begin dropping. Through nice open woods, the trail maintains a constant elevation; then it drops at about as steep a slope as is comfortable, heading for the floodplain below the dam.

Now back in boneset, ironweed, and wingstem country, the trail emerges from weeds and woods at the east end of the dam. As you walk along the dam headed for the picnic area, watch for the path that leads to the left up the hill to the Lamping Cemetery. Inside a vandalized iron fence are the badly weathered and moss-covered tombstones of the Lamping children who did not survive the harsh reality of the Ohio frontier. It is a short walk from here back to the parking area. As you go, reflect if you will on the hardships suffered by those who came before us to carve from the Ohio wilderness the civilization we enjoy at this turn of a new century.

31

Wayne National Forest (Morgan Sisters Trail)

Total distance: 2, 4, or 8 miles (3.2, 6.4, or 12.8 km)

Hiking time: 1, 2, or 4 hours

Maximum elevation: 934 feet

Vertical rise: 294 feet

Maps: USGS 7½' Patriot;
USFS Wayne National Forest hiking and backpacking trails map

The Symmes Creek trails are a joy to walk. They pass pine plantings, spectacular tall native hardwoods, floodplain forests, and open fields. It is a challenge to read the landscape to determine what occurred on the land before it became National Forest. You can take a short, medium, or long hike ending up at your vehicle. Best of all, this is a remote wilderness area with no airport flight pattern overhead or interstate highway within earshot. You can pitch your bivy sack or tent wherever you wish, as long as you leave no imprint upon the land. Where can you go wrong?

The trail for this hike is, as you might speculate, named for a pair of spinsters named Morgan who lived for many years near the end of Morgan Sisters Road, close to the center of the trail.

How to Get There

To reach the Morgan Sisters trailhead parking lot, take US 35 east from Chillicothe past Jackson to the Rio Grande exit, OH 325. Travel south on this road to OH 141, then west to OH 233. About 3 miles from this intersection, where OH 233 makes a hard left turn, Pumpkintown Road (County Road 25) goes to the right (north). One mile up this road, a drive leaving to the right leads to Kenton Lake and a parking area for the Morgan Sisters Trail system. The distance from Columbus is about 120 miles. This is the place to park if you plan to walk the Coal Branch Loop, that loop plus the Ridge Loop, or the entire trail. There is another spot where I have parked a number of times to access the Schoolhouse and Ridge Loops.

A viceroy sips nectar on joe-pye weed.

This is at the end of Morgan Sisters Road, which runs north from OH 233 not quite 1 mile east of Pumpkintown Road.

The Trail

The driveway to the Kenton Lake trailhead is fairly steep; it can be muddy, deeply rutted, and treacherous to drive during and after prolonged bad weather. Take it easy as you enter. Park at the far end of the drive to the left of the old road (to the right of the parking area), where the trail begins. It is clearly marked. The blazing for this trail is the forest service's white diamond with a yellow disk attached, but many of the yellow disks have fallen off. Whoever nailed them up drove the nails all the way in; as the trees have grown, the disks, and in some cases the diamonds, have popped off. The trail will need to be re-marked in a few years.

From the trailhead it is a steady but reasonable climb up what the topo map calls a jeep trail. As the trail reaches the ridge, it swings to the left and a blaze warns of a turn ahead. Do not turn too soon. After a hard right leaving the jeep trail, it is easy to be fooled into believing that the trail climbs uphill through the grass and among the pines. It does not. One diamond is visible from the turn. Go to it, then look beyond it to the left for a hole in the edge of the woods where the trail enters. Once inside the young woods, look down the trail to find the next blaze. If you see one nailed to a tree, you are on the trail. There are lots of brambles and greenbriers along your way in this Appalachian oak forest. The trail follows around the side of the hill at about the same elevation for a few hundred yards; then, as it passes some exposed sandstone, it drops to Coal Branch. The slope is gentle at first but steep toward the bottom. Along much of this hillside trail the route is not well defined; it is a good idea to spot the next blaze each time one is passed.

On the floodplain of Coal Branch, the herbaceous growth sometimes falls over the trail by the end of the summer, again requiring careful sighting of the next blaze. Eventually the trail works its way to the bank of Coal Branch, where it is necessary to wade or step across the water. Once across the stream, the trail turns to the right (southwest) and moves alongside the creek for several hundred yards. Very shortly you will pass the junction with the Ridge Loop. It goes to the left straight up the end of a hill. The option to take it is yours; it adds less than 2 miles to your hike.

There is a nearly pure stand of tuliptrees along the Coal Branch Loop here. If you continue on that loop, the trail will pass the open end of a valley and cross a very small side stream and the end of the ridge before reaching the other side of the Ridge Loop. It goes to the left up an old township or logging road. Again, the option is yours. On the Coal Branch Loop, the trail crosses another small creek, then passes a nice stand of treelike club moss, the second species of club moss seen along this trail. Blazes are a bit scarce or hard to see through here, but after a short distance the trail crosses Coal Branch at a sandbar, making the crossing easier. On the other side of the stream, the trail goes to the left, where it begins climbing along an old logging skid, but soon gets out of the gully and goes right up the spine of the ridge for a way before returning to a shallower skid.

Where the logging trail appears to head toward Pumpkintown Road, the trail leaves it to hang on the side of the hill, passing groves of white pines as it does so. It crosses the head of a small gully and soon passes a diamond with an arrow pointing to the right, indicating a sharp right turn ahead. Beyond the turn, the road arcs to the left and soon goes down the hillside through a beautiful stand of white pine trees. This would be my choice of locations to camp along this trail. Remember to follow the blazes carefully so that you don't miss the trail's drop to a streambed to the right. It will be but a minute before the trail reaches the driveway to Lake Kenton and the short walk to the parking lot.

The forest in the valley between the two arms of the Ridge Loop is among the nicest in southeastern Ohio. It is a Forest Service Special Interest Area and is a candidate for recognition as an outstanding old-growth forest. The trail along the northeast side runs right up the hill from Coal Branch, sometimes hanging onto the side of the hill, but usually staying right along the ridge. Eventually it intersects with an old road or jeep trail that carries on toward the Schoolhouse Loop. To include the Schoolhouse Loop in a hike, turn left. To complete the Ridge Loop, turn right and travel the combined trails for a very short distance, watching for an exit to the right. It is marked with a white diamond (the yellow disk having disappeared). The trail begins to go downhill as soon as it leaves the road. It then skirts around the upper end of a hollow, working its way to the ridge on the southwestern side. The blazes are difficult to find but if you head for the ridge, then take the ridge downhill, you should be on the trail. Part of the way it utilizes an old logging skid as it travels in a nearly straight line to its intersection with the Coal Branch Loop. Once at the bottom, turn left to head to the white pine woods and Kenton Lake, or right to complete the Ridge Loop or to go to Kenton Lake via the other side of the Coal Branch Loop.

The Schoolhouse Loop can be accessed by foot from Lake Kenton via the Coal Branch and Ridge Loops, by vehicle from a parking lot at the end of Morgan Sisters Road (it crosses the end of the road), or by foot and a connector trail from Symmes Creek Road.

From the end of Morgan Sisters Road (or from either intersection of the Ridge Trail with the Schoolhouse Loop), head north on the old township road following the white diamonds (often with yellow disks) until you see an arrow pointing to the right. The trail heads uphill at an angle to the left, reaching the top of the ridge after a couple of hundred feet. It then starts its downhill trend through a valley filled with hardwood forest. The blazes are far apart, but pieces of red engineering tape that were tied to trees when the trail was laid out are still visible, helping you follow the intended route. It will be almost a mile of hiking—over several ravines and creeks, over one ridge, and around a knob—before the trail reaches the floodplain and an intersection with the connector to the Symmes Creek Trail. Sometimes the trail uses what looks like the logging skids of the last timber harvest; other times it uses new trail whose tread is not too obvious. The connector trail (identified as such on a carsonite post) goes straight ahead toward Symmes Creek Road, a distance of about 1/3 mile. To connect with the 6-mile-long Symmes Creek Trail (another loop), turn right on the road; soon after crossing the creek on a bridge, follow the connector trail that exits the road on the left (north) and climbs to a trail junction. The Symmes Creek Trail is blazed with white diamonds with red dots, but many of the latter are missing as well.

At the junction with the connector, the Schoolhouse Loop trail turns right to cross two bridges; then it turns left across another short bridge and begins climbing on a narrow "goat trail" that hugs the hillside above a sandstone cliff. Mosses, lichens, club mosses, mountain laurel, and rattle-

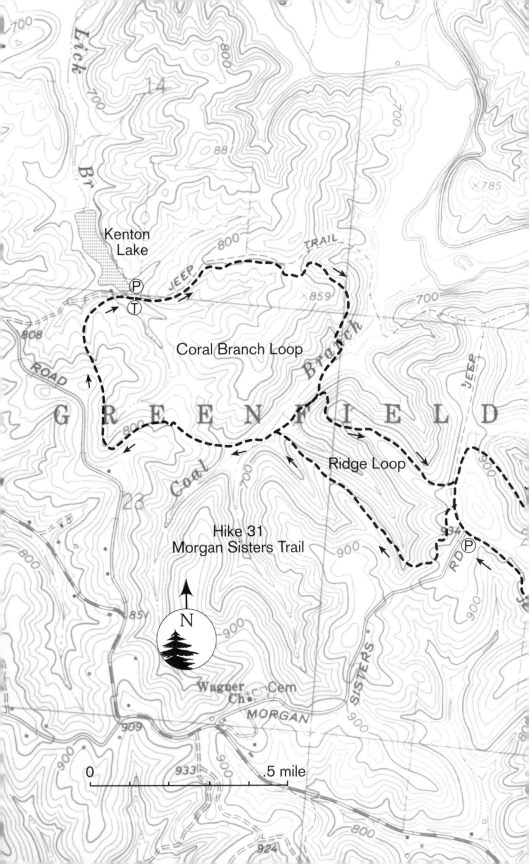

Kenton
Lake

Coral Branch Loop

Ridge Loop

GREENFIELD

Hike 31
Morgan Sisters Trail

N

Wagner Ch. Cem
MORGAN

0   .5 mile

Hike 32
Symmes Creek Trail

Connector

School House Loop

➤ The Land Speaks

Reading the landscape along the trail becomes a game, in a way (and it's much more exciting than reading license plates along the highway!). You assemble various clues in your mind on the basis of what intuitive knowledge you possess or what you have learned from printed material or other sources. Then, as you walk along the trail, you try to unravel the mystery of what took place on the land in years gone by. It may be the natural history or the cultural history that you are trying to understand, or both. The process is essentially the same for either.

For example, from its size or shape, you can usually identify a crumbling structure that was once a one-room schoolhouse. If there is no building, but an old map indicates that a schoolhouse once stood in the vicinity, you may identify the site by finding a rusty pump, the remains of privies, non-native plants such as jonquils growing in the woods, or old trees that look as if they once stood in the open. You can bet that a homestead once stood along a long-abandoned road where lilacs, daffodils, and daylilies still persist.

Roads that 100 years ago were the routes of shortline railroads are easily detected by their gentle grades and sweeping curves (and sometimes their names—Wally Road, for instance, which was once the route of the Walhonding Railroad southeast of Loudonville). In southeastern Ohio, the presence of a foundation made of hand-cut sandstone blocks (limestone in the western half of the state) under a steel bridge often means that a covered wooden span once stood there. The presence of tall redcedar trees with dying crowns growing just below the canopy in a hardwood forest is a good indicator that the area was at one time a field or pasture, and that limestone or dolomite bedrock is close to the surface. After being abandoned, old fields progress to cedar thickets before serving as nurseries for hardwood species that eventually overtop the cedars. See how many stories you can read in the land around you.

---

snake plantain are but a few of the plants that greet you on this sandstone-boulder-strewn hillside. The trail soon returns to the floodplain at a location where early maps show a road forded Symmes Creek. In the late winter, this broad floodplain is a breeding spot for hundreds of spring peepers and mountain chorus frogs. The trail turns left on the old roadbed, now carpeted with moss. After a rise of 160 feet, it reaches a grassy area about an acre in size in a col. To the left are the ruins of a building, its stone fireplace and chimney still standing. It is difficult to tell what the structure was built of, but brick was used in what looks like a wall around the building. Perhaps this is the schoolhouse of Schoolhouse Ridge, but I could find no symbol for a flag-bearing structure on this ridge on either the 7½' or 15' quadrangle map of the area.

It is difficult to find any blazes or a well-defined pathway in this opening, but the trail goes to the right past the ruins of another building and onto another old road at the

---

base of the hillside. Just beyond the building, the trail turns up the hill to the right from the road to pass through an opening in the thicket and reach another roadbed. This would be an easy turn to miss. From here the trail follows the old track around the hillside for perhaps ½ mile, at first with the hill on the right. After the trail passes through a saddle, the higher elevation (an 800-foot knob) is to the left.

Until World War II, there were lots of cabins, shacks, and shanties up these valleys and on the ridges, but they are nearly all gone now. When young soldiers and sailors came home from the war, most were not content to return to this land. They moved to the cities to work in factories, drive trucks, and, in some cases, use the GI Bill for a college education. When they could, they moved the old folks left behind to better homes. The houses fell in, the roads were closed, and nature reclaimed the small pastures, corn- and potato fields, and gardens. In the last 15 years, the National Forest Service has been aggressively acquiring the land to consolidate its holdings into large blocks of solid ownership. From this point on the trail, only one farmhouse is visible, and that one far in the distance.

There are a few pines and an occasional redcedar along this ridge, and at one point there is a great bed of myrtle on the forest floor indicating that there probably was once a dwelling, church, or cemetery nearby. The hardwoods are mixed, with some nice tall tuliptrees among the oaks; in places, there are stands of scrub pine. At a white triangle with an arrow pointing right, the trail turns right onto the abandoned Bethel Road. One-half mile to the left the road is still open to the Bethel Cemetery and the abandoned Bethel Church.

Along the trail there is an open area of grass under large trees where daffodils bloom in the spring. This area seems more likely to be the site of the "schoolhouse" that gives the loop trail its name. Can you imagine trudging along this road on foot or in a horse-drawn sleigh headed for school on a dark, cold winter morning?

Beyond here the old road appears to hook to the left off the hill, with jeep trails going straight ahead and slightly to the right. The trail follows the right fork. Along here, the forest is of very poor quality with lots of greenbrier beneath it. The trail emerges from the woods to pass a meadow on the left and then reach the end of Morgan Sisters Road. If your vehicle is at Kenton Lake, head right on the abandoned road to take either leg of the Ridge Loop and the Coal Branch Loop.

32

Wayne National Forest (Symmes Creek Trail)

Total distance: 6 miles (10 km)

Hiking time 3½ hours

Maximum elevation: 883 feet

Vertical rise: 247 feet

Maps: USGS 7½' Patriot; USFS Wayne National Forest hiking and backpacking trails map. (See page 160–161.)

The narrow, 356-square-mile Symmes Creek watershed includes parts of Lawrence, Gallia, and Jackson Counties. The stream originates near Oak Hill and flows south, emptying into the Ohio River at Chesapeake. It was not always this way. Though deep in the heart of southern Ohio's unglaciated plateau, this stream is one that was affected by the coming of the ice age to Ohio. Prior to the advance of glacial ice across Ohio, the stream that occupies the northern two-thirds of the Symmes Creek watershed was a northward-flowing tributary of the Teayes River. During the glacial advances, ice advancing from the north overran the Teayes River system and blocked movement of water to the north. The river valley became a lake, and when it rose high enough it flowed through a col in the hills to the south and made a new outlet to the developing Ohio River system. Today, in the southern part of its watershed, you can see where Symmes Creek flows through a "narrows," marking the point where the stream made the cut that reversed its direction of flow. In the northern parts of the watershed, the valley is wider and the pattern of tributaries clearly indicates that at one time it drained to the north.

Though many miles north of the narrows of Symmes Creek, the area where the Symmes Creek Trail is located is also narrow. Here, eons ago, the stream had to cut its way through massive sandstone that at this point was at the earth's surface. Upstream and downstream from the area of the trail, the wide valley of the preglacial stream is clearly seen. When you hike the

Symmes Creek Trail, you walk along the now southward-flowing stream below huge sandstone cliffs in a cut made millennia ago by a stream that was flowing to the north.

How to Get There

To explore this bit of geological history, travel east from Chillicothe on US 35 past Jackson to the Rio Grande exit, OH 325. At about 4.25 miles south of US 35, turn right on Roush Road and follow it slightly less than 3 miles to where it makes a T with Symmes Creek Road. Turn to the right and drive a little over 0.5 mile to where there is a gravel drive on the right leading to a parking area. (There is a second parking area about 1.75 miles farther west, but it is only a small grassy area alongside the road.)

The Trail

At the back edge of the parking lot, a single trail enters the woods, crosses a creek on a bridge, and goes up the hill on an old road to take you to the Symmes Creek Trail. Entrance to this road by vehicles has been blocked at a number of places by strategically placed piles of dirt that you must walk around. The Symmes Creek loop begins where the white-diamond-with-red-disk blazes indicate a trail going left and a trail going straight on up the hill on the old road. The trail to the left is the return route. It has not been many years since the road was abandoned, so the trail straight ahead is easy to follow. I suggest going that way, making the loop in a counterclockwise manner.

After hanging onto the left side of one hill, the trail climbs up a ridge and passes to

the right of the summit on the next hill. It then goes up and over the top of an 803-foot crest. Turning west now along this brushy ridge, the trail rises and dips for about ½ mile before it exits left in a saddle to follow a foot trail at a fairly level elevation around the hill ahead. A half mile later it returns to the road, turns left, and heads west again. Shortly the trail passes a track to the right that leads to a grassy area at the end of a gravel road still open and reachable by car from the north. Though you could drive to here, it does not appear to be a good place to leave a car. There was freshly dumped trash on the day I visited the area, and it is a remote place where a vehicle might easily be vandalized while its driver is absent. The forest service does not recommend it.

The trail, still on the old road, soon begins to swing to the left, dropping off the end of a brushy ridge. Hugging the hillside with older trees uphill to the right, it travels at about the same elevation for a way, then drops down the hillside toward Symmes Creek. Fifty or 60 feet above the floodplain that lies out in front of it, the old road makes a hard right turn. With sandstone cliffs above and scattered slump blocks nearby, it travels downhill to the west, reaching a pile of dirt, the parking area, and Symmes Creek Road after about 100 yards. The intersection back up the slope is the junction of the incoming Symmes Creek Trail, with the outgoing leg headed along the creek toward the trailhead parking lot. It is well marked, with diamonds and arrows pointing out each leg of the trail. Unless you have a vehicle parked along the road, turn to the left at the corner of the trail and begin following the white-diamond-with-red-disk blazes to the north.

From the intersection the trail, following yet another old road, runs alongside what is probably an old boundary fence as it drops to the floodplain. There, the sugar maples of the hillside are replaced by box elders; in the summer, wingstem, nettles, spotted jewelweed, multiflora rose, tickseed, asters, and other herbaceous plants overhang the trail. A hundred feet of boardwalk right down near stream level carries you to a white pine plantation. The water may have risen in this valley high enough to float that boardwalk away in the storm of early March 1997. In any case, the trail should be passable. The trail turns around the hill, then heads uphill a bit among the pines, then back to the floodplain. It weaves and bobs among box elders and planted pines along the base of the hill, and is soon traveling with sandstone cliffs close by on the left and slump blocks with their feet in the creek to the right. There are hemlock trees here, and polypody, or rockcap fern, covers the slump block. The beautiful, short, sky blue relative of joe-pye weed known as mist flower blooms along the trail here. Like all of its relatives (the Eupatoriums) it attracts butterflies; a pearl crescent was nectaring on a blossom when I passed by. The gorgeous red lobelia commonly called cardinal flower also blooms here. It is one of only five species of native Ohio wildflowers with bright red blossoms.

For the next ¼ mile the trail travels on the floodplain below spectacular sandstone cliffs with rock shelters varying from close to the creek to 10 or 15 feet up the hillside. The stream meanders back and forth between hillside and road. Pileated woodpeckers called out while I explored this spectacular area. Eventually the trail leaves the valley floor to rise above the sandstone and return to the oak woods. There are more moss- and fern-covered slump blocks where the trail crosses the mouth of the side ravine. Now more than 100 feet above the floodplain, the trail reaches a point where it makes a sharp turn to the left with the blazes clearly indicating that it goes uphill. At this point there is also a diamond with an arrow pointing straight ahead. This is the route of the connector trail to the Morgan Sisters Trail. No flat carsonite post here. How would you pound it into the ground when all beneath your feet is solid sandstone?

Once on the upland, the trail turns to the right and begins winding its way through woods and brambles. There are some massive white oaks and maples in these woods. The only way to follow the trail is to find the blazes. The map would lead you to believe that the only reason for these perambulations would be to lengthen the trail, but if you follow it you will understand that its bends and turns allow views of some of the monarchs of the forest. After a while, the trail descends at an angle to meet up with the road that carries the outgoing trail. At that intersection, diamonds with arrows point both right and left. Between there and the parking lot, look for a large post oak tree with a carpenter ant–eaten bole. The leaves are similar to those of a white oak, except that the lobes are in the shape of a cross. The trail crosses the creek and ends where it began, at the parking lot. Hikers who do not want to carry their camping gear with them might opt to camp here. Like other parking lots in the National Forest, this one is used by hunters during turkey and deer seasons.

33

Wayne National Forest (Vesuvius Recreation Area)

Total distance: 8 miles (12.8 km)

Hiking time: 5 hours

Maximum elevation: 920 feet

Vertical rise: 338 feet

Maps: USGS 7½' Kitts Hill; USGS 7½' Sherrits; USGS 7½' Ironton; USGS 7½' Pedro; USGS 15' Ironton (OH and KY); USFS Wayne National Forest Lake Vesuvius Trail Guide

The production of iron in the area that became known as the Hanging Rock Iron Region began with the construction of the Union Furnace in western Lawrence County by John Means in 1826. Before the whistle signaling the last cast of charcoal iron sounded at a furnace near Oak Hill in December 1916, a total of 46 furnaces had been built in Ohio, and 24 on the Kentucky side of the river. Each furnace was capable of producing from 2000 to 3000 tons of iron per year. They helped arm the Union forces during the Civil War and took part in America's industrial revolution. Now, a century after their heyday, only 17 of the old furnaces still stand in the region, surrounded by the crumbling ghosts of what were once thriving communities with homes, stores, rail spurs, and the many ancillary buildings needed to keep the furnaces in production. A map detailing the locations of the Ohio furnaces is available from the Ohio Historical Society in Columbus, and the same agency maintains the restored Buckeye Furnace in Jackson County.

Vesuvius Furnace, at the heart of the Lake Vesuvius Recreation Area within the Wayne National Forest, is one of the best preserved. Though it looks like the other furnaces, it has a special claim to fame: It was supposedly the first hot-blast furnace erected in America. John Campbell, who along with Robert Hamilton built the nearby Mount Vernon Furnace (later known only as Vernon), had experimented with his cold-blast operation by placing the boilers and blast over the tunnel head to provide a hot blast. In 1837 Campbell and three other ironmasters agreed to cover any loss incurred if William Firmstone would test the hot-blast principle on his new Vesuvius Furnace. This hot-blast furnace continued in operation until 1906, but iron production inflicted a heavy toll on the land. Not only were the hillsides carved up to extract iron ore, but also between 300 and 350 acres of timber were cut and converted to charcoal each year for each furnace, thereby effectively denuding the land. By the time the furnaces were finally silenced by competition from richer ores and more productive furnaces in other parts of the country, the land had been cut over many times.

The trails of the Lake Vesuvius Recreation Area take you through beautiful countryside. The mixed hardwood forests of the east-facing slopes, the oaks of the ridgetops and southern exposures, and the hemlock of the sandstone-lined ravines give variety to the landscape. Ruins of old roads, homes, industries, and early park development turn back the pages of time for the visitor. With trails that are well designed without severe climbs, the area is especially good for beginning backpackers. Options that allow for 1 to several days on the trail make it one of Ohio's choice hiking areas.

The 8-mile Lakeshore Trail is perfect for a day hike or a short backpack hike. The area also features a 16-mile Backpack Trail, which begins and ends on the Lakeshore Trail and is one of Ohio's best trails for a 1- or 2-night trek. Both are laid out using gentle gradients, and there are no really hard climbs. Like the other units within the Wayne Forest complex, camping is allowed anywhere along the trail. However, in this area, no camping is permitted within the designated Vesuvius Recreation Area: this means before mile 2½ and after mile 5 on the Lakeshore Trail, and before mile 2 and after mile 13½ on the Backpack Trail. There

are no convenient sources of drinking water, so you need to either carry water or cache your supply at a road crossing. Open fires are discouraged, and are prohibited at times of high fire danger, so be prepared to use stoves for cooking. Human waste must be buried properly, and all trash must be carried out.

How to Get There

To reach the Vesuvius Recreation Area, travel US 23 from Columbus, or OH 32 and US 23 from Cincinnati, to Portsmouth. Take US 52 east to OH 93 in Ironton (about 120 miles from Columbus and 130 from Cincinnati). At Ironton, travel just over 6 miles north on OH 93 to where highway and forest service signs direct you right onto County Road 29. After about 1 mile on County Road 29, turn left on a forest service road just before reaching the dam and furnace. Travel this road not quite 0.5 mile to the dock and trailhead parking lot on the right. For a day hike, park and lock your car here. For overnighters, it is probably safer to leave your car at the forest service maintenance area. After unloading your gear, return to County Road 29, turn left, and then turn right into the land marked PRIVATE DRIVE just beyond the first house on the right. Drive past another house to the shop area, and park on the left side of the road out of the way of forest service vehicles and equipment. The walk back to the trailhead is a short one.

The Trail

The trail begins from a trailhead kiosk at the lake end of the parking lot. The Lakeshore Trail is marked with white diamond blazes, the Backpack Trail with yellow ones. The miles are marked on both trails. Since the two trails intersect at the far end of the lake near Backpack Trail marker 12 and Lake-

0   1.0 mile

N

Backpack Trail

Backpack
Trail

Lakeshore Trail

③

④

⑤

Lake
Vesuvius

R

W

②

Big Bend Beach

LAKE VESUVIUS

①

VESUVIUS RECREATION AREA

⑥ VESUVIUS
RECREATION AREA

Backpack Trail

Oak Hill
Campground

Iron Ridge
Campground

Sand Hill

P

⑦

Whiskey Run
Trail

P

P T

E L I Z A B E T H

shore Trail marker 4, it is possible to utilize parts of each trail for hikes of different lengths. It is also possible to use a canoe or other boat on the lake to bypass part of the trail or to shuttle gear to the above-mentioned checkpoints.

The combined trail leaves the boathouse to climb a short distance into the woods and into what is the first of many pine plantings encountered along the way. The views along the first mile of this trail are extraordinary, especially in the autumn. A large sandstone promontory across the lake creates a picture-postcard scene.

Following the shore of the lake, the trail passes a now abandoned beach left from Civilian Conservation Corps days, then goes by a building and intake structure from a water system abandoned in 1980. Moving slightly away from the shore, you follow an old road for a short way before crossing a side stream. About 100 feet beyond this crossing the trail splits, with the Backpack Trail leaving to the left. There should be a sign between the two trails, but if it has been vandalized, it is easy to miss the split.

Continuing straight ahead, the Lakeshore Trail soon passes mile marker 1. It continues along the shore until just before the Big Bend Beach area, where it cuts left. It crosses a wooden bridge and follows the fence around the bathhouse. Rest rooms and water are available here during the warm part of the year. The trail passes a 50-foot-long sandstone outcrop before climbing the side of the ridge at a moderate angle. At one point along this section of trail, it is possible to see the lake on both sides of this peninsula. After passing mile marker 2, the trail doubles back to drop toward the shoreline. After passing a rather swampy area and just before turning left up a small hollow, the trail leaves the Vesuvius Recreation Area. There is no sign, but beyond this point trail camping is permitted.

After crossing the creek, the trail turns right to travel again near the shoreline. A small pond lies between the trail and the lake. Climbing away from the lake on the slope, you pass through more stands of planted pines and then pass above a rock exposure with a 25-foot cliff below. Just beyond is mile marker 3. The trail next turns right as it climbs a ridge that goes toward the lake. Though there is a footpath out to the point overlooking the lake, your hiking trail does not follow it but turns left to drop down to the shoreline. From here, the trail stays at lake level until it begins its return route on the opposite shore. The lake is very narrow at this point. The trail soon joins a service road to continue upstream. Just after crossing a small side stream, signs identify the junction with the Backpack Trail coming in from upstream, and the combined trails cross Storms Creek.

This crossing is usually no problem, but in periods of high water it can be difficult if not impossible to make. After the crossing, the trail turns right through an old field and reenters the woods. At a fork in the trail, the combined Lakeshore/Backpack Trail stays right along the forest edge and soon passes mile marker 4. It then leaves the lakeshore to travel up the left side of a side ravine. The two trails then split, with the Lakeshore Trail making a right turn across the creek bed before climbing the hillside. The Lakeshore Trail descends to cross another incoming stream, then makes a fairly steep climb to overlook the lake once again. After passing mile marker 5 (and reentering the Vesuvius Recreation Area, where trail camping is prohibited), you swing left to go around yet another inlet. Next, dropping to near lake level to cross two streambeds, you climb to one of the nicest viewpoints along the trail. Following a clockwise swing around a much longer inlet, you will meet a trail coming in from the left. This path is the ½-mile Whiskey Run Trail, labeled with green diamond blazes. It makes a loop that begins at the Iron Ridge Campground. A short, steep climb up the Whiskey Run Trail will lead you to a rock shelter said to have held a moonshine still at one time. Beyond and on uphill is the campground.

The combined Lakeshore/Whiskey Run Trail travels north to round a point nearly opposite the Big Bend Beach before heading due south for the next ⅔ mile. After it enters another pine stand, the trail splits as the Whiskey Run Trail departs to the left. The old beach and water intake become visible across the lake on the right, and there are sandstone outcroppings on the hill above the trail on the left. After passing mile marker 7, the trail comes to another rock shelter, this one vandalized with spray-paint graffiti. The trail then drops closer to the lake and rounds the sandstone cliff face that was visible in the early part of the hike.

Now rounding the last inlet before the dam, the trail stays close to the lake and crosses two small streambeds. After rising slightly, it returns to near lake level and passes below a rock cliff with nearly square slump blocks on the hillside below. One cannot help but wonder if the sandstone used to build the Vesuvius Furnace was quarried here. The trail follows the lake edge and arrives shortly at the dam spillway. There it makes a left turn, to be joined by the Backpack Trail. You descend concrete steps alongside a chain-link fence to arrive at the lawn and road within sight of the Vesuvius Furnace.

The trail follows Storms Creek through pine plantings to the County Road 29 bridge, which it crosses. Turning right beyond the bridge, it climbs to the top of the dam and then heads toward the road, which it takes to the trailhead at the boat dock area.

34

Wayne National Forest
(Wildcat Hollow Trail)

Total distance: 4½ or 13 miles
(7.25 or 21 km)

Hiking time: 3 or 8 hours
(with a possible overnight)

Maximum elevation: 1080 feet

Vertical rise: 350 feet

Maps: USGS 7½' Corning;
USGS 7½' Beavertown; USFS Wildcat
Hollow brochure

It has been many years since a bona fide sighting of a wildcat in Ohio was reported, but the secretive felines were at one time found in most of the state, especially in the rocky hollows of the southeast. History does not record how Wildcat Hollow on the Morgan/Perry county line got its name, but it would probably be safe to guess that a den of the elusive cats was thought to have been in the area.

Located in what is now the massive Wayne National Forest, Wildcat Hollow is the site of one of Ohio's better hiking trails. The 13-mile route is laid out entirely on Wayne National Forest land, mostly on high land between drainage systems. The trail is typical of those developed by the United States Forest Service. It is well designed, with gentle grades and switchbacks as needed. It is also well marked with square white masonite or wood blazes nailed to trees. The miles are marked off most of the way, and the standard federal agency BACK-PACKER signs are used in many places. A connecting trail of just over ¼ mile allows the trail to be shortened to 4½ miles for a nice day hike. Camping is permitted anywhere along the trail. Stoves are suggested as an alternative to open fires. Because there are no water sources along the trail, water must be carried. Human waste must be buried, and trash carried out. No permit is required. A map that includes rules for use can be obtained from Wayne National Forest (see the introduction for the complete address).

Since Wildcat Hollow Trail is located adjacent to Burr Oak State Park, this hike can

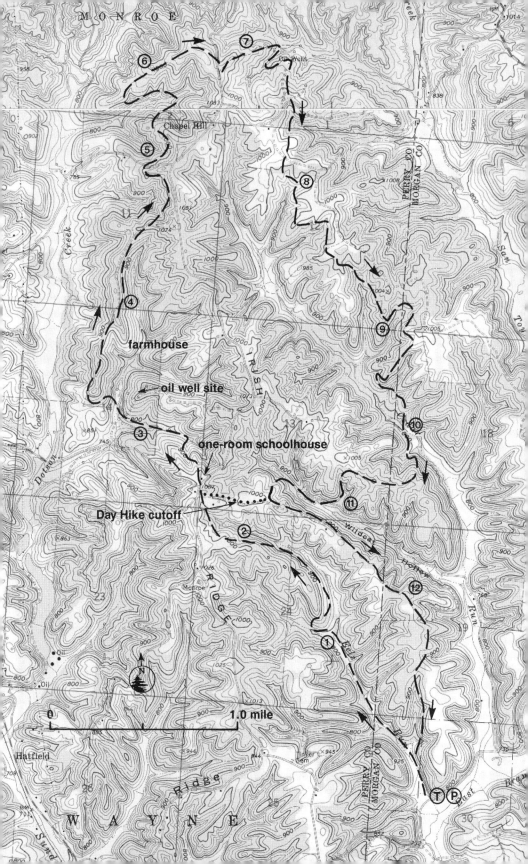

be combined with the Burr Oak Backpack Trail for a trek of about 43 miles. Such a hike would form an hourglass route: The Wildcat Hollow parking lot would be at the pinch of the hourglass, and parking here would allow you to dispose of your trash and pick up supplies and water midway through the hike. The Burr Oak Trail is laid out differently from the Wildcat Hollow Trail, so extra considerations are necessary when planning such a hike. Much of the Burr Oak Trail is close to the water's edge, and lake conditions must be accounted for. There are also steeper climbs in the state park.

This trail is an excellent choice for the fledgling backpacker or for a weekend trek. It is not heavily used, so crowding is not a problem. It is, however, within an area designated for hunting with primitive weapons, so bright red or orange apparel is appropriate during open season.

How to Get There

To reach Wildcat Hollow from the central Ohio area, travel US 33 southeast to Nelsonville. Take OH 78 east to Glouster, and then turn left (north) onto OH 13 and travel 5 miles to Township Road 289. Turn right (east) there and follow the forest service signs for 3 miles to the trailhead, using Irish Ridge and Dew Roads. The drive takes about 2 hours from Columbus.

From Cleveland, travel I-77 south to I-70. Take I-70 west to exit 154 in Zanesville. Turn south on OH 60, then turn onto southbound OH 93 in Zanesville. When OH 93 intersects OH 13, 21 miles south of Zanesville, turn left (south) on OH 13. Take it 13.5 miles to Township Road 289, turn left, and follow the signs as in the instructions for drivers coming from Columbus. The distance from Cleveland is about 180 miles.

From Cincinnati, travel OH 32 east to Athens. Take US 33 north to Nelsonville,

OH 78 east to Glouster, and OH 13 north to reach Township Road 289, also a trip distance of about 180 miles.

The Trail

Departing the open area around the parking lot from the left rear corner, the trail immediately enters a lovely pine grove as it heads up the Eels Run valley. For the next mile, the trail goes in and out of these pines and back and forth across the stream several times. Just beyond the first creek crossing, a sign points both ahead and to the left. Here is where the return trail completes the loop. The trail is designed to be walked clockwise, with the outbound trail going left at this juncture.

When Eels Run splits, the trail follows the left branch. Mile marker 1 is just beyond this point. A few yards after the mile marker, the trail heads up the right slope to move counterclockwise around the end of the ridge. It hangs on the left slope of the valley, gently climbing toward Irish Ridge. Beech/maple and mixed mesophytic forest cover these hillsides, along with a healthy shrub layer of bush honeysuckle, evidence of a former homestead. Apple trees not surrounded by the secondary succession forest give further evidence of human activity in the area. As the trail moves higher up the hillside heading toward the ridge, it enters an open area where it passes mile marker 2. There, at an elevation of 1000 feet, the trail has risen almost exactly 200 feet in 2 miles—a nice, gentle gradient for backpacking.

As the trail swings to the right toward its intersection with Irish Ridge Road, it passes more tall white pines, here with ground cedar covering the forest floor. Just after the trail joins Irish Ridge Road, a dirt road enters from the right. Obviously built for some other purpose, the ¼-mile track is the connector to the returning trail, creating a short loop of about 4½ miles. The connector needs no description since it is an almost straight, level trail through brush and successional forest.

The main trail continues on Irish Ridge Road to its intersection with County Road 70, or Waterworks Road. The trail turns left to travel very briefly on Waterworks Road, shortly to drop off the right side of the road into white pines and young successional-growth hardwood. After leaving the road, the trail turns left to parallel it for a short distance. It then turns to the right, passes directly under a power line, and uses switchbacks to drop into the head of a ravine, which it follows downstream. As you pass mile marker 3, more whispery white pines appear alongside the trail.

Where the ravine widens and forms a hollow, a large number of old oil well shacks and collection pipes can be seen. The trail is not easy to follow as it turns to the right up the hollow. It ducks under a cable, joins an oil well service road to cross the creek, and passes under an overhead collection pipe before turning left to reenter the woods. A sign for the Wildcat Hollow Backpack Trail reassures you of the correct route. The trail curves to the left on the side of the hill as it climbs, using switchbacks, to reach the ridge. Passing through more pines as it swings right, it eventually hits an old dirt road that it takes to the right. Still climbing, the trail ignores another dirt road leaving to the left and continues to the top, where it turns left to follow the ridge. Less than 1 mile beyond, you pass mile marker 4.

The trail continues on this narrow ridge for another ½ mile, passing a recent clear-cut area on the left. At this point the trail becomes a haul road, providing access to Irish Ridge Road. The trail makes an easily missed left turn several hundred yards before this sometimes muddy road reaches the gravel road. After leaving the haul road, the path circles to the left above a hollow, passes an oil well, then climbs to Chapel Hill Road. There it turns right, going up the road about 100 feet to where, just before the road curves left, it exits left into the woods. Mile marker 5 is but a short way beyond.

Following the hillside to the right, the trail crosses several washes, then turns left on an old track. As you head downslope, there is a good view of the Perry County countryside. Leaving the old road, the trail winds its way past a series of white pipes that denote the presence of a gas transmission line. Using switchbacks, the trail reaches the valley floor and heads downstream. Still within sight of gas-line markers, the path curves right to begin climbing the hillside beside more pipeline markers. After it passes mile marker 6, it makes a single, curving switchback to the right before gaining the ridgetop. Continue to ascend the ridge, eventually reaching 1060 feet and curving to the right to meet Irish Ridge Road for the last time.

Turning right onto the gravel road, the trail goes up the road about 100 feet to where a BACKPACKER sign indicates its exit to the left. Still following the ridgetop, you pass mile marker 7 about 250 feet after leaving Irish Ridge Road. The trail then leaves the ridge, swinging right as it drops into a hollow. At a split in the trail, the blazed route takes the right fork. It then goes in and out of a side hollow before turning right and starting to climb back to higher ground. The ascent begins with a short, fairly steep climb, then continues at a gentler grade, passing through another white pine planting and near a wildlife watering hole. Reaching Township Road 13, the trail cuts diagonally right to climb some log steps. It soon crosses a gas-line right-of-way, and then emerges onto another gravel road. This road

(Township Road 297 in Perry County and Township Road 113 in Morgan County), which rides the ridges southeast through the National Forest land, is closed less than 1 mile to the left of this crossing. It is now used as a bridle trail and footpath.

Across the road from where the trail emerges, a dirt track enters. The trail does not take this track but exits just to its left. Shortly, it passes another wildlife watering hole. For the next 1½ miles, the trail stays high on the hillside east of Cedar Run, passing by or through four areas where timber was recently harvested by clear-cutting. Because the regrowth from live tree stumps is rapid, many blazes are obscured by vegetation during the growing season and are difficult to find. Keep a constant watch for markings. At one point the trail uses another old roadbed for a short stretch but soon leaves it, turning to the left. Not all the woods along this ridge have been cut, and in the area where mile marker 9 should be there is a very nice mature mixed oak forest. There the trail swings around the heads of ravines as it approaches the last of the recently clear-cut areas. With the timber harvest area on the right, the trail descends, using a single switchback, to Cedar Run Hollow. Once in the valley, the trail crosses the main stem and then a small side stream of Cedar Run using log bridges. This crossing is close to the 10-mile mark.

The trail turns downstream on the low hillside, but, after crossing another dry wash in a side ravine, it makes a sharp right turn to begin ascending the ridge. Using only one switchback, the path swings gently to the right as it climbs the ridge. As it approaches a fence between National Forest land and an inholding still being farmed, the trail turns to the left and begins to descend into a small side ravine of Wildcat Hollow. As it leaves the woods, it crosses Township Road 300, then turns right to move upstream parallel to the road. The path then goes past a swampy area and another old oil collection area. After crossing the creek, you rise up the side of the valley wall, still headed upstream. You then make a left turn to climb 100 feet to the ridge in less than 1000 feet. The trail has come over 11 miles and, at this point, meets the connecting track for the shorter day hike. There are blazes going to the left and right.

To complete the 13-mile loop trail, turn to the left at this intersection. Shortly, the dirt road divides, with the trail taking the left fork. A fairly open area on the right affords a view back into Wildcat Hollow. The trail continues along the left side of the ridge, eventually reaching a brushy area where it crosses an old cement floor. This spot is near the 12-mile point of the trail. For a brief time the trail returns to the woods, but it soon enters a second open area. You then follow the tracks of another early road along the left side of the ridgetop for just under ½ mile. After turning to the right off the old road, the route goes through the middle of another open area, then returns to the woods as it drops gently off the right side of the ridge to the valley floor. Following a dry wash downstream for a few hundred feet, it meets the outbound trail about 500 feet up Eels Run from the trailhead parking lot.

There could hardly be a more fitting finish than the grove of pines through which the Wildcat Hollow Trail passes as it comes to an end.

35

Zaleski State Forest

*Total distance: 10 to 23½ miles
(14 to 32.9 km)*

*Hiking time: 6 hours (day hike) to 3 days
(backpack)*

Maximum elevation: 1030 feet

Vertical rise: 307 feet

*Maps: USGS 7½' Mineral; USGS 7½'
Union Furnace; ODNR Zaleski State
Forest and Backpack Trail map*

Count Peter Zaleski never saw the land in southeastern Ohio that bears his name. An exile from Poland, Zaleski was active in the Paris banking scene. Using investment monies largely received from Polish émigrés, he formed the Zaleski Mining Company to exploit the resources of Vinton County. In 1856 the town of Zaleski was laid out, and a charcoal-fired iron furnace known as the Zaleski Furnace was constructed just north of the settlement.

It was not the first furnace in the area. Hope Furnace on Sandy Run a few miles to the north had been in blast for two years, producing high-quality iron from the local ore and limestone, and burning charcoal made from the abundant timber of the area. Nor was Zaleski's industrial enterprise the first to come to Vinton County since settlement by European whites. In the first half of the century, millstones had been produced from native rock at a site now under the waters of Lake Hope.

Zaleski's town is still here, but the furnace is gone. Like most of the furnaces of the area, it survived long enough to flourish during the Civil War but was shut down within 10 years of the end of that bitter conflict. The operations had denuded the hills for miles around, and what remained of the already thin iron-bearing veins were now so far under the hills that it was unprofitable to mine them. New sources of high-grade ore and better smelting processes doomed the furnaces. The only remaining evidence of the iron industry here are Hope Furnace, preserved in Lake Hope State Park, and traces of haul roads along which ore, lime-

A hundred years ago, activity in the Zaleski State Forest area was centered on the Hope Furnace.

stone, and wood were carted to the furnace.

Prosperity never really returned to Vinton County. In the mid-20th century the thin veins of high-sulfur coal were exploited, mostly by drift mining. That process left many of the small valleys of the area awash with "yellow boy," a yellowish deposit leached from mines, and the streams and rivers unable to sustain life because of high acidity. Where there is yellow boy, the pH of the water is very low from sulphuric acid, and it spells death to all creatures great and small. Today, strip-mining for coal, logging of secondary forests, and tourism are the main industries of the area.

Established during the early 1930s, 26,867-acre Zaleski State Forest was the site of a Civilian Conservation Corps camp during the Depression. It also holds Ohio's first resort-type park development, the Lake Hope Lodge and Cabins. Lake Hope State Park, now 3223 acres, was carved from the state forest in 1949 when the Department of Natural Resources came into being. It includes all the recreational facilities of the state-owned land except the Backpack and bridle trails.

The Zaleski Backpack Trail was established in the mid-1970s. It is laid out in a long loop (a connecting side trail at its "waist"), with a smaller loop attached to it by a two-way trail. This layout allows the trail to be walked in several combinations. A hike on just the southern part of the large loop covers 10 miles and can be walked as a day hike or an overnight, since there are two designated campgrounds along the way. Adding the rest of the central loop brings the hike to 17 miles (or 19 miles if a third campsite a mile beyond is used). If desired, the northern loop (not described here) can be added to bring the total mileage to 23½

Campsite 3

Campsite 1

Campsite 2

connecting route

Hope Furnace

0   1.0 mile

miles, with three campsites, although it can be hiked using only two overnights.

Camping is permitted at the designated sites only. Each of these has a privy and a fire ring, with fresh water close by. There is no fee for hiking, but preregistration at the trailhead bulletin board is required. This backpack trail is the only one in Ohio with self-guided interpretive information on the map. The publication, the "Zaleski State Forest and Backpack Trail" map, is available from the ODNR publications office, but it can usually be found at the trailhead. The interpretive information is keyed to numbered signs along the trail. The trail is divided into short sections between points designated by letters. The main trail is blazed with orange paint, the side trails with white.

Whether done in its entirety over several days or in pieces as day walks, hiking the Zaleski Trail is an exhilarating experience. The wildflowers of both woods and open areas are lovely during the growing season, and wildlife is common throughout the year. Because of the vast expanse of woodland, Zaleski is good breeding country for the woodland birds that make their way to Ohio each spring. Amphibians and reptiles, including copperheads and timber rattlesnakes, are also found in this wilderness area. The Zaleski Backpack Trail is an ideal trail for the naturalist-hiker at any time of year.

How to Get There

The trailhead can be reached from the Columbus area by traveling southeast on US 33 past Logan. Turn right (south) on OH 328, then left (east) on US 56. At OH 278, turn right (south) and travel 4 miles to the upper end of Lake Hope. The trailhead is located at a parking lot on the east side of OH 278 opposite the Hope Furnace parking lot. At the trailhead is an information kiosk where registration forms are to be completed. An alternative from Columbus is to take US 23 south to Circleville and then OH 56 east to OH 278, where you turn right. The trip takes 2 hours either way.

From western and southwestern Ohio, take US 35 east to Chillicothe from I-71. From Chillicothe, travel US 50 east through McArthur to OH 677. Turn left (north), and at OH 278 turn left (north) and drive to the parking lot about 1 mile north of the Lake Hope dam (3 hours' traveling time).

From Cleveland, the trip takes about 4½ hours via the Columbus route.

The Trail

A sign located on the east side of OH 278, across the Sandy Run bridge from the parking lot, identifies the shared entrance to the Zaleski Backpack Trail and the 2-mile Olds Hollow Trail. The trails begin by crossing a metal bridge built by students from nearby Hocking Technical College. A series of wooden block steps carries you above the floodplain. Shortly, the two trails go their separate ways. Either trail can be taken here to continue on the Backpack Trail, since they come back together about a mile down the trail. Although the Olds Hollow Trail is a bit more rigorous and just a tiny bit longer, it is an interesting alternate route. It passes by the cemetery that once served the community of Hope, the town now covered by the lake of that name, and by a small but interesting rock shelter. The Olds Hollow Trail goes right at the juncture, and the Backpack Trail goes to the left.

The Backpack Trail immediately enters a lovely pine grove that has a cathedral-like quality. It then drops back to the swampy land along Sandy Run and crosses a wooden footbridge. Climbing to a fork, an arrow indicates that the left branch is the route to follow. After passing through another stand of pine, the trail drops to another footbridge and to the junction with the returning Olds Hollow Trail. The rock shelter on the Olds Hollow Trail is just a few yards straight ahead.

The Backpack Trail turns left and begins to climb the hillside. It swings down and then back up before dropping to King Hollow. To the left is a bridge for the return trail from Point F. The main trail turns right and almost at once begins climbing the ridge, gaining 840 feet in a little over ⅓ mile. As it reaches the ridge, the trail joins an old road to travel the high ground through a wonderful mixed oak forest. The trail stays on or just off the ridge, curving gently to the left. A sign announces Point B and the first water, located downhill to the right. The trail has come 1½ miles.

You continue on the old ridge road as it swings to the south. After less than ¼ mile you will arrive at Point C, where a white-blazed side trail leads out a side ridge to the first campground. Since the next campground is less than 4½ miles down the trail, this one is usually used only by hikers who got a late start.

Still following the ridgetop road, the trail turns east from Point C, then curves to the right and heads south once again. About ½ mile after Point C, you reach the first sign keyed to the interpretive material on the ODNR map. The text tells that the trail is traveling on the old Marietta-to-Chillicothe road that passed through Athens. The route was used by prehistoric Native Americans of the Fort Ancient culture as well as by settlers and was abandoned in 1870. A half mile beyond this sign, the old road leaves the ridge to the right as the trail continues straight ahead. After another ½ mile, the trail descends over rocky outcrops to arrive at interpretive Stop 2, the Moonville overlook. According to legend, the portion of the B&O Railroad track in the valley below is haunted by the ghost of Moonville.

As the story goes, at the turn of the century a brakeman was killed near the Moonville tunnel as he waved his lantern to stop a train. Being exceedingly drunk, he apparently swayed into the path of the oncoming locomotive. He is reportedly buried in the Moonville graveyard and, on some nights, his lantern can be seen "a-glimmerin' and a-wavin'," still trying to stop that train. Unfortunately, it is difficult to see Moonville or even the railroad track when the trees are in leaf, so I did not attempt to verify the presence of the ghost at night.

After leaving Stop 2, the trail turns left over the ridge, drops slightly, and crosses another ridge before descending a ravine into Bear Hollow. At an intersection with another old road, the trail turns right to head down the hollow. Following the old road, the trail makes a couple of stream crossings and passes a beaver pond full of standing dead trees. After climbing the hillside a bit it arrives at Stop 3, the main street of an early mining town known as Ingham Station. Though it takes a sharp eye to see any evidence of the town that existed here over 100 years ago, the settlement supported a store, a train depot, and several families in the 1870s. An old cellar hole is visible alongside the trail. Ancient apple trees and ornamental shrubs betray the past occupation. Closed off and difficult to locate, the entrance to the old Ingham coal mine is farther up the trail on the left.

Leaving Ingham Station, do not follow the old road up the ridge, although it appears as if most hikers go this way. The trail actually turns right, off the road it was following. It passes through heavy herbaceous vegetation, then hits another old road, which it soon leaves to the left to pass the closed drift mine. Next it makes a very steep climb. As it begins to level off, the trail takes a

➤ Return of the Turkey

The wild turkey (Meleagris gallopavo) is said to have been abundant in Ohio at the time of European settlement. Throughout the state, flocks of 30 to 50 were regularly encountered during the winter, and they were seen as scattered individuals the rest of the year. But unregulated hunting and changes in habitat sent the population into a downward spiral. Wild turkeys were extirpated from Ohio by the end of the 19th century. After a short, unsuccessful attempt at pen-rearing wild turkeys for release into the wild, in the mid-1950s the Division of Wildlife obtained some trapped wild birds from a game agency in another state. In February 1956, 10 were released in Vinton County. Between 1956 and 1971, another 397 turkeys were released in southeastern Ohio. By 1983, wild turkeys were known to be in 32 counties, and there were estimated to be 7677 individuals.

With the Division of Wildlife continuing its trap-and-release program, wild turkeys are now found in most areas of the state where suitable habitat exists. There are hunting seasons in both fall and spring, with various restrictions to allow the population to continue to expand. I see turkeys often as I hike the trails around the state, in sizable flocks in the forest in the winter and females with their broods in fields near the edge of the woods in late spring or early summer. It's a thrill to see them at any time of year.

switchback to pass a sandstone outcrop, then turns right to reach and climb steps that lead to a juncture with the old road up the ridge. Stop 4 on the interpretive trail is at the overlook at the top of the hill. It describes yet another old town, this one called King Station. According to the guide, the stretch of railroad track from Moonville through Ingham to Mineral is considered by many to be "the loneliest in the state of Ohio."

From Stop 4, the trail follows an old road along the ridge. About ½ mile beyond Stop 4 it arrives at Stop 5, an archaeological site. To the right of the trail is a small, doughnut-shaped ceremonial ring built and used by Native Americans of the Adena culture, who were active in southern Ohio between 800 B.C. and A.D. 700. Underfoot on the trail, you can see chips of the dark Zaleski flint they worked. Native to Vinton County, this type of flint was the third most important flint to Natives in Ohio.

Swinging right but still following the ridge, in about ½ mile the trail comes to Stop 6, where it once again travels the old Marietta-to-Chillicothe road, this time going east. Another ½ mile along the ridge brings you to Point D, where a CAMPSITE sign points right to a white-blazed trail down the old road. A water hydrant is off the trail to the left.

The main trail now makes two quick left turns, then begins descending into King Hollow. Using the water haul road part of the way, it drops into a ravine and then climbs to the King Hollow Trail. It shortly arrives at Point E, about 6½ miles from the start. Leaving the King Hollow Trail to reenter the woods at Point E, the trail begins a ½-mile, 221-foot climb, using one switchback, to reach a ridge spur that it follows for a short distance. At the main ridge, the trail turns left on a logging haul road, which it follows until it runs into a dirt road at Stop 7. A sign alongside the road identifies this part of the state forest as the Zaleski Turkey Management Area. This venture is a cooperative effort of the Divisions of Forestry and Wildlife to provide suitable habitat for the propagation of wild turkeys. It apparently has been successful, for when I stayed at the campsite at point H, I was awakened in the morning by the gobbling of turkeys close by.

After crossing the dirt road, the trail soon intersects a gas well service road, then turns left to drop into Harbargar Hollow. After a sandstone cliff with a small recess cave on the left, a sign along the right side of the trail directs you straight ahead to Points G and H. The main Backpack Trail turns to the right just beyond this sign. Another sign dead ahead reads DAY LOOP RETURN TO POINT A. If you plan to return to Point A and complete the 10-mile loop, take this side trail straight ahead.

The side trail soon turns left around the end of a ridge, then goes into and out of a small hollow that has sandstone outcrops and several recess caves. Approaching Sandy Run, it swings to the left to parallel the stream and OH 278. Once more it turns into and out of a short hollow, passing over the top of another rock shelter. As you leave the woods, you pass through tall bottomland weeds and reach the King Hollow Trail. A short distance beyond the road, the trail crosses a wooden footbridge, then climbs to a junction with the outgoing trail. Turning right, it returns to the trailhead after about another ¾ mile of travel through pine groves.

For those continuing on the longer trails, head up the east side of the Sandy Run valley from Point F. The trail crosses dry washes in the heads of several ravines and over one ridge before dropping into Mizner Hollow. From there, it angles up the hillside to the left and turns right up the ridge. Turning left, you move counterclockwise around the hillside before turning right to angle down the slope into Ogg Hollow. In the hollow, the trail turns upstream. You leave the creek shortly, going left and heading up the hillside. Gaining 250 feet in less than ¼ mile, the climb is one of the more strenuous on the trail. Reaching the ridge, the trail follows it, rising and falling slightly for not quite ½ mile, until it reaches a knob with a panoramic view. This is Stop 8, and the printed guide is not really needed to interpret the scene. A quick look straight ahead reveals that the 20 acres to the north have been designated a Regeneration Harvest Area. Merchantable sawtimber has been removed, and the woody growth of over 5 feet in height was cut down. Though often defended by wildlife agencies as being of benefit to game species such as ruffed grouse, the technique has increasingly come under attack by environmentalists, who believe it to be detrimental to the preservation of overall biological diversity.

From Stop 8, the trail turns sharply left, still on the ridge. A short distance after it makes a curve to the right, it begins its descent into Morgan Hollow. You drop to the creek using only one switchback. There is a short, rather steep section near the bottom. Point G, where the southern loop goes to the left and the connector to the campground at Point H, and the northern loop goes right, is only a few steps beyond the creek. OH 278 is only a few hundred feet down the valley to the left.

From this intersection (Point G) to the campground at Point L, the trail covers just over 1 mile. This section is the only part of the main Zaleski Backpack Trail that must be hiked in both directions. The connecting trail heads right upstream for several hundred feet, then turns left to climb the ridge. There, turning to the right, it begins following another old road. Stop 12 tells the story of this road, which was used during the 1860s to haul charcoal to Hope Furnace. The charcoal, used to fire the iron furnace, was made by piling wood in large stacks, lighting it, covering it with wet earth and leaves, and leaving it to burn for 10 to 12 days. (The interpretive numbers are out of sequence here because the trail has been rerouted since its original layout.)

Just beyond the interpretive stop, the trail turns left. The path entering from the right is the former trail; this was once Point G. A few hundred yards of nearly level ridgetop trail leads to the gravel road used to supply water to the tank just ahead. Follow the gravel road, soon reaching the sign for Point L. Across the road on the right is the drinking water hydrant, and the campsite is only moments away. Less than 100 feet ahead on the road is Point H, where the nice, wooded campsite is within view. The privies are several hundred feet beyond the campfire area.

After camping, you must now rehike the L-to-G segment, again passing Stop 12, this time in its proper sequence. Shortly after Stop 12, the old road leaves the ridge, going down the slope to the right. The trail continues ahead to drop off the left side of the ridge into Morgan Hollow. Follow the stream out of the hollow, passing Point G, shortly to arrive at Sandy Run, Point M.

After crossing Sandy Run and reaching OH 278, the trail turns left to follow the highway for 1/10 mile. A corrugated steel building on the left side of the road is Stop 13, a metering station utilized in the Lake Hope mine-sealing demonstration project. It contains instruments that monitor water quality and flow. The objective of the project is to prevent acid mine drainage from old drift mines upstream from entering the Lake Hope area.

Point N, where the trail leaves the highway, is at the end of the guardrail on the left side of the road. The trail climbs quite steeply, gaining 200 feet in elevation in a very short distance. It passes Stop 14 shortly after leaving the highway. This stop originally pointed out an exposed drift mine. The mine has since been closed up as part of the mine-sealing project and is no longer visible. The exposed vein of coal here was extracted by hand and cart. The vein was mined wherever it drifted, thus the name.

As the trail continues up Starrett Ridge, it becomes obvious that it is following an old road. Stop 15 tells that the township road was used until about 1920, when the last few farms in what is now Zaleski State Forest were abandoned. After Stop 15, the road and the trail follow the ridge for about 1/2 mile, gently rising as they gain elevation. The trail turns left to climb to an area now overgrown with shrubs, which Stop 16 identifies as the site of a former farm. The foundation stones, old wells, and cellars have all but disappeared, but fencerows and ornamental, shade, and fruit trees reveal its past use. From the homestead site, the trail follows old roads as it heads south on Long Ridge. At one point, where the trail meets another trail, the blazes are somewhat unclear. You make a left turn, then almost immediately make a right turn. After paralleling Road 11B along Long Ridge for about 3/4 mile, the trail meets with Irish Ridge Road at Point O.

The next section of trail takes you through perhaps the longest and one of the loveliest hollows in the area. After crossing Irish Ridge Road, the trail goes out a lightly wooded side ridge, then drops into the upper end of Stony Hollow. Reaching the bottom first in a side ravine, the trail turns right to enter the main hollow and turn left downstream. For the next 1¾ miles, the trail follows the stream as it makes its way toward Sandy Run. For the most part it stays on the left side of the hollow, at three points climbing partway up the hillside only to return to the valley. You cross the stream eight or nine times, but the crossings are easy except in bad weather. You will pass by a rock shelter big enough to walk into before reaching the Stop 17 sign. The reference here is to an old slab pile that formerly marked where a portable sawmill operated during the early 1950s. Apparently Mother Nature has erased the evidence, for I could see no signs of this activity. After several more stream crossings, the trail again climbs the hillside, traveling between a sandstone cliff and a slump block. After climbing above a wide curve in the creek below, the trail drops to meet the campground entry road at Point P.

Following the hard-surfaced road to the left, the trail quickly reaches OH 278, where it turns right. After just over ¼ mile, you pass Hope Furnace on the right and arrive at the trailhead parking lot.

36

Brukner Nature Center

Total distance: 4⅔ miles (7.4 km)

Hiking time: 2½ hours

Maximum elevation: 926 feet

Vertical rise: 131 feet

Maps: USGS 7½'; Pleasant Hill; Brukner Nature Center trail map

Steps cut by a chain saw solve the problem of a deadfall across the boardwalk.

When Clayton J. Brukner, Miami County industrialist and inventor, heard that the Aullwood Audubon Center near Englewood was turning away classes of children for lack of room, he wondered whether the land he owned along the Stillwater River would be suitable for a similar environmental education center. Having received a favorable opinion from National Audubon Society consultants, he set about making it happen. Brukner Nature Center was incorporated on June 17, 1967, to be developed on 165 acres of property owned by Brukner, land that he had maintained as a wildlife refuge for many years. As a nonprofit organization, the center endeavors to provide meaningful experiences that emphasize natural history and the environment for the people in and beyond Miami County. It functions as both a nature study and an environmental education center.

Situated adjacent to Horseshoe Bend on the Stillwater River, the center includes both upland and riverbottom land and holds tracts with pine woods, prairie, thickets, deciduous forest, swamp, pond, stream, and river. Six miles of trails beckon you to explore all these habitats. Exhibits and programs at the interpretive center have been designed to help you better know and understand what you see.

Brukner Nature Center is one of a number of private, not-for-profit nature centers located throughout Ohio that have many miles of trails suitable for hiking. Take advantage of the great variety of educational programs that they offer, enjoy their quiet trails, and give them your support.

The trails of Brukner Nature Center are open during daylight hours throughout the year. There is no charge for admission to the grounds, but a fee is collected for entry into the Interpretive Building on weekends. Picnicking, gathering of natural materials, camping, pets, and alcoholic beverages are not permitted.

How to Get There

The center is reached by taking I-75 to Troy, then OH 55 west 3.5 miles to Horseshoe Bend Road. The entrance is on the right side of Horseshoe Bend Road about 1.5 miles west of OH 55. All trails start from the Interpretive Building. There is a map on an outdoor bulletin board, and free trail maps are available in the center.

The Trail

Start this hike from the far southwest corner of the parking lot, to the left of the Interpretive Building. Here you will find the Pineland Trail going due south. The path skirts the west side of a cattail pond and turns right to cross the earthen dam of another pond. Take a hard right turn beyond that pond onto the Hickory Ridge Trail. You pass a meadow on the left and young woodland on the right before entering older woods. The wood-chip trail then heads out Hickory Ridge, where it goes downslope toward the riverbottom. Hickory and young oaks dominate the ridge on the left. There is a deep gully on the right. The slopes are covered with older trees and associated wildflowers and shrubs. Where the trail reaches the stream, a second trail enters from the left. This is the other end of the Hickory Ridge Loop Trail. Do not take it, but continue downhill. After 100 feet, there is a bridge to the right. Do not take it at this time, but continue straight ahead.

Here the gravel that was on the trail as it descended the hill stops. A sign on a tall honey locust tree identifies the beginning of the Stillwater Loop Trail. Take the path to the right into the riverine forest of the Stillwater bottoms. Cottonwood, sycamore, box elder, and elms dominate this frequently flooded area. Listen for the clucking sound of the ever-present red-bellied woodpecker. The river can be heard to the right, and the trail moves close to it. Because the center is managed as a natural area, dead trees are not removed, and the flotsam and jetsam of high water are allowed to accumulate where they drop. An island close by is dominated by large cottonwoods and hackberry. The trail swings to the left across 100 feet of floodplain before turning upstream along the base of the steep hillside. Cross a culvert, then follow the bark-covered trail back to its junction at the sign on the locust.

Turn right up the valley to the first trail to the left. Cross the bridge, then turn left (west). This is the Wren Trail. One hundred feet ahead, the trail splits. Leave the Wren Trail, taking the path to the left. To the left of the trail is a large sycamore covered with poison ivy. A sign on the right tells of the construction of the boardwalk ahead by the Miami-Shelby County Youth Conservation Corps and the Brukner staff in 1977, using funds given by the Container Corporation of America. The wet woods along the boardwalk are dominated by silver maple at this point. Two deadfalls across the trail have steps cut in them to allow hikers to pass.

After traveling on nearly 500 feet of boardwalk, you will come to a dividing point. Take the boardwalk, to the right. It passes an alder thicket, a skunk cabbage patch, and an observation tower. At the end of the boardwalk, steps lead to higher ground, where after 150 feet the path rejoins the Wren Trail. Continue straight ahead, going clockwise on the Wren Trail. Chinquapin oak, hackberry, basswood, and redbud indi-

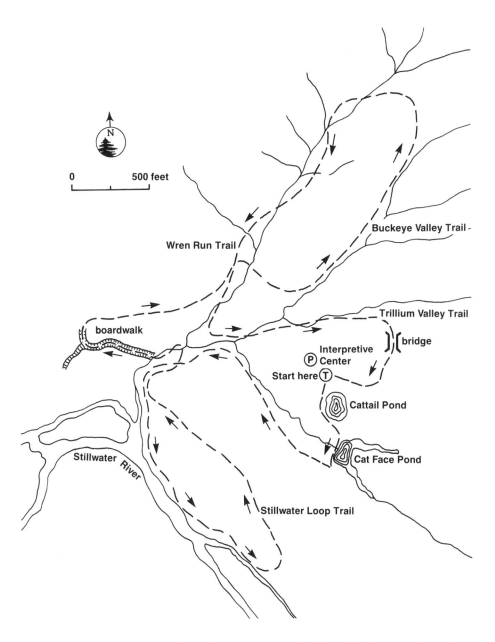

cate the presence of limestone bedrock not far below the surface.

Two hundred feet of gentle climbing brings the trail back to the upland. The boundary fence and farm fields are about 40 feet to the left along here. Glacial errat-ics are piled along the fence and in ravines; Brukner is in an area of Ohio where boulders were scattered on the surface of the land by continental glaciation. Redcedars, an early invader in old fields in this part of Ohio, indicate the presence of thin soil over dolomite or limestone. There are lots of grapevines, and the forest appears to be dominated by sugar maple and white oak here. There is a huge shagbark hickory "wolf tree" in the ravine to the right that somehow missed the lumberman's saw. Over the fence line, farm trash has been discarded in the fashion so typical of earlier years. With several feet of glacial drift on top of the bedrock here, the groundhogs have found easy digging in this upland area. There are large shagbark hickories on both sides of the trail as it returns to the stream valley. Look for the rectangular holes of the pileated woodpeckers that reside here year-round.

Dropping to a valley, the Wren Trail comes to a T intersection, where it turns right to complete its loop. Your route turns left to follow a connecting trail upstream to the Buckeye Valley Trail. After 75 feet you will meet that loop trail. Turn right on it, cross the stream, and make a 100-foot climb out of the valley on 41 steps. The trail swings right and crosses into another watershed, where it heads upstream along the rim of a deeply cut ravine to its right. The forest is again oak/hickory. After a few hundred yards, the trail curves left (north) across the ridge to reenter the valley it had crossed earlier. As it drops downhill into a moister environment, beech and sugar maple reappear. Buckeye trees appear along the stream. A sign indicates the trail's end. Continue down the valley on the connecting trail to where it meets the Wren Trail, then turn left and travel on the Wren Trail until it comes to another connecting trail that goes left across a bridge. After crossing the stream, stay on the trail to the left. Benches along the trail provide opportunities for rest and quiet nature study.

As the connecting trail heads up the valley, it splits. The right fork, which appears to be an old road, goes toward the Interpretive Building. Along this trail, the outdoor cages of the wildlife rehabilitation program run by the center staff are located. Take the left path, however. This is the Trillium Trail.

On the point that stands out to the right of the trail as it begins its climb up the valley, snow trillium—for which the trail is named—can be found in bloom in the very early springtime. Back now on wood chips, the trail passes a patch of scouring rush or horsetail along the stream. The trail climbs the valley along its right flank. Limestone slump blocks lie to your right. A great horned owl was calling on the day I walked this trail, probably one of a mated pair that already had young in their nearby nest. Listen for their soft *whoo, whoo, whoo*. Trees with shiny bark below large holes tell of active raccoon dens. Tall oaks give way to a forest of young trees in the valley to the right. The trail crosses a bridge and turns to gravel as it climbs a set of steps to the upland. Now heading due south, it crosses a deep ravine on a bridge built on oversized steel I-beams.

After crossing the entry road, turn right onto the Pineland Trail, which enters a 30-year-old planting of white and red pine. Something about white pines makes such spots great places to stop for contemplation. In the late afternoon, listen for the mournful calls of the screech owls that live nearby. The trail now returns to the parking lot.

37

Charleston Falls Preserve

Total distance: 2 miles (3.2 km)

Hiking time: 1½ hours

Maximum elevation: 900 feet

Vertical rise: 65 feet

Maps: USGS 7½' Tipp City; MCPD Charleston Falls Preserve map

Charleston Falls Preserve is a 169-acre sanctuary located above Dayton, 3 miles south of Tipp City. It is a facility of the Miami County Park District. Charleston Creek and the falls on that stream get their names from the small community of West Charleston that lies a mile to the east. The central feature of this petite preserve is, as the name implies, the beautiful waterfall that tumbles over a 37-foot limestone escarpment into a cool shale valley. Here, rocks of lower Silurian age, formed from material deposited in the bottom of warm, shallow seas perhaps 400 to 440 million years ago, lie at the surface, where a small stream is making its way downhill to the nearest river.

The rock exposed at Charleston Falls is essentially the same age as that exposed at the escarpment at the eastern end of Lake Erie. The formation near the surface at the top of the falls is the Brassfield limestone. Here it is especially blocky and tough; it is referred to as Bioclastic Brassfield, because it is rich in fossils. Below it are limestones of the Belfast Beds, which are layered and cross-bedded, allowing water to penetrate easily. Freezing and thawing action breaks this rock apart, leaving the layer above it. The next stratum down in this valley head is the Elkhorn shale, an Ordovician-aged (440 to 500 million years since deposition) member of the Cincinnatian shale. Loose, crumbly, and relatively impenetrable to water, the shale forms a slope away from the base of the rocks above. This remarkable little gorge was cut by the massive amounts of glacial meltwater that flowed along this drainage as the last glacier melted, until it was gone from the divide located 33 miles to the north.

Managed not as a park for active recreation but as a natural area, Charleston Falls has a system of trails that allow visitors to observe without destroying its special natural features. The only picnic area is located close to the road, away from the falls and stream. Rest rooms are located at the rear of the parking lot.

How to Get There

Take OH 202 north off I-70 (exit 36). Travel 3 miles until you reach Ross Road. Turn left (west) here; the preserve entrance is on the right. Park at the only lot.

The Trail

Walk east 100 feet to a trail running north and south along a shaded old fence line. To the right (south) toward the road is the picnic area and an entrance to another trail to the falls that goes across an open meadow. In the late summer, when the goldenrod and New England asters are in bloom and monarchs are nectaring in preparation for another flight toward Mexico, choose this trail. There is an observation deck where you look out over the top of the vegetation. At other times of the year, turn left and follow the ⅓-mile trail north and then east through the woods to the falls.

In all but the driest of summers, the falls will be heard before it is seen. Walk to the top of the falls for a careful look from above. Then backtrack 50 feet to a short trail to the right that leads to wooden and natural stone steps going into the ravine below the falls. Take care, for there are no handrails on the steps or boardwalk below. An observation area allows a closer look at the escarpment. Water comes over the rim in at least two places. In the right light, the falls will produce a beautiful rainbow. Because of the slumping shale at the base of the cliff, no

real plunge pool exists. Instead, the water falls onto a rocky talus slope.

Continue across the boardwalk, then climb more wooden steps to another observation platform for a look at the falls from the left side. From there, scramble up the natural rock "steps" to the base of the dolomite cliff. Follow the trail for about 700 feet below the cliff face, passing a small limestone cave, until it climbs on a few wooden steps to double back on itself. The calcareous soils derived from the limestones of this gorge are especially conducive to the growth of such plants as Virginia bluebell, purple cliff brake, walking fern, and columbine. Look for them along the way. Turn left at a sign that says RETURN LOOP. Take this trail about 200 feet to where it intersects another trail. Turn left to go to the Thorny Badlands. In the past, a self-guided trail brochure was available, and the numbers are still in place along the trail. Consideration was being given to incorporating the information into the trail guide, so you might want to pick one up as you enter the preserve. If available, the information provided will add meaning to the hike.

The first post you encounter after you join the main trail is No. 3, which is meant to stimulate thoughts about the four essentials for life on our planet: soil, water, sunlight, and air. Compare the variable availability of these elements at various stops along the trail, and note what different life-forms exist when the mixture is changed.

The trail now dips to cross a bridge, then rises to an area where white pines were once planted to halt an erosion problem on the abused slope to the left. Here many special year-round residents like barred owls and chickadees and transients like purple finches and pine warblers can be seen. You can easily discern when the pines were planted, because each whorl of branches

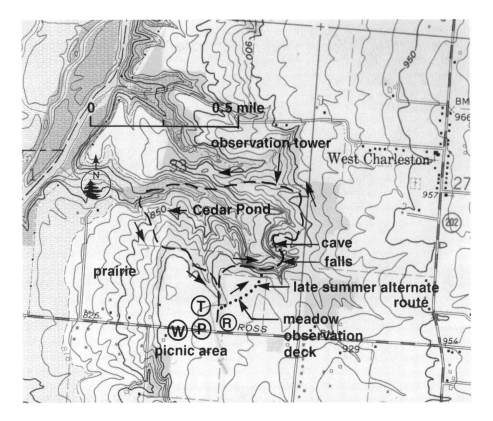

represents one year's growth. These trees are lovely now and have served their purpose in controlling erosion. In due time they will die out as they become overtopped by invading deciduous trees. This is hardwood country.

At the high point on the trail stands a wooden observation tower where you can look over the tops of the hawthorns, cedars, and grasses on the hill below. (The name Thorny Badlands came from the presence of these hawthorns.) Wooded at the time of settlement, this slope was clear-cut for lumber, planted in corn, and later heavily grazed. It will take many years to heal the scars left from these three activities. The invasion of hawthorns is the first step in the succession from old field grasses and forbs to eastern hardwood forest.

At Post No. 6, take time to notice the change in environment upon entering the forest tunnel. Too dark for many plants, this place is ideal for fungi, the decomposers of the natural world.

At the trail juncture, continue straight ahead. After a short distance, there is a spur trail to the left that leads to a bench overlooking the stream. This is a good place to rest body and soul, to contemplate the words of others such as Henry David Thoreau, who wrote, "I went to the woods because I wished to live deliberately, to front only the essential facts of life, and see if I could not learn what it had to teach, and not, when I came to die, discover that I had not lived."

Back on the main trail, continue downstream. The trail soon crosses Charleston Creek on man-made stepping-stones. The

The sign at Cedar Pond must be read in its reflection.

path climbs uphill from the stream, and in about 100 feet comes out into the open at the edge of a small planted prairie. Using seeds gathered from within 50 miles of here, the park staff—under the leadership of former Miami County Park District director the late Scott L. Huston—created a prairie where one never before existed. The eroded slope, given its thin soil over limestone, was a good place to plant native prairie grasses and forbs. Small patches of original prairie occur along the Stillwater River not far from here in Miami County, on a variety of mesic and xeric sites. (A good example can be seen in the Miami Park District's Stillwater Prairie Reserve off OH 185, 9 miles west of Piqua.) Leave the main trail and walk the narrow path uphill through the prairie, noting how it looks in this season. Be certain to return to this site during the last week of July or the first week of August for a spectacular show of native prairie flora.

Returning to the main trail, walk uphill. Look to the left at the serene setting of the small, man-made Cedar Pond. Here is a sign that reads correctly only in its reflection. Stay long enough to let the green frogs or cricket frogs return to their calling and to contemplate how the dragon- and damselflies and the red-winged blackbirds and swallows fit into the natural world.

Heading due south, follow the main trail to where it turns east (left) along an old fencerow. Ignore the side trail to the Locust Grove that leaves the main trail to the right at this corner. After traveling about 600 feet, take the trail to the right as it swings southeast past a small meadow, then heads to the shaded trail leading to the parking lot. Plans are to convert the meadow west of the parking lot to more tallgrass prairie over the next several years. You may want to visit the area frequently to watch the progress of this restoration project, which is being partially underwritten by a grant from the Ohio Division of Wildlife. Meanwhile, take home lots of good memories and leave only a few footprints.

38

Clifton Gorge State Nature Preserve and John Bryan State Park

Total distance: 5½ miles (8.8 km)

Hiking time: 3½ hours

Maximum elevation: 990 feet

Vertical rise: 150 feet

*Maps: USGS 7½' Clifton;
ODNR Clifton Gorge State Nature
Preserve brochure and map;
ODNR John Bryan State Park map*

The Clifton Gorge/John Bryan complex is rich in early Ohio history. As a year-round flowing river, the Little Miami powered the wheels of frontier industry. Dozens of mills running all sorts of industrial operations sprang up along the Little Miami, from Clifton to Cincinnati. Because of the narrow gorge at Clifton, those located there were among the best. A stagecoach road running from Pittsburgh to Cincinnati came through Clifton, dropped into the gorge, and returned to higher ground to head downriver. Its purpose was to pick up goods from the mills along the way. All the mill industries have now vanished except for the long-lived Clifton Mill. The ruins of these structures and the road that served them can still be seen in the preserve and the park.

Considered one of Ohio's premier nature preserves, Clifton Gorge and the adjoining John Bryan State Park should be visited at all seasons to enjoy their full beauty. No visit to the area is complete without a stop at the historic Clifton Mill, located one block east of the trailhead in Clifton on the bank of the Little Miami River. Antioch University's Glen Helen Nature Preserve (see Hike 42) is located 5 miles west, in the village of Yellow Springs. Its 26 miles of trails, including the Glen Helen Scout Trail, offer additional hiking opportunities in this area.

How to Get There

The main entrance to Clifton Gorge State Nature Preserve is located along OH 343, 0.5 mile west of Clifton and OH 72; however, a secondary parking lot located at the corner of Jackson and Water Streets on the edge of the village offers a better starting point and is where this 5½-mile hike begins. To reach the trailhead from Columbus, travel I-70 about 50 miles west to OH 72. Then go 8 miles south to OH 343 in Clifton. Turn right (west). Jackson is the second street to the left. It meets Water Street in two blocks. From Cincinnati, travel north on I-71, and then north on OH 72 to Clifton. From Dayton, travel east on US 35, north on I-675, east (right) on Dayton–Yellow Springs Road, shortly north (left) on US 68, and then east (right) on OH 343.

The Trail

The trail begins just to the right of the information kiosk. To the left of the kiosk is a glacial erratic bearing a bronze plaque that commemorates Clifton Gorge as a National Natural Landmark. The trail heads directly to the gorge, about 100 feet from the parking lot. There, an overlook allows a first glance of the river, and an interpretive sign tells of the creation of the gorge by meltwater from the last glacier. The gravel-filled bed of this ancient river, known as the Kennard outwash, has been traced 33 miles from Logan County to the head of Clifton Gorge.

The trail immediately turns to the right to follow the rim of the gorge downstream. Passing between old "wolf trees" along the gorge and regenerating fields, the trail soon comes to two bridges built by the present-day Ohio Division of Civilian Conservation workers. The tops of northern white cedar (arborvitae) trees growing in the gorge are visible, and on the upland, redcedars (eastern junipers) grow. Just beyond, at a bend in the river, is an overlook at the site of the old Patterson Mill. This mill site was not the first in the area. Owen Davis and Benjamin Whiteman built a gristmill and inn on the present site of Clifton in about 1803. By

1809, however, Robert Patterson, the founder of Lexington, Kentucky, cofounder of Cincinnati, and an early settler of Dayton, had built this mill to make cotton and wool cloth. The four-story mill spanned the gorge like a bridge. Its 22-foot overshot wheel nestled in an alcove in the rock. During the War of 1812, the mill provided cloth for the uniforms of American soldiers fighting in Ohio. In 1870, a flood demolished the mill. Another flood in 1876 destroyed the dam. All that can be seen today are the square holes in the rock at the bottom of the gorge that held the beams that supported the mill.

This overlook provides an excellent view of the narrows of the gorge just downstream. The trail continues to follow the rim of the gorge downstream. Several ancient arborvitae lean out from the gorge wall and reach for the sky along here. At the "pool overlook," a sign tells the story of Darnell's leap. In 1778, a party of men led by Daniel Boone was captured at Blue Licks, Kentucky, by a band of Shawnee Indians and taken to the principal Shawnee town of Chillicothe (now Oldtown, Ohio) on the Little Miami River. A few months later Boone managed to escape, and returned to Boonesborough in time to warn of an impending Indian attack. Cornelius Darnell, another member of Boone's party, escaped some time later, but the Indians soon discovered his flight and gave chase. They caught up with him at this spot on the north bank of the "narrows." Facing certain death by torture, Darnell chose instead to leap the chasm. Although he fell short of the far side, he managed to grasp hold of the trees that mantled the cliffs and so halt his fall. From there he was able to climb to the clifftop and escape.

The trail soon swings to the right, headed toward the highway. At a fork in the trail, take the left fork, which leads to the Cedar

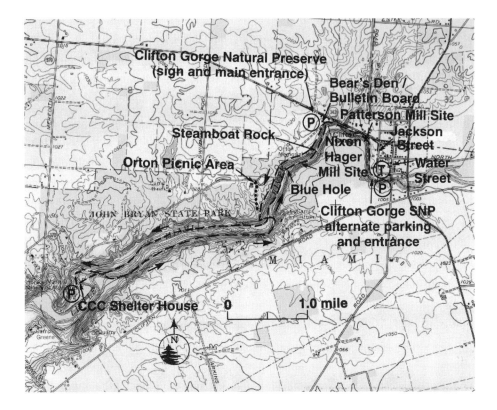

Garden overlook. A sign tells of the varied habitats visible from there, each supporting its own collection of plants. In the thin soil along the clifftops, prairie plants such as whorled milkweed can be found. On the vertical cliff faces grow white cedars, a northern species brought here by the last glacier. The riverbanks below encourage tree species, such as sycamore and cottonwood, that do well in moist situations. The shaded cliffs across the river harbor several plant species rare to the state, including mountain maple, Canada yew, and red baneberry. The trail follows the cliff edge to go out to the road and cross a side stream on a walkway on the river side of the highway bridge. It then returns to the woods and immediately crosses another side stream on a wood and steel bridge parallel to a stone

arch bridge on OH 343. The highway department wanted to replace the stone bridge with a more modern one but was prevented from doing so by local outcry.

The trail now rises slightly to arrive at a grassy area that was once a parking lot for the Clifton Gorge refreshment stand operated by the Grindall family. The site at one time also contained a cage that for 55 years held Muggins, a black bear captured as a cub in Canada and brought to this place as a tourist attraction. The cage, store, and home are gone, but one outbuilding is still being used as a shop by the Division of Natural Areas and Preserves. Old, open-grown maple trees mark the former house site.

At this point, a set of steps lead into the gorge. Do not take them. You will return that

Clifton Gorge

way. Instead, go straight on the North Rim Trail. This is probably the route used by the old Cincinnati-to-Pittsburgh stagecoach road as it approached its drop into the valley of the Little Miami a few hundred yards west of here. At the right of the trail is an alcove called the Bear's Den, a place to gather for conducted walks. Near the information kiosk is a slice of a white oak tree that began growing in 1691 and died in 1985 in what is now the state park campground. Its annual rings have been labeled with the natural and historical events that occurred during the tree's lifetime. Just beyond on the right is a gravel trail that leads to the main parking lot on OH 343, where there are rest rooms.

The trail passes through a gate and continues on the stage road, now called the Orton Trail. Immediately thereafter, a trail goes to the left, following closely along the cliff edge. Take this trail along the top of the cliffs. Until early 1990, this was a favorite area for rock climbers and rappellers, but that activity has now been banned to preserve the plants and rock features of the gorge. Hardwoods and white cedars line the rim to the left of our trail. Old fields with invading sumac and redcedar are on the right. From one of the overlooks, Steamboat Rock, a large slump block that originated along the cliffs, is visible in the river below. A cut in the cliff once held a switchbacked road that led to a straw-board mill below. A hundred feet beyond, a grassy side trail comes in from the right. As you continue on the rim trail, the stage road soon appears in the woods to the right. The hiking trail moves on and off the stagecoach track several times before finally merging with it. About 100 feet beyond that point, the trail swings left toward the rim of the gorge. A newer side trail exits right to continue into the park on the upland. Still following close

to the rim, the trail soon passes two overlooks, then reaches a junction with a side trail that goes to the right toward the Orton Picnic Area. Your path soon reaches the point where the stagecoach road descends to the valley. (This is where you cross the boundary between the park and the preserve.) A narrower trail, which you do not take, leaves to the right to continue along the rim. After crossing a new wooden footbridge, the stagecoach road you are following travels over cobblestone paving as it drops rapidly to the gorge. It uses only one switchback on its route through the opening in the cliff and down the talus slope. What a rough ride it must have been in a leaf-sprung stagecoach!

The trail coming off the hillside meets the river at an open area where the upriver Little Miami footbridge is located. Here, it turns right to continue following the Cincinnati-to-Pittsburgh stage road along the north side of the river. For the next mile it stays at a fairly level elevation at the bottom of the talus slope, sometimes passing between large slump blocks and occasionally fording a spring-fed side stream. Though the forest is mature now, the dead redcedars in the woods indicate that this flat land was once cleared. The redcedars were the pioneering species that invaded the area when agriculture was halted.

Eventually the trail arrives at the downriver footbridge. The path labeled CAMP TRAIL close to the river will be your return route. Continue your hike by following the stage road as it angles uphill toward the blacktopped road that leads from the main park area to the lower picnic area. The break in the cliff face where the stagecoach road climbed out of the gorge is visible ahead. After a left turn onto the road, the trail runs past a pond on the right (created by the diking effect of the road) and then to the picnic area. Rest rooms are up the slope to the right of the road, and drinking fountains to the left are on during the frost-free months. A beautiful stone shelterhouse is a heritage of the Civilian Conservation Corps (CCC) days at John Bryan State Park.

The trail follows a set of 57 steps to the left of the shelterhouse built by the CCC and leading to a grassy area along the river. There stands a glacial erratic on which a National Scenic River plaque was erected in August 1973. This spot in the river is known as Kutler's Hole. It was once the location of Brewer's Mill and Distillery. The trail follows the left bank of the river upstream along the river's edge, rejoining the stagecoach road about 25 feet before the downriver footbridge across the Little Miami. Originally built by the CCC in the 1930s, this bridge and the one a mile upstream were rebuilt in the mid-1960s. This one has poured concrete abutments and piers, while the one upstream uses laid-up stone.

The hike continues by following the trail across the bridge, then turning left along the talus slope on the south side of the river. Shortly, the trail splits, with one branch going close to the river through a white cedar grove. The other branch angles gently up the slope. This hike follows the right fork, passing close to huge slump blocks and across ravines with lovely waterfalls uphill. Though there are lovely vernal wildflowers on the north side of the river, the north-facing slope here is where the real show takes place in April and May. Walking fern is common on the blocks of dolomite. Where the trail drops to the valley floor, two sections of boardwalk keep the trail from becoming mired in mud. Many of the trees on the slope are chinquapin oak, a species especially well adapted to the calcareous soils of the area. Most of the way, a high cliff stands at the top of the talus slope. At one

point, however, a road comes through a break in the cliff to a house on a piece of private property almost at the trail's edge. Just before the trail reaches the upper bridge, an interpretive sign on the right tells us that the land upstream on the south side has been designated a Scientific Preserve. The sign lists some of the rare plants to be found in this area.

The trail crosses the bridge to return to the north side of the Little Miami. There, it immediately turns right upriver. Soon another sign tells of the origin of the slump blocks on the rim of the gorge and of their slow descent down the shale slope below the cliffs. It also tells of the need for woodland spring flowers to bloom and set seed before canopy trees leaf out.

Using wooden steps and walkways to get over and around the slump blocks, the trail winds its way between the river's edge and the base of the talus slope. An exceptionally beautiful spot on the river is known as the Blue Hole. In 1851, this view of the Little Miami River inspired a young Cincinnati artist named Robert S. Duncanson. Born in New York in 1821 to an African American mother and a Scottish Canadian father, Duncanson spent his childhood in Canada. By 1842 he had settled in Cincinnati, where his paintings caught the attention of Nicolas Longworth, a prominent citizen. Longworth's commissions aided the young artist's success. Duncanson traveled widely to find subjects for his paintings. The one he did of this spot is called *Blue Hole Little Miami River;* it now hangs in the Cincinnati Museum of Art.

The trail next climbs to the site of the Nixon-Hagar Paper Mill, operated during the mid-19th century. Straw gathered from nearby farms was boiled and beaten into pulp, rolled, and drained to form cardboard and brown butcher paper. A dam across the river near Amphitheater Falls upstream created the head to drive the mill wheel. Refuse was dumped into the river. A service road down the cliff face is still visible to the left. The mill was abandoned by 1899, and its chimney came down in 1912. Bricks from the latter can still be seen in the trail. Beyond the two mill overlooks, a sign on the left of the trail tells of the origin of a small cave. It is not a true solution cave (a cavern formed when rock dissolves) but a slump-block cave. It is the only cave in the preserve that is a part of the trail system and, as such, is open for exploration. The trail climbs to the base of the Cedarville dolomite cliff and passes the former rock-climbing area. The land is now being allowed to rest in the hope that native vegetation will eventually return to the nooks and crannies of the rock face.

The trail drops toward the river between two huge slump blocks, then climbs toward Amphitheater Falls on stairs and decking. The blocklike, 7-foot-thick Euphemia dolomite that underlies the massive Cedarville dolomite and the layered Springfield dolomite gives the impression that these are carefully laid-up steps at the base of the falls. The trail heads upriver, passing Steamboat Rock. Soon moving uphill to the cliff base, the trail passes another formerly popular climbing area. Rising about halfway up the Cedarville dolomite, the trail reaches a set of 23 wooden steps that take it back to the rim trail near the Bear's Den gathering place. The trail to the right returns you to the trailhead at the Jackson Street parking lot for a total distance of about 5½ miles.

39

East Fork State Park

Total distance: 14 miles (21.2 km)

Hiking time: 8 hours or 2, 3, or 4 days

Maximum elevation: 860 feet

Vertical rise: 125 feet

Maps: USGS 7½' Batavia; USGS 7½' Bethel; USGS 7½' Williamsburg; ODNR East Fork State Park map; USACE William H. Harsha Lake, Ohio, map

William H. Harsha Lake on the East Fork of the Little Miami River in Clermont County was one of the last Army Corps of Engineers flood-control reservoirs built in Ohio. Completed in 1978, the 2160-acre impoundment locates water-based recreation within 25 miles of Cincinnati. It was named in honor of the former congressman from Portsmouth, whose 21 years in the US House of Representatives included 11 as the ranking Republican on the Public Works and Transportation Committee.

Of the project land area, the corps maintains 660 acres, the Ohio Division of Wildlife manages 2248 acres for hunting, and the Division of Parks and Recreation manages 5618 acres as East Fork State Park. State park literature calls the impoundment East Fork Lake, while the Corps of Engineers brochure refers to it as William H. Harsha Lake.

There are two major hiking trails in the park. I describe here the East Fork Backpack Trail, a 14-mile route where 5½ miles of trail are hiked in two directions and the remaining 3 miles is a loop at the far end. It is located entirely on the south side of Harsha Lake and can be walked as a day hike or as a backpack trip using the two campsites it shares with a longer trail for one, two, or three overnights. The first campsite is just over 3 miles from the trailhead. The second area is about 4 miles beyond, at the farthest point on the trail.

Though admittedly less scenic than some other backpacking trails in Ohio and nearby states, this trail is excellent as an introduction to the sport of backpacking. The climbs are

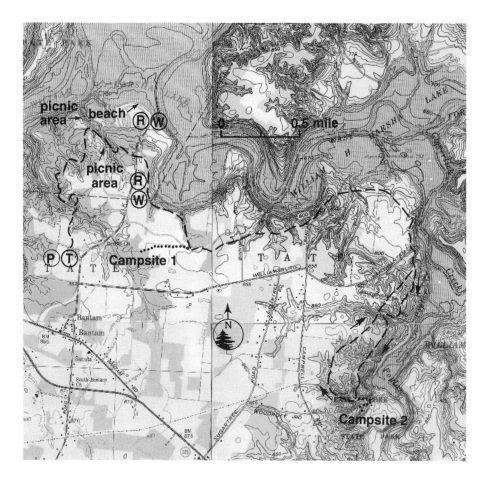

easy, the distances short and flexible, and the camping facilities good. Even with an "after work on Friday" start, hikers from the Columbus, Dayton, and Cincinnati areas can make the first campsite by dark during the summer months. With a day pack containing lunch and water, you can also make this a day hike. Remember that the area has been in public ownership for only about 18 years. Think what it will be like when it has been protected as long as places like John Bryan State Park or the parks in Hocking Hills. Enjoy watching it grow.

The state park also maintains a second trail now known as the Steve Newman Worldwalker Perimeter Trail in honor of the young man from the area who walked around the globe. This trail is 31½ miles long with four overnight sites and is open to horseback riders as well as hikers. It circumnavigates the lake and requires two unbridged river crossings that are difficult at some times of the year. It is not shown on the map. If you are interested in this hike, a brochure with a map is available from the Department of Natural Resources.

How to Get There
The Backpack Trail originates at a parking lot near the park office on the south side of

the lake. Take OH 125 east (toward Amelia) from I-275 exit 65. After about 8 miles, OH 222 enters from the left. One and a half miles beyond, OH 222 turns right. At that intersection, turn left onto Bantam Road. A half mile ahead there is a sign that points left to BACK COUNTRY TRAIL SOUTH ACCESS PARKING. The gravel drive passes between two ponds and ends at the trailhead parking lot. A bulletin board shows the route of both the Backpack and Perimeter Trails. There is provision for self-registration. No fee is charged for using the trail.

The Trail

A sign identifies the trail going north from the parking lot as the EAST FORK BACKPACK TRAIL. It is well marked along the entire route with red paint blazes on the main trail and white on side trails. (The Perimeter Trail uses green blazes.)

Recently wood-chipped in the area near the entrance by the local Scout troop as an Eagle Scout project, the trail winds its way through a brushy area. It enters the woods, headed toward the lake about 1 mile away. At a ravine, it descends downstream to the left on log steps before crossing the stream on stepping-stones. Turning right, it climbs to a ridge, then heads left toward the lake. Two smaller streams are spanned by footbridges before the trail makes a sweeping U-turn, staying on the edge of the ridge. A bench for the weary or contemplative sits along the trail. After crossing a series of smaller ravines on steps and bridges, the trail splits. The first mile marker is in this area. Take the left fork along the edge of the woods. Before dropping to the picnic area, the trail crosses an open area where there is a grand view of the lake.

Beyond the road, the trail descends on a series of log steps, then, after about 50 feet, it turns right along an old field before entering the woods. This turn is easy to miss during the growing season. Two wooden bridges span small ravines, then the trail climbs to an open field. It swings right alongside the woods, enters it, then drops to a deep ravine. Going upstream to cross without a bridge, the trail turns left and climbs to another fork. Turning right, it passes between forest on the right and brambles on the left. In about 100 feet it enters the woods, turning to the right. The second mile marker is in this vicinity.

When it emerges from the woods, it crosses the beach entrance road. Water is available there during the warmer months, and public toilets can be found there and at the picnic area just ahead on the right.

The trail now curves to the right just inside the woods from the picnic area. Pay no attention to the many side trails coming from that area. Staying on the contour around the curve, it intersects another trail, goes left, and proceeds down a set of steps. It turns right to intersect another trail before a bridge, then turns left to cross the bridge before turning right again. Fortunately, these turns are all well marked with blazes. After crossing a small wash, the trail drops to a bridge. It then climbs back to the rim of the ridge, which it follows to another bridge. Steeply climbing away from that bridge, the trail returns to level ground, where you will find mile marker 3. Soon it intersects a side trail to the right where a sign says OVERNIGHT AREA.

A white-blazed trail leads across the boat ramp road, along an old fencerow, and into a woods to the camping area shared with the Perimeter Trail. Facilities there include two low, floorless bunkhouses that will each accommodate two campers, toilets, and tables. There is no water. Tents are welcome.

Back at the intersection, continue on the trail, which soon emerges from the woods to cross the boat ramp road and reenter the woods, continuing eastward. This road is the last public road the trail crosses, although the next overnight area is within a short walk of one. Beyond here, the trail crosses a narrow, paved, abandoned road. The trail becomes more difficult to follow. Crossing ravines and washouts and moving up and down the slope, you will pass mile marker 4. Eventually the trail swings to the south near mile marker 5 to follow the rim of the now flooded valleys of Cloverlick and Poplar Creeks.

From the very start of the trail, the woods have been full of alien "nuisance plants." Japanese honeysuckle, multiflora rose, bush honeysuckle, and *Euonymus fortunei* are ever present. Add the native brambles such as blackberries, and traveling along the edge of the abandoned fields can be quite difficult. But the trail is blazed and can be followed if you watch carefully for marks. If the blazes do disappear, you've missed a turn. Just backtrack and you will be able to locate the proper route.

The trail crosses two more abandoned paved roads. Bantam Road (the northern extension of the still-open North Campbell Road) is crossed before the trail begins to swing southeast. From that crossing, the distance to the second campsite is just a little over 2 miles. About ½ mile farther down the trail, after it turns to the south, Antibantam Road is crossed.

After crossing Antibantam Road, the trail climbs slightly, passes an old fence line, then drops steeply to the left to cross a wooden bridge. Beyond the bridge, the trail rises gently to a shrubby area in the direction of the lake, then reenters the woods. Just beyond here your outbound trail goes straight ahead while the return route comes in from the right. The 6-mile marker is approximately ½ mile beyond here.

There are many ravine crossings ahead, and the trail almost gets lost in tallgrass a time or two. The blazes can be difficult to see where the trail passes through a peaceful pine planting, but the most difficult place to follow the trail is where it crosses under a high-tension power line. After coming into the right-of-way, go uphill, angling left. There are a couple of very small footbridges across the wash, so here it is still obviously "the trail." Look uphill to the next tower, where there is a blaze. After passing the tower, follow the left edge of the woods to a blaze indicating that the trail is exiting the right-of-way. Mile marker 7 is about 400 yards ahead. The campsite and the end of the loop are only minutes from here. The power line actually lies farther south than shown on the USGS map, having been moved during construction of the lake.

The trail drops to near lake level and crosses a bridge. When it intersects an old dirt road that comes downhill to the lake's edge from the southwest, the campsite is just ahead. The site is under large oak trees at the top of the hill beyond the road. White blazes lead to it. The two bunkhouses here are larger than at the other campsite and will house four persons each on plywood bunks. There are also toilets and tables, but no water. Again, this area is shared with persons using the Perimeter Trail, so there may be horses and trail riders as well as long-distance hikers. In case of an emergency, North Campbell Road is less than ½ mile away and can be reached by walking up the abandoned road below the campsite.

The entrance to the red-blazed return route is not difficult to find if you know where to look. Return to the wooden bridge (sometimes washed out) that the trail came in on. A short distance after crossing a bridge, the trail goes left, not crossing the creek but following it upstream for about 50 feet before turning left up a steep diagonal climb. The hike now becomes easier than the outbound trail since the ravine crossings are farther from the lake. Even the power-line crossing is easier—go directly across the right-of-way. You will pass through a nice grove of tall, well-spaced trees. There was a dump of old tires here when I walked the trail in 1989, and they were still here in 1996. Mile marker 8 is located nearby. After about 1 mile of walking, you will reach a familiar T. A left turn leads you back to the trailhead via a now familiar route. If you want to remain on the trail a third night, turn left at the white-blazed side trail 3 miles this side of the trailhead.

40

Fort Hill State Memorial (Deer Trail)

Total distance: 5 miles (8 km)

Hiking time: 4 hours

Maximum elevation: 1280 feet

Vertical rise: 418 feet

Maps: USGS 7½' Sinking Spring; OHS Fort Hill State Memorial brochure

Fort Hill State Memorial, located off OH 41 in Highland County about a dozen miles south of Bainbridge, contains a prehistoric Native American hilltop enclosure that is one of the best-preserved archaeological sites in Ohio. Equally important is the natural history of the area, with its rock outcrops and its great variety of plant and animal life. This tract of land is a piece of wilderness in the true sense of the word, an area not now being profoundly affected by human use. Over 10 miles of well-marked nature trails enable you to reach nearly all parts of the memorial. Deer Trail is the most rugged, taking you up and down the slopes, past most of the seven major plant communities identified there by the late E. Lucy Braun.

The presence of this ancient "fort" on this high hill in southwestern Ohio has been known by archaeologists for more than 150 years. John Locke wrote about it in 1838 in the *Second Annual Report on the Geological Survey of the State of Ohio.* The often-referenced *Ancient Monuments of the Mississippi Valley,* written by Squire and Davis in 1848, contained a detailed map of the 48-acre enclosure. No wonder, then, that when the opportunity arose in 1932 the state sought to protect it by purchasing a key 237-acre parcel. Additional purchases have enlarged it to its present 1200 acres. The Depression-era Civilian Conservation Corps did much of the development work to open the area to the public. An on-site museum was built in 1968 to provide interpretation of the natural and cultural history of the memorial.

Though the builders of the earthwork

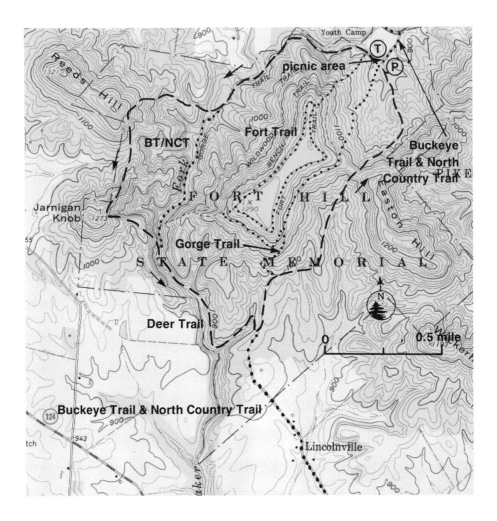

have not been identified, it is presumed that the Native Americans of the Hopewell culture that inhabited Ohio between 300 B.C. and A.D. 600 did so. Interestingly, when Locke visited here in 1838, the hill was covered with virgin timber, including large trees on the "fort" wall and in the ditch. He estimated one large chestnut on the wall to be 600 years old, and the age of a 7-foot-diameter tuliptree in the ditch to be the same. Allowing some time for abandonment and reforestation, Squire and Davis suggested that, on the basis of Locke's observation, the fort was at

least 1000 years old. Carbon-14 datings put the Hopewell time in Ohio back about twice that far.

The unusual natural history of this tract of land has a number of causes. First, the geology here is uncommon: a hill of carboniferous shale with a sandstone cap and a dolomite base, which makes for acidic soils on the hillside and alkaline soils in the stream valley. Also, the area's proximity to the edge of the advancing glaciers seemingly left it with boreal relict plants. Over 650 species of vascular plants have been found at Fort Hill. The size of the tract and the age of the trees apparently affect the number of bird species that use it for nesting (particularly the neotropical species that come north only to breed). Hiking at Fort Hill is like walking the pages of an ecology text.

This is not a hike for a hot and humid summer day, but rather a great one for spring or fall. The trails are open 8–8 daily, year-round. The museum, which has been closed for renovation as a part of the Ohio Historical Society's "Gateway Initiative," is to reopen during the 1997 vacation season. There are picnic facilities and rest rooms also available during the warm months of the year.

How to Get There

From Columbus, travel south on US 23. At Chillicothe, take US 50 west (right) through Bainbridge, after which you make a left turn onto OH 41 south. Turn right onto Fort Hill Road and travel to the memorial entrance. The best route from Cincinnati is US 32 east to OH 41. Turn left (north) onto OH 41 and travel to Fort Hill Road on the left, which leads to the memorial entrance.

The Trail

The Deer Trail starts along the left side of a mowed playing field to the west of the main parking area. The trail crosses a short plank bridge before entering the woods. A sign at the entry into the woods warns the hiker that "this is a semi-wilderness nature preserve. Trails have limited but adequate markings. Trails may be rugged and/or wet. Allow at least ½ hour per mile of trail. To avoid becoming lost: stay on trails; read all maps and signs carefully. Deer Trail 5 M. Gorge Trail 4M."

The two trails start out together. The Deer Trail is marked with blue blazes, the Gorge Trail with yellow. The North Country

➤ The Magnificent Chestnut

The American chestnut (Castanea dentata), *a large, rough-barked tree that sometimes grew to 100 feet with a trunk 10 feet in diameter, was once a dominant tree of the mixed oak forest of the dry, sandstone ridges and knobs of eastern Ohio, the Allegheny Plateau. This magnificent nut-bearing tree is virtually gone from its original North American range, the victim of a blight caused by an imported fungus,* Cryphonectria parasitica. *Introduced on Chinese chestnut, it was first reported in New York in 1904. It spread so fast among the native trees that had no resistance to the fungus that by the middle of the 20th century, the American chestnut was virtually gone. Many of the shelterhouses built in the state parks and forests in southeastern Ohio by the Civilian Conservation Corps during the 1930s were built of chestnut planks cut from salvaged victims of the blight. The search for a blight-resistant American chestnut or hybrid American/Chinese or Japanese chestnut continues to this day. Look for chestnut stumps on your walks; you may be lucky enough to find one with a few live sprouts.*

Trail also shares this route as it passes through the area. It is marked with official-looking plastic markers.

Hugging the hillside, the trail begins climbing as soon as it leaves the mowed area. Soon reaching 20 feet above Baker Fork, it follows the contour above the overhang created by the dolomite cliffs below. The trail is at the bottom of the slope created by the Ohio black shale bedrock. The

Dolomite cliffs at Fort Hill State Memorial

stream turns right (northwest), but the trail does not. Instead, it goes upslope on the side of the hill, only to drop steeply back to the same contour, allowing the stream to come back alongside it. The path continues on the hillside until it intersects a wide trail coming downhill from the left. (On old brochures this route is called the Sunset Trail.) There is a restored cabin near this juncture. The Gorge Trail now goes straight ahead, staying on the left side of the stream above the rock wall. The Deer Trail drops to the streambed, where there is a great view of the undercut dolomite cliff face of the gorge. Here grow the rare *Sullivantia* (named for William S. Sullivant, the pioneer Columbus botanist who discovered it), purple cliff brake yew, and other northern relict plants.

Crossing the stream on stepping-stones and scrambling over rock, you now begin the steepest climb of the hike. At times on log steps, and sometimes not, the trail gains about 350 feet in elevation in less than ½ mile. Leaving plants that do well on alkaline soils behind in the gorge, the trail winds its way among oak, sassafras, wild black cherry, hickory, and other acid-tolerant trees. Just before gaining the summit of Reeds Hill, the trail turns south and crosses a saddle before ascending 1273-foot Jarnigans Knob. Just prior to the ascent, you will pass a classic chestnut oak "wolf tree." A windfall in 1988 made the trail difficult to follow in this vicinity, but careful circling will get you back on the blue-blazed path. Now beginning its descent to Baker Fork, the trail drops through oak/hickory woodland, then into a grove of beech trees before reaching the stream. The final drop to the streambed is on another set of wooden steps.

After crossing the stream and being joined by the Gorge Trail coming in from the left, the Deer Trail stays on the left bank of the stream. It heads downstream using steps and a bridge to maintain footing on the rather steep slope. Not quite ½ mile after crossing the stream, it climbs a set of steps to the left away from the stream to join an old road coming in from the right. Lincolnville, ½ mile to the right down the old road, was the site of Bragg's tannery, which was built around 1860 and did a flourishing business for about 40 years using the bark from the chestnut oak trees for tanning leather. The distance from the point of this junction to the parking lot is 1½ miles on the blue-blazed Deer Trail. The trail begins climbing once again, but this time more gently. At an intersection, it turns right while the Gorge Trail goes left toward the upper slope, where it joins the Fort Trail. (The ele-vation of the fort is about 1285 feet.) To visit the fort from here, take the Gorge Trail to its intersection with the Fort Trail. Turn left on that trail, which is blazed in red, and take it to the fort. Backtrack to get down or take the trail to the parking lot off the north end of the hilltop.

Those who do not wish to visit the fort should stay on the Deer Trail. After turning right, the Deer Trail crosses several shallow ravines as it makes its way northeast to the 1140-foot saddle between Easton Hill to the east and Fort Hill. After crossing the divide, the trail stays to the right as it rounds a hill in rather rocky terrain and then drops to the picnic shelter and parking lot. A pump provides much-needed drinking water, and there are rest rooms nearby.

41

Germantown Metropark

Total distance: 6½ miles (10 km)

Hiking time: 4 hours

Maximum elevation: 900 feet

Vertical rise: 160 feet

*Maps: USGS 7½' Farmersville;
FRMD Germantown Metropark brochure;
FRMD Germantown Metropark trail map
(not to scale)*

Germantown Metropark contains Montgomery County's largest tract of mature forest. Part of the park came into the public domain in 1918 when the Miami Conservancy District bought land along Twin Creek for constructing a flood-control dam. Dayton and the Miami valley had suffered a devastating flood in 1913, and leaders of the community were not about to let it happen again. Five flood-control dams were built on the main tributaries of the Great Miami River. Of a unique design, these dams do not hold permanent pools of water, nor do they have gates that can be closed at times of high water. Only when water collects behind the dam because it cannot pass through it quickly enough does a temporary impoundment result. Because these dams were not meant to produce power or to create large, permanent lakes, the land on the floodplains behind them has remained in its natural state, with forest and fields. The valley behind Germantown Dam was mostly forested, and when the newly created Dayton and Montgomery County Park (now Five Rivers Metropark) District went looking for park sites in 1967, it was able to lease 361 acres of this flood-control property from the conservancy district. The park district subsequently added over 1400, mostly upland acres.

The woods at Germantown are exceptionally good for spring wildflowers, and because of the vast expanse of unbroken forest, it is the summer breeding grounds for many woodland birds. The nature center has recently been completely remodeled with new exhibits that explain the need for a land ethic and the concepts of good stewardship

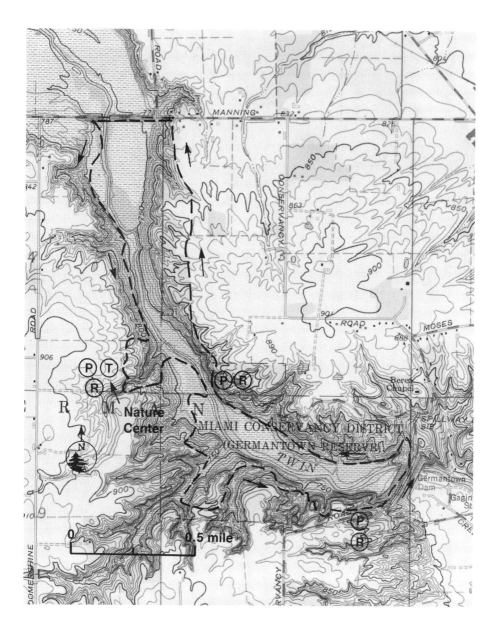

of the land. A warm fire in the stove will take the chill off winter hikers while they watch birds through an observation window.

How to Get There

Germantown Metropark is reached by traveling about 8 miles south of Dayton on I-75. Take exit 44 right (west) onto OH 725. After passing through Miamisburg and Germantown, OH 725 climbs out of the valley of Twin Creek to pass Conservancy Road and, 12 miles from I-75, to reach Boomershine Road. Turn right. The park entrance is 1 mile north of OH 725 on the right side of the road. Taking the first right turn inside the park leads to the nature center parking lot, 0.3 mile from the entrance. The park's facilities include many miles of foot trails, several picnic areas, and a unique underground nature center built into the side of a hill. Several short trails and a long trail known as the orange trail, which circumnavigates the entire park, originate at a boardwalk overlook to the right of the nature center.

The Trail

The trails in Germantown Metropark are well marked with a color coding system; 4- x 6-inch posts with colored spots or backpacker symbols mark the way, and posts with letters indicate trail junctions. The 6½-mile orange trail described here passes three parking lots, so it is possible to start or end at Points T, P, and S. The ½-mile white, 1-mile blue, and 1¾-mile yellow trails all start south from Point T. The ½-mile red and 1½-mile green trails both go north from Point T. The 1-mile silver trail originates and returns to Point S at a parking lot off Conservancy Road 1⁸⁄₁₀ miles north of OH 725. There are thus many ways to combine trails for hikes of from 1 to 6½ miles in length. Be sure to follow the orange markers for this 6½-mile hike.

Leaving the nature center to the west, the orange trail makes a short drop to pass down wooden steps through a cedar thicket to Point N. Here is where the shorter blue, yellow, and white trails loop back from the right. Along with the orange, they leave Point N to the left. After fording a small creek, they follow an old roadway alongside a cedar-lined gorge cut through Ordovician limestone and shale. The combined trails curve to the right as they climb through oak/hickory/beech forest soon to reach Point J, where the blue and white routes turn up a ridge to the right.

After a slight rise, the orange/yellow trail begins its descent to the floodplain. During times of high water, this trail may be inundated. (By following the blue trail left from Point J, past Point K to L, and then taking the yellow trail to the left to Point I, you can bypass the floodplain.) After traveling downstream for ¼ mile through a box elder/sycamore/cottonwood/ash floodplain forest, the trail swings back on itself and heads toward the hill, where it begins a moderately steep climb out of the valley. At the top of the hill, the trail reaches Point I, and the yellow trail exits right as it heads back to the trailhead.

The orange trail goes left but soon turns right to make a fairly steep descent into a ravine. It then curves right to head up a valley. After crossing two side streams, the trail crosses the main stream and climbs a set of wooden steps back to the ridge, soon reaching Point H. Here you meet the silver trail, which goes both left and right. The orange trail joins it to the left.

Now following a ridgetop among tall red oaks, the trail drops into a low saddle, then makes an abrupt right turn to drop into another ravine. At the bottom, the path turns toward Twin Creek and curves to follow the creek, staying about halfway up the hillside.

You then drop steeply into another ravine. In this area, the ravines expose sand deposited in preglacial valleys by a pre-Wisconsinan glacier. On the upland, the sands are covered by Wisconsinan-aged drift. Highly erodable, the gullies are so steep-sided that they have never been cleared for cultivation, and support mature hardwood forest. The trail climbs very steeply out of the ravine, then curves left as it regains the high ground and reaches Point G just downhill from Conservancy Road. The silver trail joins the orange trail to cross the head of a small ravine heading for Point S at a parking lot. Emerging from nice mature hardwood forest on the left side of a parking lot, the orange trail passes a bulletin board and latrines, then enters a young redcedar and maple woods.

Soon returning to mature oak/hickory/beech woods, you hike around the hillside to reach the upstream side of the earthen dam about 20 feet below the top. After crossing the dam at that level, the trail joins a gravel road just below a stand of Scotch pine. It crosses an old ridge road and drops to a T, where you make a right turn uphill to a natural material disposal area. Beyond a grass-covered fill area, the trail turns left down an old road as the service road turns right toward Conservancy Road.

The trail follows the old track to the left. Evidence of early park development in the form of disintegrated concrete picnic tables and stone posts can be seen in this area. After crossing a small creek, the trail nears a park driveway. To the left down the hill is an old borrow pit where gravel was obtained for construction of the dam. It once held water but is now filled in and overgrown with tall weeds. Near the end of the park road loop, the trail climbs uphill to the right to reach Point P. The pink loop trail originates here. Turning left, away from the road, the

orange/pink trail passes to the right of the latrine and heads through some eroded upland with redcedars. In a couple of hundred feet, the trail reaches Point F. Continue straight ahead on the trail coded orange and pink.

Following the border between old field and woods, the trail soon comes to Point E, where the pink trail leaves to the right and the orange trail proceeds straight ahead. Shortly after this intersection, the trail arrives in the open under a power line. After following the right-of-way a short distance, the trail passes through a wooded fencerow and into more open fields. About 1000 yards to the right is a platform where carcasses of road-killed animals are placed to feed vultures.

Now heading almost due north, the trail follows the forest/field boundary, soon arriving at a corner of the park property. After crossing the head of a ravine, you parallel the boundary fence, then enter more cedar thicket as you head toward a junction with Manning Road.

Turning left on the blacktop, the trail follows the road to a steel-truss bridge over Twin Creek. Two hundred feet beyond the bridge, at a wooden gate, the trail makes a hard left to turn downstream between the woods and an old field turning to thicket. After another ⅛ mile, the trail cuts across the thicket to the left to reach a hill. It angles along the hill to the left toward the rim, where it overlooks the river. Here, at a point where an unlabeled side trail enters from a grassy cedar glade to the right, an orange trail sign with arrows pointing upstream and downstream stands. You continue straight ahead. Still following the orange trail, you drop to the floodplain forest for a short stretch. Then, after crossing a side stream, turn right to climb uphill to Point D. The green trail comes in from the right and the orange/green trail leaves to the left. Again in mature hardwood forest, the combined trail travels midway along the side of the hill. Redcedars are visible at the uphill edge of the woods. Side streams are again filled with flat pieces of limestone, indicating that the Ordovician-aged bedrock is not far below the surface. After following an old trace for about ⅓ mile, the trail climbs the hillside to the right on another old road. Near the top is Point B where the green trail, joined now by red blazes, turns left into a stand of redcedars, and the orange trail, also joined by red blazes, turns right into a beautiful stand of mature hardwood. After about 100 yards, the trail passes a fire circle on the right and leaves the woods as it reaches Point C. Here, the green trail exits right and the combined orange/red/green trail heads left through grassland toward a cedar glade. After crossing over the earthen dam of a small man-made pond, the orange/red/green trail meets the other end of the red/green trail coming in from the dense cedar glade that lies to the left. This is Point A, and only a short connecting trail remains between here and the nature center/boardwalk where the trail began.

42

Glen Helen Nature Preserve

Total distance: 5 or 10 miles (8 or 16 km)

Hiking time: 3 or 6 hours

Maximum elevation: 1020 feet

Vertical rise: 180 feet

Maps: USGS 7½' Clifton; USGS 7½' Yellow Springs; GHA Glen Helen trail map; GHTC Glen Helen Scout Trail map

Antioch University's Glen Helen Nature Preserve has been described as one of Ohio's best-kept secrets. Its 26 miles of foot trails take the hiker past waterfalls, a national- and state-designated Scenic River, beautiful Silurian-aged limestone and dolomite cliffs, a butterfly preserve, a National Natural Landmark woods, a school forest, and the bountiful spring from which the nearby village of Yellow Springs got its name. There are numbered posts on many of the trails of the glen that are keyed to *A Guide to the Historical Sites in Glen Helen,* which at this writing is out of print. Maps are available at Trailside Museum, where rest rooms and drinking water can also be found. It is open 9:30–4:30 Wednesday through Saturday, and 1–4:30 Tuesday and Sunday. Glen Helen was given to Antioch in 1929 by Hugh Taylor Birch as a living memorial to his daughter, Helen Birch Bartlett. More land has since been added, bringing the total close to 1000 acres.

In 1969, the local Boy Scout Troop 78 established the Glen Helen Scout Hiking Trail in the preserve. It is one of the few such trails in the state that are entirely off-road. Like all the trails in Glen Helen, it is open free to the public year-round during daylight hours. An attractive commemorative patch is available to Scouts and Scouters who hike the trail, provided they do so with a Scout unit that has made advance arrangements with the Trailmaster, Milton S. Lord. His address is 1360 Rice Road, Yellow Springs, OH 45387; 513-767-1288.

Trailside Museum is where preregistered Scout units meet Mr. Lord and where folks hiking the trail on their own can park. Neither camping nor picnicking is permitted in Glen Helen, but facilities for both are available in adjoining John Bryan State Park.

Glen Helen is especially well known for its nearly continuous show of native wildflowers. Each season offers a new collage of nature. Hike and enjoy this gem often.

How to Get There

The trailhead for the Glen Helen Scout Trail is at Trailside Museum, the visitors center for Glen Helen, located at 505 Corry Street in Yellow Springs. From central Ohio, travel I-70 west to US 68 (the 52A exit). Turn left (south) and travel 8 miles to Yellow Springs. Make a left turn at Corry Street, the northernmost traffic light in town, then drive 0.6 mile to the parking lot on the left. From the Cincinnati area, travel I-75 north to I-675. Take I-675 east toward Columbus. Turn right (east) at the Dayton–Yellow Springs Road exit and go 6 miles into Yellow Springs. The third traffic light after entering the village is at Corry Street. Turn right, go one block to cross US 68, then travel 0.6 mile farther on Corry Street to the parking lot on the left.

The Trail

The trail begins on the Inman Terrace outside the museum. It takes off south along the Yellow Springs Creek valley, staying on the rim at first. Shortly it passes through a break in the dolomite cliffs to drop to the top of the talus slope. The heavily wooded slope has a large number of sizable chinquapin oaks, along with other hardwoods, and is rich in vernal wildflowers. The occasional alien plant, abandoned roadway, or crumbling stone fence reveals a dwelling site of earlier times.

Two miles downstream, the trail crosses Grinnell Road and then goes over Yellow

Springs Creek on a 100-year-old covered bridge. Actually, this bridge is a rebuilt 60-foot section of the 120-foot-long Cemetery Road Bridge that formerly spanned Anderson Fork near the southern edge of the county. This section was moved to its present location in 1974 when construction of Caesar Creek Reservoir necessitated removal of the bridge.

Turn right off the east end of the old bridge and follow a path along the meadow's edge, until you reach a log stile that carries the trail over the fence along Grinnell Road. When you reach the berm of the road, turn right and cross the Little Miami River on the southwest (right) edge of the bridge. If you are going to hike the full 10-mile trail, continue to the far end of the highway bridge and turn right just beyond the guardrail. It is possible to shorten the hike to 5 miles by crossing the road before going over the bridge and picking up the return trail at the left abutment. At that point, the trail drops down the bank from the road berm and crosses a footbridge. Directions for the remainder of the return trip follow those for the loop into the southern glen.

Shortly after turning from the road into the woods, you will enter a meadow where the trail begins following the bank of the river downstream. Huge sycamore trees stand like silent sentinels along the river's edge. For the next 2 miles, the trail passes through a succession of woods and fields, hugging sometimes the riverbank, at other times the base of the talus slope. After passing an old milldam and skirting the edge of a marsh, the path comes out at the east abutments of the long-gone Jacoby Road covered bridge. Destroyed by vandals in 1970, this Howe truss bridge with a Burr arch was the last covered bridge spanning the main stem of the Little Miami River. All along the trail through the southern glen,

The Cascades at Antioch's Glen Helen Nature Preserve

artifacts of 200 years of habitation by people of European descent are in evidence. Milldam and raceway, riprap, barbed wire fences, barn, osage orange trees used for living fences, multiflora used for the same purpose, and gas-line rights-of-way—they all tell their own stories.

After a rest room and water stop, and perhaps a lunch break at the Greene County Park District's Jacoby Road Little Miami Access Park, reenter the glen over the wooden stile that crosses the fence oppo- site the park entrance. For the next 1½ miles, the trail follows the base of the talus slope, crossing streams and springs and passing along the other edge of the marsh at a spot where wild iris bloom in the late spring.

A hydraulic dam located in a streambed close to the trail is often heard before it is seen. Using part of the natural energy of water flowing downhill as power, it pumps water uphill to a barnyard on Clifton Road, nearly ¼ mile away. Farther up the valley

Yellow Springs

Yellow Springs

Orator's Mound

Raptor Center

cascades

Pine Forest

Five-mile cutoff

Jacoby Road Miami River Access

0   0.5 mile

N

there is a tile springhouse where water from a free-flowing spring is collected for use in nearby residences.

The man-made pools that are seen to the left of the trail north of the springhouse were a part of the artificially created landscape for the home Mr. Birch built on a nearby site above the cliff line. Large patches of skunk cabbage in the valley below the trail give away the location of seeps from the base of the talus slope. After clinging to the hillside, the trail drops to the forested valley floor. It then makes an abrupt right turn up a small ravine that enters the main valley from the southeast.

At the head of this ravine, the trail crosses the stream and turns left to follow the multiflora rose hedge to the northeast. The upper pasture, as this area is known, has not had livestock in it since 1974. In 1975, native hardwoods were planted in an effort to reforest in advance of the spread of the rosebushes. To the left of a large sycamore tree that stands alone in the far end of this upland area, the trail reenters the woods. It descends to the valley via an old farm lane. Back on the floodplain, the trail turns right on a service road that passes a barn built in 1954. It is no longer in use. Please do not enter it.

Beyond the barn, the trail turns left off the service road to cross a stream and go up a rise to the Ralph Ramey Butterfly Preserve, named for me after I served as director of Glen Helen from July 1973 to April 1990. Fields in this area are managed to attract native butterflies. Beyond the butterfly preserve, the trail goes through an opening in the fence and turns right to leave the southern glen the way it entered.

To catch the inbound trail heading upriver, cross the Little Miami River Bridge at an angle, heading for the abutment at the far right end. The trail leaves the road on the wing of the abutment, dropping to a footbridge across the overflow from the millrace for the nearby mill. It then travels upstream on an overgrown island, emerging from the woods at the milldam. The entire mill complex is a National Historical Landmark known as the Grinnell Mill Historic District. Now owned by Antioch, the mill originally ground grain for local farmers. Harmless northern water snakes make their home in the holes in the surface of the deteriorating dam. Please do not disturb them.

At the dam, the trail turns left to cross the millrace, then turns right and heads up the valley in riverine forest. At a fork in the trail, where a side trail heads right to the riverbank, go left and begin angling uphill. Where there are other trail choices, always take the left choice. About two-thirds of the way up the hill, a wild trail goes straight ahead, across the glen's boundary fence. It ends in an old park dump area where an incinerator from Civilian Conservation Corps days still stands. If you mistakenly reach that area, backtrack through the fence to the first trail to the right and continue uphill.

You should make two more switchbacks before reaching the top of the hill and the monument to Horace Mann, Antioch's first president. This bronze casting is a duplicate of the one that stands on the Massachusetts capitol grounds. The one in Glen Helen was erected in 1936 as part of a nationwide celebration of 100 years of public education in America. To the right of the Mann statue there is a pink marble obelisk with a bas-relief of Erastus Birch, father of Hugh Taylor Birch and member of Antioch's Board of Trustees during the time of Mann's presidency. A second obelisk was planned to memorialize the younger Birch, but it was never built.

The trail now goes due north, following

the driveway, to Bryan Park Road, where it angles across the road to the right to enter the glen's school forest gate. This area is where Yellow Springs High School students plant and raise Christmas trees, which are put on sale each December.

You now follow a cinder road heading north along the boundary between Glen Helen and the park. Soon, the trail comes alongside an area where pine and spruce trees were planted in 1926, at a time when this part of the glen was a part of John Bryan's Riverside Farm, which had been given to the state.

At the north end of the Pine Forest, the trail turns sharply left. From here it follows the route of the old Yellow Springs–Clifton stagecoach road, now a fire lane, to the Glen Helen Outdoor Education Center (OEC) area. Several ponds to the left, just downhill from the Pine Forest, are known as the Birch Pools. Most of the woods between this point and the OEC have been reestablished since Antioch acquired the property more than 60 years ago. Where the cinder path divides, take the right fork and follow it for nearly 1 mile. After the trail passes a cable gate and crosses an old stone bridge about 100 feet later, turn left. This short trail leads to the bridge over the Cascades on Birch Creek. The view from below, looking upstream at the Cascades, is the most picturesque and best-known scene in Glen Helen.

The OEC lies to the right of the fire lane, opposite the entrance to the path to the Cascades. It is the location of the glen's year-round school camp program and, during the summer, of Ecocamp, a natural-history-oriented camp for youngsters of all ages. At the Glen Helen Raptor Center, located at the OEC, ill, orphaned, and injured birds of prey are treated in an effort to return them to the Ohio sky. To visit the Raptor Center, go straight ahead on the fire lane instead of turning toward the Cascades bridge.

Birch Creek marks the eastern edge of the 250-acre National Natural Landmark section of the glen. At the west end of the Cascades bridge, enter the woods on the middle trail, directly ahead. Soon you will pass Helen's Stone, which bears a poem written by the glen's namesake. Directly south of here, but not visible, is the site of an 1826 Owenite settlement. In quick succession, the trail passes a Hopewell Indian mound; a kiosk telling the story of a white oak that fell nearby; the site of the late-18th-century Neff House resort hotel; the spot where in 1803 pioneer Lewis Davis built the first cabin in the area; and, lastly, the famous spring from which the village gets its name. Flowing year-round at 52 degrees and 70 gallons per minute, the spring is not really yellow, but rust-colored from the iron impurities in the bedrock through which the water travels before reaching the surface. Neither this nor any other spring in Glen Helen is approved as a source of public drinking water.

Beyond the human-landscaped spring is Bone Cave, a small cavern that can hold a dozen or more schoolchildren scrunched together. Just beyond the cave the trail turns north, following the base of the cliff. Before reaching US 68, the trail drops to Yellow Springs Creek, which it crosses on a bridge. You then cross an old sidewalk that once led from an interurban stop to a dance hall overlooking a lake in the glen. From here the Scout Trail crosses a small ravine, then follows the rim of the gorge to Trailside Museum. Just before reaching the museum you pass the Glen Helen Building, which houses the Glen Helen office and is where many Glen-sponsored programs are held. It is served by the same parking lot as the museum.

43

Hueston Woods State Park and Nature Preserve

Total distance: 2 to 5 miles (3 to 9 km)

Hiking time: 1 to 3 hours

Maximum elevation: 960 feet

Vertical rise: 140 feet

Maps: USGS 7½' College Corner; USGS 7½' Oxford; ODNR Hueston Woods State Nature Preserve brochure; ODNR Hueston Woods State Park map

In 1797, Matthew Hueston returned to the fertile ground in southwestern Ohio that he had seen as a soldier marching with General "Mad" Anthony Wayne to the Battle of Fallen Timbers. Eventually, the pioneer farmer owned several thousand acres in Butler and Preble Counties. Though most of Hueston's land was soon cleared for farming, a 200-acre tract of beech/maple forest along Four Mile Creek missed the ring of the ax. Perhaps it was too steep to farm, or maybe, since cane sugar was not available on the frontier, Hueston considered the sap of the sugar maples too valuable to lose. For whatever reasons, the hilly tract of timber remained untouched by successive generations of the family. When the last Hueston family member died in 1935, local banker Morris Taylor recognized the educational and scientific value of the virgin woods. He purchased it and protected it until 1941, when the state of Ohio bought it as a forest park. Additional land around the "big woods" was acquired by the state, and eventually Hueston Woods State Park was developed. In 1969, the original tract of virgin forest was declared a National Natural Landmark, and in 1973 it was dedicated as a State Nature Preserve.

Hueston Woods is especially lovely in the autumn. The Main Loop Road affords good vistas on the reds and golds of the beech/maple forest. Deer are often seen in the meadows and at the edge of the woods along the road.

Hueston Woods State Park, in which Hueston Woods State Nature Preserve is located, is a full resort park with cabins, lodge, campground, beach, marina, pioneer museum, nature center, hawk and owl rehabilitation center, and golf course. Information about the park facilities can be obtained from the Division of Travel and Tourism or the Department of Natural Resources.

How to Get There

Hueston Woods is located on the Butler/Preble county line about 5 miles north of the college town of Oxford. From all of Ohio except Cincinnati, it is most readily reached by traveling west on I-70 to US 127, 10 miles from the Ohio-Indiana line. Travel south 6 miles on US 127 to Eaton, then south 15 miles on OH 732 to the park entrance. From Cincinnati, follow US 27 north 38 miles to Oxford. Then take OH 732 north 5 miles to the park entrance.

The nature preserve trailhead is located at a cul-de-sac off the Main Loop Road, approximately 5 miles from the park entrance. At the split in the road about 0.6 mile past the park entrance, take the left fork. This road leads around 625-acre Acton Lake in a clockwise direction, passing the spillway and then following the boundary between the state park golf course and the nature preserve. A little over 0.5 mile after crossing Brown Road, a cul-de-sac appears on the right side of the road. Here is the trailhead for the Big Woods Trail. Rest rooms and a drinking fountain are also located here.

The Trail

The trailhead is on the right side of the parking lot. After passing through an opening in a rail fence, the trail immediately plunges into tall timber. About 44 percent of the canopy of Hueston Woods is made up of gray-barked beech trees, 28 percent is sugar maple, and 19 percent is white ash. A variety of other hardwoods, including red

and white oaks, make up the remaining 9 percent. In this mature and reasonably undisturbed woods, a distinctive layered effect is visible. Under the canopy is an understory of saplings such as the shade-tolerant sugar maple. Beneath that is a layer of shrubs such as spicebush. Close to the ground is a layer of herbaceous plants. There is a similar stratification in the animal populations, with birds such as the Cooper's hawk nesting in the canopy and smaller birds like the red-eyed vireo in the understory. Many visitors to the woods are treated to the noisy call of the pileated woodpecker, a species once thought in danger of extinction but now common in large tracts of Ohio woodland. Also, because it is protected from grazing, the forest hosts a wide variety of wildflowers, and it is known to have a good population of terrestrial amphibians.

Sap buckets hang on sugar maples in Hueston Woods State Nature Preserve.

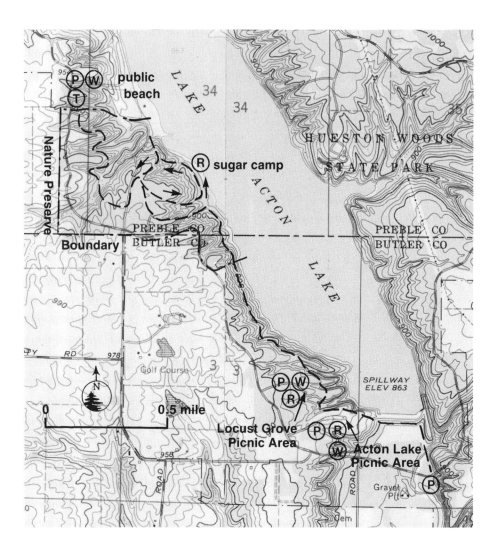

Once in the woods, the trail goes in and out of three ravines, crossing streams on bridges or flat rocks. Steps have been installed on steep slopes to help prevent erosion. Just before the trail climbs to an old paved road, note the large burl on a white oak tree. Where the trail reaches the road, ⅔ mile from the trailhead, there is a water fountain. Before the construction of Acton Lake in 1956, the road crossed the valley of Four Mile Creek. It has now been rerouted and goes only to a demonstration sugaring operation on the edge of the woods near the lakeshore. At the road, it is necessary to turn left and follow the paving for just over ¹/₁₀ mile. The Sugar Bush Trail crosses the road about 150 feet beyond the curve to the right. Turning right onto this ⁸/₁₀-mile loop trail leads you into the large timber. There, after 150 feet, take the Blue Heron Trail, which exits to the right. All of this 200-acre tract slopes rather steeply to the valley of

Four Mile Creek, now flooded to form Acton Lake. The trail is now passing through the area of highest elevation in the woods. Following the Blue Heron Trail leads to another cul-de-sac parking lot, which the trail skirts.

Shortly after the trail leaves this second lot, it crosses a stream on stepping-stones and climbs to a ridge, which it then follows downhill to the lake. After crossing another steam on stepping-stones, this hike turns left onto the West Shore Trail. There is also a trail straight ahead that leads to a fisherman's trail along the lakeshore. Following the West Shore Trail/Blue Heron Trail brings you to the south end of the open grass around the Sugar House. During Maple Syrup Weekends toward the end of winter, the woods are strung with sap-collecting lines, and the sweet smell of steaming hot sap hangs heavy in the air. Park naturalists and volunteers are on hand to re-create the age-old method of making sugar by boiling down the sweet maple sap.

Rest rooms are available at the sugar camp.

It is possible to complete the loop back to the Big Woods Trail either by following the blacktopped road up the hill or by taking the combined West Shore/Sugar Bush Trail from the north end of the parking lot. After a couple of hundred feet, the latter moves gently upslope to reach a knob, where the West Shore Trail goes straight to return to the lakeshore and the Sugar Bush Trail goes left up the ridge to eventually reach the road. Continue on the Sugar Bush Trail to the road, where you turn right to follow it back to the head of the Big Woods Trail. Follow the ⅔-mile trail back to the trailhead.

An additional 3 miles can be added to the hike by turning right where the Blue Heron Trail meets the West Shore Trail. It is an easy 1½-mile walk to the dam and spillway. Picnic facilities and drinking water are located at the Locust Grove and Acton Lake picnic areas, easily reached by side trails to the right.

44

Goll Woods State Nature Preserve

Total distance: 3 miles (4.8 km)

Hiking time: 2 hours

Maximum elevation: 715 feet

Vertical rise: 10 feet

Maps: USGS 7½' Archbold; ODNR Goll Woods State Nature Preserve booklet

A giant of a bur oak stands as a silent sentinel along the Goll Woods Trail.

The first European to explore the northwest corner of Ohio was, in all probability, the French fur trader Robert Cavelier La Salle. He visited the valley of the Maumee River in 1679, finding it inhabited by Chippewas, Ottawas, Wyandottes, Delawares, and Pottowatamies. More than 150 years later, German pioneer families became the first whites to settle in what is now German Township in Fulton County. By 1834, the Native American tribes that La Salle had encountered had been pushed out of Ohio, the Shawnee who replaced them had long since been defeated, and only a handful of Wyandottes remained on a reservation near Upper Sandusky.

In June 1836, Peter F. Goll, his wife, Catherine, and their young son, Peter Jr., emigrated to America from Dobs, France. The next summer, Peter Goll Sr. made his way to the federal land office in Lima, where he purchased 80 acres of what we now know as Goll Woods for $1.25 an acre. Goll's farm prospered, and he continued to buy land, eventually owning 600 acres.

The timber at that time was described as "dense throughout the whole area: it was tall and the whole of an extremely vigorous growth. The varieties included Elm in abundance, Basswood, Oak of several varieties, Hickory, Black Walnut, Whitewood [tuliptree], Butternut, Sugar Maple, and a sprinkling of beech in some parts, and in the lowest lands Black Ash, and White Ash prevails throughout the township." Timber wolves howled in the forest close to settlements and cougars roamed here, as did bison, elk, black bear, Canada lynx, and other mammals that have long since vanished.

The area was the wet forest of Ohio's Great Black Swamp, land that was under the western extension of Lake Erie after the exodus of the Wisconsinan ice sheet from the Ohio. The land was flat with soils that did not drain well. The soils were black from the decay of vegetation that flourished in the shallow, postglacial lake basin. They were rich soils that grew big timber.

Settlers needed that timber when they first arrived—to build houses, barns, and wagons. But they needed more than trees to survive and raise families. They needed tillable land, and every farmer knew that any land that could raise such trees as these of the Black Swamp could surely raise great corn and wheat. In 1859, therefore, a law providing for extensive ditching was passed by the county commissioners, and in a few decades the swamp that once covered two-thirds of the county was almost gone.

Almost, that is, except for this 80-acre tract we call Goll Woods. The Goll family stayed on the land for four generations. The land was passed on from Peter F. Goll Sr. to Peter Goll Jr. to George F. Goll, and then to his son and to his daughter, Mrs. Charles Louys. Although Goll and his descendants were farmers, they loved the big trees, and they carefully guarded the Big Woods from the timber operators. At the urging of citizens and conservation groups from northwestern Ohio, the Ohio Department of Natural Resources (ODNR) purchased 321 acres of land, including Goll's 80-acre Big Woods, from Mrs. Louys in 1966. It was dedicated to the people of Ohio as Goll Woods in 1969 and in 1975 became Goll Woods State Nature Preserve.

The closest thing to a stand of old-growth woods in northwestern Ohio, Goll Woods holds visitors in awe. Many of its magnificent trees were large when the

Pilgrims landed at Plymouth Rock. Trees commonly found in three different types of forest—elm/ash/maple swamp forest, mixed mesophytic, and beech/maple—are found here. Swamp forest is found in the wet area, beech/maple grows on the moist but well-drained sites, and mixed mesophytic, a blend of many species, frequents the transition areas between.

Goll Woods is a place of beauty during all seasons. Lots of special creatures such as tree frogs, barred owls, red-headed woodpeckers, red foxes, and several species of salamanders make their homes here. So, too, do many kinds of ferns and wildflowers, including the delicate purple, white, and yellow Canada violet and the three-bird orchid. Unfortunately, it is but a small remnant of the once vast forest of this part of Ohio.

We can only hope that some of the countries of the world just now undergoing "development" will do better than we did protecting larger tracts of these original forests.

How to Get There

Travel I-80/I-90 (the Ohio Turnpike) west from Toledo to exit 3. Turn left (south) on OH 108 and go 1.5 miles to Alternate US 20. Turn right (west) and travel 8.3 miles to OH 66 in Burlington. Here, turn left (south) and go 1 mile to Township Road F. Turn right (west) and travel 3 miles to Township Road 26, where you turn left (south) to the preserve entrance.

The Trail

A walk through Goll Woods is a walk through a precious remnant of the primeval forest characteristic of northwestern Ohio's Great Black Swamp. Start exploring by heading into the eastern 160-acre tract. Take the right fork at post 1 on the Goll Woods self-guided nature trail. A guidebook is available from the ODNR's Division of

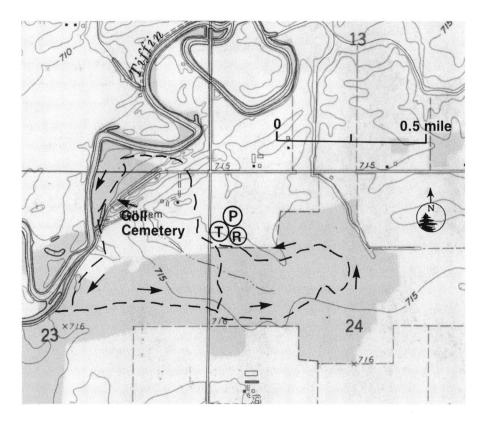

Natural Areas and Preserves office in Columbus. The area near post 2 was probably swamp forest at one time, but with the water table dropping in recent years, it is undergoing a transition. The red maple and ash are still there, but so, too, are trees that do not tolerate being in standing water all year, such as tuliptree, basswood, bur oak, chinquapin oak, sugar maple, and shagbark hickory. This is the transitional mixed mesophytic area.

Goll Woods' vernal flora is special. On a May trip, I was struck by the light color of the wild blue phlox compared to what I have seen in central Ohio, where I grew up. The trail guidebook provides a checklist of the more common flowers of the preserve. Remember, "Let them live in your eye ... not die in your hand." Between post 3 and the next

stop on the trail, a side trail enters from the right. This will be your inbound trail at the end of our hike.

At post 4, let the statistics speak for themselves. Bur oak, *Quercus macrocarpa*, diameter at breast height (DBH): 56"; height: 112'; estimated board feet: 4270. A bur oak that stood at post 5 was struck by lightning in 1970 and has now fallen. The lightning scar is still visible along the full length of the trunk. The trail now turns east to explore more of the Big Woods. Every Ohioan should know the tree at post 6. This is the buckeye from the Native American word *hetuck*—"the eye of a buck deer"—and it is the official state tree.

Perhaps by this point you will have discovered one of the nuisances that plagued early settlers in the black swamp region—

mosquitoes. A good warm-weather walker is always prepared with a head net or repellent close at hand. In early Ohio, mosquitoes were more than a nuisance; they were a hazard because they carried malaria. The papaws at post 7 are Temperate Zone members of the largely tropical custard-apple family. Dark maroon flowers in May change to yellowish green, banana-like fruits in the fall—food for opossums and raccoons. Before reaching the next stop, you'll pass a trail to the left that takes a short route back to the trailhead. Continuing on this hike, however, you will come to post 8, where the "Elder of the Woods," a 122-foot-tall bur oak, has occupied the site for close to 500 years. It died in 1984, but when I last visited the woods it was still standing. What stories it could tell! No hiker needs to be told about the poison ivy pointed out by post 9. "Leaves three, let it be."

Nature is the grand recycler. Post 10 reminds the visitor that letting dead trees rot and return to the soil allows their nutrients to be used again. That philosophy is central to the management of nature preserves. White ash like the one at post 11 provide the wood for such products as baseball bats, tool handles, and furniture. This giant is 104 feet tall with a 32-inch DBH. Four of North America's 18 species of ash grow in Goll Woods.

The cross-section of the bur oak that fell during the winter of 1968 at post 12 is nature's time capsule. From the growth rings, you can read of dry years and wet ones, lightning strikes, fires, and the disease and death of the old oak.

All along, the elevation of the trail has been changing very subtly. At post 13, the forest has changed to true swamp forest with black ash, red maples, and silver maples dominating. Swamp white oak also occurs, but the American elm has been gone for nearly 40 years. The trail rises now, only a few feet, to a well-drained sandy knoll, and once again the composition of the forest changes. At post 14, American beech and sugar maple dominate. In time, as the area becomes better drained, this combination will probably dominate Goll Woods.

People who live downwind from a cottonwood like the one at post 15 have at times probably wondered aloud about the worth of these trees. The "cotton" can be a real nuisance! The red squirrels that live in this one, however, could easily sing the cottonwood's praises, as could the other mammals and many birds that are cavity dwellers. The much larger fox squirrel also abounds in this woods. By examining the toothmarks on the opened acorns, you should be able to distinguish which of the two squirrel species found in Goll Woods made them: the smaller or the larger species?

Now heading west, the trail reaches post 16. This is the location of a tall tuliptree, a living fossil. Geologists have found evidence that this genus has existed for as long as 100 million years. Because it grows tall and self-prunes its lower branches, it was often used by pioneers for log structures in this part of Ohio. A relative of the magnolia, its green and orange, tuliplike blossoms grow on the top of the tree, usually out of sight. Small ponds such as that at post 17 support life of all sorts, including frogs, salamanders, dragonflies, and mosquitoes, which only spend one phase of their life there. Others, like fairy shrimp, are tied to the pond throughout their lives. Bigger creatures like raccoons and skunks feed off the turtles and frogs that are found in ponds.

Ferns similar to those at post 18 have been around for 400 million years. They need moist environments like the one found here to survive. Lichens, like the greenish white Parmelia lichen on the trunk of the

➤ Lichens: Complex Organisms

Lichens are the pioneers of the plant world. They grow on rocks, soil, and wood in the harshest weather conditions; and they are found in forests, fields, backyards, and urban park. They are sensitive to acid rain and air pollution, a characteristic that allows them to be used as monitors of air quality.

Found in unique shapes and colors, they are not really a single organism but two, comprising a photosynthetic organism and a fungus that have formed a symbiotic mutualism. Each organism gains some advantage from this cooperative living arrangement. In most lichens, the photosynthetic partner (or photobiont) is a green alga and/or a cyanobacterium (what we used to call blue-green algae). The other partner is a fungus and is referred to as the mycobiont.

There are estimated to be 13,500 species of lichens. They grow in four general forms: crustose, growing closely attached to the substrate; squamulose, which are scale-shaped with a free edge; foliose, which are flattened from top to bottom or leaf-like; and fruticose, which are bushy and most often attached at the base. The familiar reindeer moss is an example of the last.

To photograph lichens, you need a good macro lens. I prefer to use a 90 mm to 105 mm focal length, so as not to make a shadow with my camera. Their study requires a hand lens and a reference book or two. How to Know the Lichens *by Mason E. Hale (Wm. C. Brown Co.) has good keys, and* Michigan Lichens *by Julie Jones Medlin (Cranbrook Institute of Science) has top-notch color illustrations. How many different lichens can you find on your next wilderness walk?*

tree at post 19, are examples of two different life-forms that coexist to their mutual benefit. The plant is composed of both a fungus and green alga cells, living harmoniously as one structure. Hummingbirds and eastern wood pewees use bits of this species of lichen for lining the insides and outsides of their nests.

The shortcut side trail enters from the left as you approach post 20. The giant white oak at this stop would provide enough wood to construct half of a small frame house. This tree is 44 inches in DBH. At the time of settlement, thousands of trees like this one were felled and burned in huge piles to clear the land for agriculture. Forests like that at post 21 were often burned by Native Americans to keep the brush from growing up and hindering hunting. When pioneers found these burned areas, they called them oak openings.

As this interpretive trail ends, continue exploring the other environments of Goll Woods by taking the trail across the road from the other end of the parking lot. While passing through the pine planting east of the manager's residence, try to figure out what year it was planted. The planting will probably be crowded out by hardwoods eventually. Here the trail crosses the road toward the Tiffin River. There is an especially large patch of toadshade, the maroon sessile trillium, here in April and May. The trail goes through a stand of beech/maple and tuliptree between the river and the Goll Cemetery. Take time to read the tombstones in the graveyard and to reconstruct the lives of those buried here from the facts gleaned from the stones.

The trail reenters the woods on the east side of the road 200 feet to the right (south) of where it emerged. From there it swings to the south through more pines and secondary-succession scrubland. It passes a parking lot before turning left (east) past more large trees. After ½ mile, the trail reaches the road that bisects the preserve. Angle across the road to the right to enter the trail and connect with the east woods loop. Upon reaching the T intersection with the nature trail, turn left to return to the parking lot.

45

Kelleys Island

Total distance: 9 miles (14.5 km)

Hiking time: 6 hours

Maximum elevation: 615 feet

Vertical rise: 40 feet

*Maps: USGS 7½' Kelley's Island;
ODNR Lake Erie Islands State Parks map;
KICC Kelleys Island map*

Early maps call it Cunningham Island, but for more than a century the 2800-acre solid limestone island that lies in Lake Erie, 11 miles north of the mainland city of Sandusky, has been known as Kelleys Island. Between 1833 and 1841 the Kelley brothers of Cleveland, Datus and Irad, purchased the entire island for $1.50 per acre. The name Cunningham—that of a squatter who had built a house on the island in 1808—was lost to geographers forever. With the establishment of the Kelleys Island Stone Company, quarrying—the industry that was to bring people and fame to the island—was under way in earnest.

By 1842, grape cuttings had been set out on the island, marking the beginning of the second industry that was to carry the name far and wide. Fermented from grapes grown on the sweet soils of the island, the products of the Kelleys Island Wine Company were widely known for their quality. The 1990 census listed 200 residents for Kelleys Island, where there were once several thousand people working in jobs related to the fishing, quarrying, and winemaking industries. Though now supplemented by air service, the principal way to reach Kelleys Island remains, as it was in the 1830s, by boat. The ferries do haul cars and trucks to and from the island year-round (weather willing), but the number of vehicles on the island remains small. It is thus a wonderful place to explore on foot.

In addition to the artifacts from the early industries, the island has other points of interest. Inscription Rock, on the south shore, is covered with Native American drawings.

Hikers pause to view the famous glacial grooves along the trail on Kelleys Island.

The glacial grooves scratched in the limestone bedrock that are visible at Glacial Grooves State Memorial are world famous. There are homes and churches left from the island's heyday to be admired. The Ohio Department of Natural Resources (ODNR) operates a 661-acre state park with a beach, boat-launching ramp, and campground on the island. Local merchants and restaurateurs ply their goods to tourists during the vacation season. The Kelleys Island Chamber of Commerce will gladly send you a packet of material with a map and information about local businesses, including accommodations. Its phone number is 419-746-2360.

How to Get There

There are ferry operators serving Kelleys Island. The Neuman Boat Line operates ferries out of Marblehead from April 1 through mid-November, and from Sandusky during July and August. Its current schedule can be obtained by calling 419-626-5557. The Kelleys Island Ferry Boat Line runs from another dock at Marblehead year-round, with an expanded schedule from early May until late September. Its toll-free number is 1-888-225-4325. The Sandusky Boat Line operates out of Sandusky. Its number is 419-627-0198. Sandusky is 54 miles east of Toledo via I-80/I-90 and US 6; 105 miles north of Columbus via US 23 and OH 4; and 64 miles west of Cleveland via I-80/I-90 and US 250. To get to Marblehead, which is only 3.5 miles from the island, take OH 2 west from Sandusky across the Sandusky Bay Bridge. Turn right (north) on OH 269, then right (east) on OH 163. Free parking is available at all three terminals. All three of the ferries will bring you to the south shore of Kelleys Island and Water Street. When you get off the ferry, be sure to note the time of the last returning boat. If you plan to take the last one, get to the dock early, as it is often crowded.

If you are carrying camping gear, you will want to proceed to the Kelleys Island State Park at the north end of Division Street to obtain a campsite and to stow gear. From the Neuman dock, walk east 1 mile, then turn north on Division Street. The Sandusky Boat Line docks at the foot of Division Street. The Kelleys Island Ferry comes into the Seaway Marina, less than ½ mile east of Division Street, the center of town. The park campground entrance is not quite 1 ½ miles north on Division Street on the right side. Use the sidewalk and take time to study the homes and other structures along the route. You may want to stop at the Kelleys Island Historical Society's stone church museum on the right side of the road just north of the business district. Be sure to walk through the cemetery, studying the names and inscriptions. Don't miss the Butterfly Box, where you can walk amid live butterflies in a plastic hoop house and shop for butterfly- and beetle-related gifts. Islanders have had a long love affair with butterflies, especially the monarch, as the island is an overnight resting place for that long-distance flier in the fall. The chamber of commerce can provide details about the butterfly festival held each September.

After setting up camp (or leaving your luggage at some other accommodation), walk north from the campground entrance to the Glacial Grooves. I suggest that you stop at the park office to purchase an inexpensive booklet entitled *A Glacial Grooves Fossil Walk on Kelleys Island*. The grooves are nothing short of awesome—400 feet long, 30 feet wide, and 15 feet deep. They are scars that were scratched along the surface of the limestone bedrock by the mile-deep glacial ice as it advanced to the south many millennia ago.

The Trail

The ¾-mile-long North Shore Loop nature trail originates just north of the grooves. It goes into the quarry only briefly, then swings to the right to travel through the woods to the rocky shoreline. As you would suspect on an island that is solid limestone, the woods are composed of trees that do well on sweet soils: hackberry, redbud, blue ash, water ash, basswood, chinquapin oak, and, early in succession, redcedar. Where the trail continues west, paralleling the shoreline, the sparse vegetation on the rock surfaces between the trail and the lake is an unusual natural community known as a stone alvar. (One of the best examples of this kind of habitat is found at Lakeside Daisy State Nature Preserve just south of the village of Marblehead on the mainland. It is open to the public during May, when the plant that is its namesake is in full bloom.) The trail eventually swings south and east to return to the parking lot. I walked it in the evening and saw many deer in the scrubby area along the way.

Return to Division Street on the driveway and turn right at the intersection just outside the park. This is Titus Road. Follow the road about 1 mile across the neck of the island to the west shore. The land to the left along Titus Road was under water when the lake level was higher during glacial retreat. At that time, the ice would have melted from this area of the lake basin, but the St. Lawrence outlet to the sea would not have been cleared yet. The meltwater from the retreating glacier flowed to the sea via New York's Mohawk River and Hudson River valleys. Thus, the lake level was high enough to divide Kelleys Island into two islands.

Turn left, headed south along the shore, and enjoy the changing views of the lake, cottages, and farms as you walk to Carpenter Point at the western tip of the island.

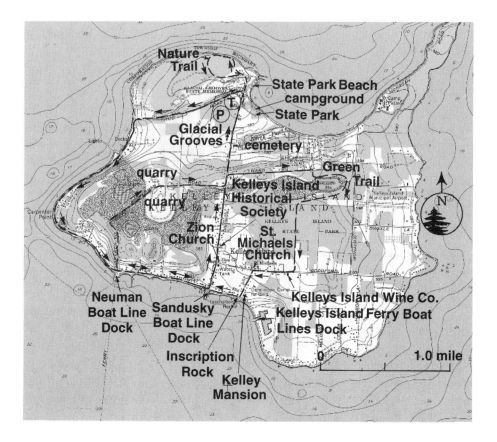

Huge stone loading docks that stood along this shore for years have been removed, to be replaced with a smaller modern loading facility. You will pass one of the island's finer eating establishments, the West Bay Inn, before you reach the westernmost end of the island.

Continuing on OH 575, the island's only highway, walk east to Cameron Road. You will have come a little over 2½ miles from the park entrance. Turn left (north), and follow Cameron to where it changes into Bookerman Road and turns east past the quarries. Though they stood idle for many years, one of them is now being operated by Kellstone. When Bookerman reaches Division Street, turn north a short distance to

Ward Road, which goes to the right. One-half mile east there is a trailhead sign on the right side of the road that shows the layout of trails in the East Quarry Area of the state park that lies to the south of Ward Road. Turn onto the trail, and follow the green blazes around the east end of Horseshoe Lake and through the brush and pine plantings to an exit onto Woodford Road, a distance of about 1 mile. A self-guided trail brochure for the East Quarry Trail is available free at the park office.

At Woodford Street, turn right. The new Kelleys Island Wine Company is on the left. At Addison Road, St. Michael's Church stands on the right. Turn left toward the lake. The Kelley Mansion, built in 1863, sits on the left corner of Addison and Water Streets. Seventy-eight archaeological sites and 316 buildings, including this mansion, associated with the settlement and history of the largest American island in Lake Erie were recently added to the National Register of Historic Places as the Kelleys Island Historic District. Prehistoric sites on the island show evidence of human occupation from Paleo-Indian times through the Late Woodland period, or from 12,000 B.C. to A.D. 1300. Among those sites is Inscription Rock, which sits to the right across Water Street from the mansion under a protective shelter.

There are many more places to explore and things to see on Kelleys Island. ODNR's Division of Natural Areas and Preserves is considering dedication of the unusual stone alvar habitat along the North Shore Loop Trail as a natural area, and there is discussion of possible construction of a wildlife observation platform overlooking North Pond, which lies to the south of the campground. There are excellent eating establishments on the island, and fishing trips can be arranged on the waters of Lake Erie. The route that I have suggested is about 9 miles long, but you can easily pick your route to suit your interests. Bicycles can also be rented on the island. For a day, a weekend, or a week of walking, leave your automobile on the mainland and visit Kelleys Island.

46

Lockington Reserve

*Total distance: 3½ to 6½ miles
(5.7 to 10.7 km)*

Hiking time: 2 to 3½ hours

Maximum elevation: 960 feet

Vertical rise: 70 feet

*Maps: USGS 7½' Piqua East and Piqua
West; SCPD Lockington Reserve map;
BTA Buckeye Trail map; St. Marys
section map*

The 1913 flood devastated the Great Miami River valley. Nothing on the floodplain was spared, and farmers and city folk alike suffered. Downtown Dayton was awash with water like no one had ever seen. City fathers decided that such a flood should never recur. The Miami Conservancy District was thus created, and five flood-control dams were built on the great Miami and four of its principal tributaries. These dams are unique because they impound no permanent pools and have no gates to close, even in time of flood. Only when the rainfall upstream exceeds the amount of water that can pass through the dam does water pool behind it. As the rain lets up and the water drains out, the water level drops. When no floodwater is being retained, which is most of the time, the hundreds of acres behind the dams are available for recreation.

In Montgomery County, those lands form the heart of four park district reserves. Lockington Dam on Loramie Creek, in southern Shelby County, is the fifth of the conservancy's flood-control reservoirs. The Shelby County Park District now manages 200 acres of the land around the reservoir as Lockington Reserve. Because it is a flood-control area, at times of heavy rainfall the trails may be inundated. If in doubt, call the park district office at 513-773-4818.

Loramie Creek, the West Branch of the Great Miami, originates on the flatland of Shelby County between the Lake Erie and Ohio River watersheds. It gets its name from Pierre Loramie, a Frenchman who operated an Indian trading post, Loramie's Station, at the present site of Fort Loramie from 1769

Open lock at Lockington Reserve

until 1782. In the early 1840s, the headwaters of Loramie Creek were dammed to make Loramie Reservoir, which fed the Miami and Erie Canal. The summit at Loramie was 512 feet above the level of the Ohio River at Cincinnati, so a series of locks was needed to allow boats to make the 99-mile trip. The first of these, Locks 1–5, were at the village of Lockington, 18 miles from the feeder that brought water from Loramie Reservoir to the canal. During the late 1800s, Lockington thrived, and in its heyday it boasted 19 industries. The 1880 census reported a population of 219, and those are only the ones who got counted. But by 1913, when floods sounded the death knell for the canal system statewide, water traffic had already ceased in Lockington. The locks, located in the middle of the village, are preserved by the Ohio Historical Society in cooperation with the Shelby County Park District. The canal towpath, north of the town, is the route of the Buckeye Trail (BT).

When the flood-control reservoir was built on Loramie Creek, it was named for the closest town on the 15' USGS quadrangle, Lockington (those were the days before every reservoir was named for a politician). The area includes trails for hiking and cross-country skiing, several bird blinds, a camping area available for a fee by reservation, and two picnic shelters. The park district offers an already assembled "Rent-a-camp" if you do not have or do not want to bring your own gear. The Buckeye Trail passes along the eastern edge of the preserve, and there is a connecting trail to the BT from the shelter and rest room area. Due to the vagaries of public wells, carrying water from home is advisable.

How to Get There

Lockington Reserve is reached by taking US 36 west from I-75 into Piqua. Turn right

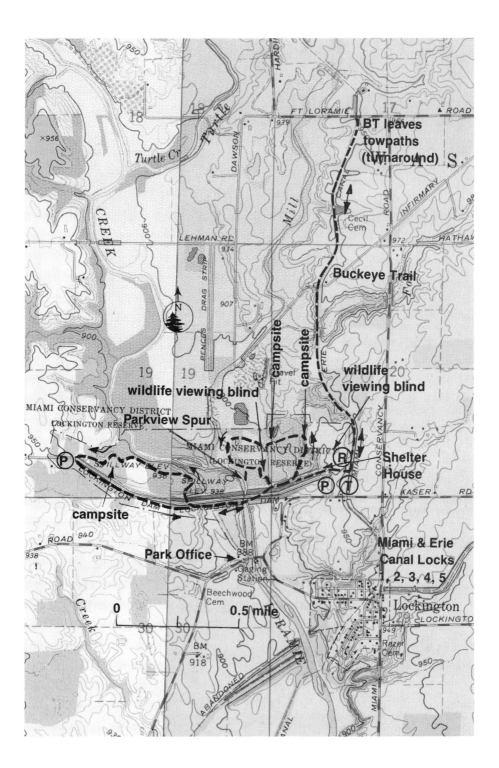

(north) on OH 66 and follow it 4 miles to Hardin Road, where you turn right. At a T with Fessler-Buxton Road, turn right. After crossing Loramie Creek, turn left onto Kaser Road, which leads to the park entrance at Lockington Dam Road.

The Trail

The Buckeye Trail and the trails of the reserve start at this parking lot at the east end of the dam. To walk the section of the BT north of here along the Miami and Erie Canal towpath, go east from the parking lot 200 yards, following the blue blazes. Turn left at the towpath. For the next 1½ miles, the BT follows the path once trod by horses and mules as they towed canal boats between Cincinnati and Toledo. At Dawson–Fort Loramie Road, the BT leaves the towpath for pavement. Turn around here, and return to the reserve area.

To continue the hike for another 3 miles, head downhill on the service road at the base of the dam. Turn right and go down a set of steps. After crossing a bridge that spans a stream between a small pond on the right and a large borrow pit pond on the left, the trail crosses a smaller bridge. As it reaches a pine growth, it splits. Follow the right fork as it goes uphill and curves left through the pines. It soon reaches a point where a trail to the right leads to the group camping area. Make a half-right turn. There will be a meadow on the left and woods on the right. Watch for a wildlife-viewing area that overlooks the meadow. You may want to spend some time there.

Soon, a quarry pond on private property to the right becomes visible. After 100 feet, the trail reaches a spot where you can see a meadow a short distance ahead through the woods. Upon reaching the meadow, follow its left edge. Shortly, the trail splits. The right fork is a spur that leads through the woods to Loramie Creek for a good view of the dam. After studying the unusual open dam, return on the same spur trail and turn right to continue on the main trail. After 100 feet, the trail turns into the woods and approaches two bird blinds, where you can view birds at feeders.

Departing the bird blinds, continue toward the dam. Where the trail reaches an old road, turn right. The borrow pit pond will be on the left. When this trail reaches the base of the dam, turn left up the slope to where you can climb to the abandoned road on top of the dam. Travel this path west for 1 mile, across the dam and over the spillway to the west parking lot. There, turn right at the colored marker indicating the trail. It crosses a boardwalk between two ponds, then passes another pine planting as it heads to the 90-foot-high bluff overlooking the creek. Upon reaching the edge of the bluff, the trail turns right to loop back to the trail along the foot of the dam. This west loop trail is not heavily used and may be a little difficult to follow; however, the dam is always in view, so there is no chance of becoming lost even if you end up bushwhacking around a deadfall or a place where the trail has grown over. Return to the trailhead parking lot via the old road atop the dam.

A visit to the Lockington Reserve area would not be complete without spending some time in the village viewing the locks and the 150-year-old homes that remain from the canal days.

47

Maumee Bay State Park

Total distance: 2¼ miles (3.6 km)

Hiking time: 2 hours (if you are looking at things along the way)

Maximum elevation: 575 feet

Vertical rise: 5 feet

Maps: USGS 7½' Reno Beach and Oregon; ODNR Maumee State Park brochure; Maumee Bay Boardwalk map

Note: *This trail and its ancillary facilities meet the standards of the federal Americans with Disabilities Act (ADA).*

Ohio is said to be second only to California in its loss of natural wetland habitat. Since settlement, millions of acres of fens, bogs, swamps, wet prairies, and marshlands have been drained for agriculture or to make managed "duck marshes." At Maumee Bay State Park, a small expanse of Lake Erie marsh has been preserved and a boardwalk constructed to allow visitors to have a closer look at this rare habitat. The Milton B. Trautman Nature Center, with exhibits that interpret the natural and cultural history of the Lake Erie marshes, is located at the entrance to the boardwalk. No matter how many times you walk this trail, you will always have a different experience. Visit it in different seasons when different land birds and waterbirds are using the area. Experience the many moods of the great variety of weather Mother Nature throws at the boardwalk. See how many different species of dragonflies, damselflies, and butterflies you can see on a summer walk. Come when the male frogs are singing their "aren't I pretty, come mate with me" call over the months of spring. Learn the blossoms of the plants of the wetlands by visiting often during the growing season, with short-focusing binoculars, a 100 mm macro lens on your camera, and a wildflower book in your pack. And remember, it's a wetland, so be prepared for the six-legged hummers. These female mosquitoes need a blood meal to ensure that there will be a next generation to help feed the birds and other insects.

How to Get There

To reach Maumee Bay State Park with its lodge, cabins, campground, Milton B. Trautman Nature Center, and the Maumee Bay Boardwalk, take OH 2 east from I-280 on the east side of Toledo. At North Curtice Road, turn north (left, toward Lake Erie). This road will lead you into the park, where signs will direct you to the nature center.

The Trail

Before you start your trip on the boardwalk, visit the Nature Center. Pause on the bridge to admire the cutout steel artwork in the pond to the right. The center is dedicated to the memory of the late Drs. Milton B. and Mary A. Trautman. Milton was the author of the monumental treatise *Fishes of Ohio,* and Mary was his steadfast helpmeet during the writing of this book and the completion of many other projects. They were dear friends of mine and of the community of naturalists in Ohio and beyond. How fortunate we all are that they passed our way. There is an exhibit related to their lives in the nature center. The hours of the Nature Center are 10–5 Monday through Friday and 10–6 Saturday and Sunday. The Nature Center and the boardwalk were opened in 1992. The 6-foot-wide boardwalk is the proud work of the young people of the Ohio Civilian Conservation Corps.

There are stations along the trail with benches and signs interpreting the natural history of the area. At one time there was a self-guided trail folder available that was keyed to numbers along the trail, but since the signs are now in place, it may no longer be in use. Ask at the nature center.

The trail leaves from the back door of the center, entering a short piece of swamp forest. It quickly turns due north toward the lake and a split in the trail. In the summer, swamp rose mallow and the invasive alien purple loosestrife grow near there and many other places along the trail.

I suggest turning to the left at the first intersection and taking the loop that brings you back to the main trail after about ⅓ mile. Along the trail are a number of standing dead trees used by cavity-nesting birds such as tree swallows and woodpeckers. Buttonbush grows close to the boardwalk in many places. Both common and narrow-leafed cattail grow in the marsh. The tall, common reed grass is patchy in the marsh. I saw several viceroy butterflies along the trail, and photographed one that was basking. This is typical habitat for that monarch-look-alike species: There are cottonwoods and willows here, both species that are known to be host plants for viceroy larvae. In the early spring, male red-winged blackbirds can be seen swaying back and forth near the tops of last year's reed grass as they advertise for a mate with their squeaky *kong-ka-ree* song.

After passing a side trail to the lodge, the boardwalk rises slightly onto what is probably a sandy beach ridge. There is a bench here and a sign that explains, among other things, why, in the construction of the park facilities, the beach was "armored" with riprap. The view of the lake is spectacular. The boardwalk then turns away from the lake to shortly intersect with the trail back to the nature center and the trail to the east end of the marsh. During much of the spring and into the summer, male bullfrogs sing their basic *jug-of-rum* call. Other species of frogs utilize the marsh during mating season, each in its own season and each singing its own distinct song.

Turning left (east) to explore more of the marsh, the boardwalk passes through perhaps 200 feet of woods that include pin

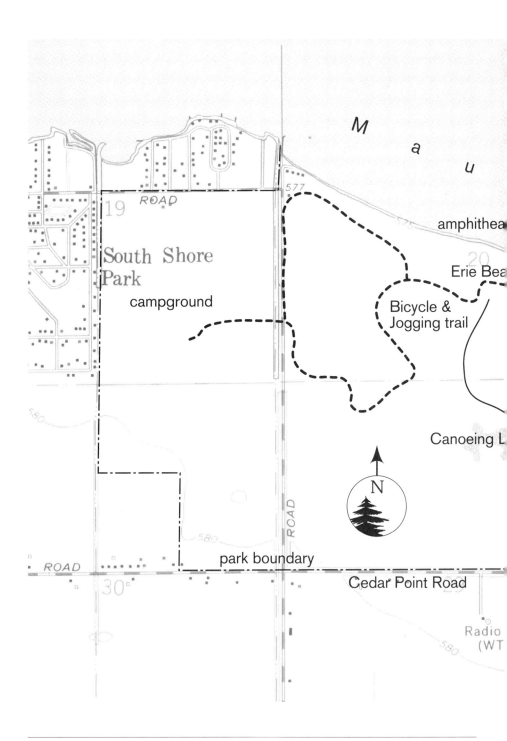

M
a
u

amphithea

19 ROAD

South Shore
Park

577

campground

20

Erie Bea

Bicycle &
Jogging trail

Canoeing L

N

580

park boundary

ROAD

ROAD

30°

Cedar Point Road

Radio
(WT

580

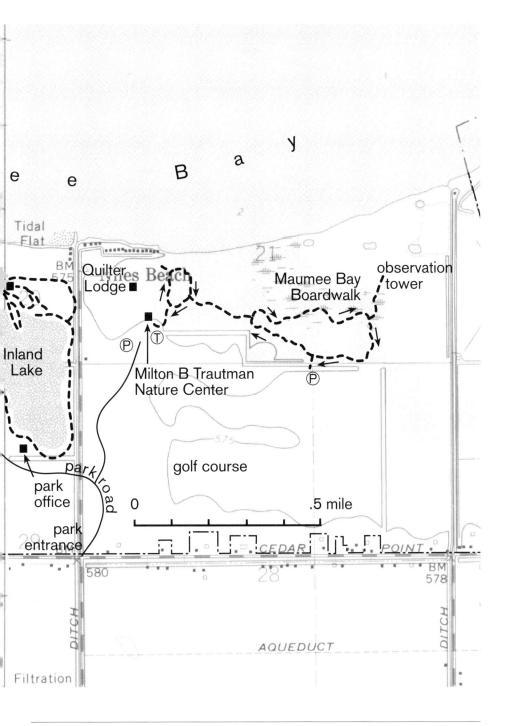

Maumee Bay State Park

➤ Dutch Elm Disease

The American or white elm was once an important part of Ohio's forests. A part of the elm/ash/maple forests of poorly drained bottomlands, it was also part of the mesic woodlands in the northern part of the state. Forest-grown American elms had tall columnar trunks. For many years, the largest known white elm grew at Marietta. It was 26 feet, 6½ inches in circumference at breast height. American elms, with their wineglass shape, once lined the streets of most Ohio cities and villages. The Dutch elm disease is a fungus, Ceratocystis ulmi, carried by the European bark beetle. It was first discovered to be affecting elms in Cleveland in 1930. By 1933 it was being seen at the port of New York, but by then no amount of quarantining could prevent its spread across eastern North America.

At the same time, a second disease was attacking the elms in Ohio. Originally called phloem necrosis, but now referred to as elm yellows, this phytoplasm-caused disease was first seen in Ironton, Ohio, in 1918. It was likely as devastating to Ohio's elms as Dutch elm disease. In any case, by the late 1940s, Ohio towns had lost nearly all of their lawn and street shade trees, and the elm was gone from the swamp forests.

Today, an occasional young elm tree can be seen in places like Cedar Bog (where giant elms once stood), but they hardly ever make it past the 6-inch-diameter size. A few municipalities in the East still use the American elm as a street tree, but they have to use an aggressive spraying program to halt the spread of the two diseases that all but wiped out the species in the Ohio woods.

---

oak, bur oak, cottonwood, and hickory. Common yellowthroat males remind you of their presence with their wichity-wichity-wich.

Dragonflies dart and damselflies flutter in their efforts to catch meals on the wing. Sometimes the dragonflies sit on the top handrail, awaiting a passing meal. It was along this section of the trail that I looked to the right and saw two does cooling themselves in the shade about 20 feet from the boardwalk.

At another intersection, read the signs, rest awhile if you wish, then go left on the trail closer to the lake. The trail passes through a virtual forest of common reed grass (often called by its specific scientific epithet, phragmites). Beyond a small clump of hardwoods, the vegetation to the right of the trail is nearly a monoculture of buttonbush with an occasional loosestrife protruding in midsummer. Footprints in sand close to the boardwalk reveal the presence of the ubiquitous raccoon, a species also willing to make a meal of the smaller creatures of the marsh.

After nearly ½ mile of travel, the boardwalk reaches a side trail to the left that leads to an observation tower. On its way to the tower, the trail passes through a veritable sea of cattails. From the trail you can see to the lake and across the marsh to the east into the Cedar Point National Wildlife Refuge. There was a great egret fishing in the marsh beyond the tower on the summer day when I visited. The view of the lake is what-ever the weather allows it to be.

After backtracking the ½ mile to the T that sits in a jumble of dead trees with loose-strife and cattails below, turn left to continue on the trail. A swamp sparrow crossed the boardwalk in front of me along here, remind-ing me that that species is a likely breeding bird in the marsh. There is a patch of reed canary grass, shorter and finer than the phragmites along here. At a glance, I could not tell if it was the native wet prairie species or the invasive European species. Swamp white and bur oaks grow close to the trail where it enters another wooded area. There are still American elms in the swamp forest mix, but they do not grow to be very large before they succumb to the ever-present Dutch elm disease. There are more dying or dead than healthy along the trail.

A side trail to the left leads through more woods to a blind with open water beyond—a good place to spot sunning turtles. Return-ing to the trail and turning left carries you through swamp forest with emergent plants beneath. A wood pewee was calling here, one of the species that continue to sing long after the nuptial season.

The trail passes an exit to the left (south) that leads to the cabin area, a parking lot and rest rooms. There is a bench at this junction and another one not far on along the trail on the inside of the loop. As the habitat gets a little drier, it becomes suitable for spotted jewelweed in among the trees. It covers nearly all the ground along here in the late summer. Another bench reminds me that this area is probably a great spot to sit and observe neotropical migrants resting and preparing for the trip across the lake on their way north in late April and May. The nature center has a list of which birds are seen at which periods through the spring migration.

Arriving back at the intersection (labeled Junction 3) of the eastern loop with the connector, turn left to backtrack toward the nature center. At the next intersection (Junction 2), turn to the left. In no time you will be at Junction 1, where another left turn will return you to the nature center and the walk to your vehicle. Now that you have had an introduction to wetlands, return often for your next lesson; this time, on your own.

48

Oak Openings Preserve Metropark

Total distance: 17 miles (27.3 km)

Hiking time: 10 hours or 2 days

Maximum elevation: 690 feet

Vertical rise: 50 feet

Maps: USGS 7½' Swanton; USGS 7½' Whitehouse; MPDTA Oak Openings Preserve Metropark map

The Oak Openings is a sandy tract of land, about 130 square miles in area, in western Lucas County and extending into adjoining Fulton and Henry Counties. Though it is mostly flat, sand dunes as high as 25 feet are scattered throughout the area. Underlain by an impenetrable Wisconsinan-aged clayey till, the land is covered with a loose, permeable sand deposited on or near the shoreline of glacial Lake Warren, a precursor of present-day Lake Erie. The underlying glacial till is alkaline, but the sand is acidic. Rainwater that collects in low places and soaks into the soil becomes alkaline when it contacts the underlying limy till. The sand dunes and dry hills, however, remain acidic. In addition, the local accumulation of organic material in ancient swamps has led to locally acidic sites. Many native tree species that require rich soils or a neutral soil are thus absent from the area. On the other hand, there do occur many patches of wet prairie of presettlement days, and the area is home to many rare and endangered species of plants and animals.

The incredible diversity of habitat and the presence of many species of plants and animals not commonly found elsewhere in the state make this trail especially attractive to naturalists. From mid-February, when the skunk cabbage comes into bloom, until late October, when heavy frost knocks down the last of the gentians, there is always an unusual flower in bloom somewhere in the Oak Openings. Among that number are at least a dozen species of native orchids. In the open areas where prairie and old field species occur, butterflies are common, and

Evergreen Lake, along the 17-mile Oak Openings Preserve Metropark

many species of mammals and birds reside in this vast park year-round. Reptiles with habitat requirements as different as those of the spotted turtle and the hog-nosed snake reside here. It's a place to come often with your senses tuned to the wonderful world of nature that abounds here.

In 1939, when the Metropolitan Park District of the Toledo Area was formed, plans were made to "revitalize" the sandy area west of Toledo. An initial 67 acres was acquired, and the planting of thousands of pines and other evergreens that were to stabilize the soil was begun. One major sand dune area was conserved within the park so that future generations of visitors could see this type of Ohio habitat. The original development, known as Springbrook Park, is now only a small part of the 3800-acre Oak Openings Preserve Metropark. The complex includes a reservable lodge, picnic areas,

and many miles of bicycle, horse, and foot trails, including a 17-mile loop trail that goes around the perimeter of the park.

The Seventeen Mile Trail at Oak Openings was originally developed as a Scout hiking trail and is still used for that purpose. Scout units wishing to walk the trail should contact the Trails Committee, Toledo Area Council, BSA, 1 Stranahan Square, Toledo, OH 43604, for information on reservations, awards, and camping. The trail can be hiked as a single 17-mile loop, or, by adding a 2½-mile connector that utilizes roads and the parkway, it can be done as two 10-mile segments. There are no campsites available to the general public, and camping is not permitted along the trail. There are, however, two privately operated campgrounds within a mile or two of the trailhead. There is a group camping area at the trailhead available to youth groups only, on a reservation basis.

Dogs are not allowed on the trails. This is a wet area, and during some seasons of the year insects will be bad. A prudent hiker will be prepared. Be especially careful about matches and cigarettes because of the flammability of the prairie grasses and pine needles. Water is available at pumps located at picnic areas along the trail. There are no concessions serving food anywhere within the park.

How to Get There

To reach the entrance to Oak Openings, take OH 2 west from I-475/US 23 at exit 8 on the west side of Toledo. Travel 8.5 miles to Wilkins Road. Turn left (south) and travel 2.75 miles to the park entrance on the right side of the road. Park on the Mallard Lake Picnic Area lot on the right side of Oak Openings Parkway, 1.25 miles beyond the entrance.

The Trail

The trail is well signed and marked with yellow blazes—although the occasional mile markers do not relate to how the hike is now walked but to an earlier time when the starting point was located at the present midpoint group camping area.

To begin the hike, walk east from the Mallard Lake parking lot to the old picnic shelter, which is now the Buehner Walking Center. This is the trailhead for all hikes in the park; exhibit panels interpret the natural history of the park, and a large map table shows the routes of the many bike, horse, and foot trails of the park. Go east to the lake edge, then turn right to follow the trail around the southern end of the lake. Follow the trail along the left side of the parkway to its intersection with the orange-blazed Evergreen Trail. Turn right and cross the parkway to a kiosk in front of the lodge. There, turn left (east) and begin following the yellow-blazed Seventeen Mile Trail.

After 200 feet, the trail crosses the road and enters a deciduous woods. Here, the trail passes the area designated for group camping. It is used by Scout groups that arrive at the area on a Friday so they can camp near the trailhead and get on the trail early the next morning. After you have walked about ¼ mile, the trail divides into inbound and outbound forks. I suggest hiking the southern loop first, but the choice is yours.

Turning right, for ¾ mile the trail travels between Swan Creek and the parkway, soon reaching OH 295. After a right turn, follow the berm of the road across Swan Creek toward the entrance to the Evergreen Lake Picnic Area. About two-thirds of the way between the creek and park entrance, the trail turns right on a path through the woods. The trail soon joins the paved all-purpose trail just a few feet from the trailhead signs alongside the parkway. Turn right on the all-purpose trail and follow it across Evergreen Lake Dam. Don't miss the turn at the far end of the dam. The all-purpose trail goes straight, the hiking trail left.

Now following the shoreline, the trail passes a stand of hemlock where a horse trail comes in from the right and follows it along the lakeshore. Where the two trails enter a pine grove, a shelterhouse, horse stalls, and rest rooms serve those using the bridle trail. Having almost reached the southern boundary of the park, the trail crosses the bridle trail to the left, then makes a tight clockwise turn as it begins heading northwest. As it passes through a narrow pine plantation, it crosses an east-west-running fire lane. After leaving the pines and entering a wet woody area, it crosses a second fire lane. A quarter mile later, the hiking trail turns west, crosses a horse trail, then travels along the edge of a deciduous woods for another ¼ mile. Next it crosses an old road and angles left, beginning a sweeping semicircular arc through pine and regenerating fields. There is a fire lane going straight ahead that is easily mistaken for the footpath. This is the Pine Ridge Area, where prairie forbs such as Carolina puccoon can be found in the grassy openings. A quarter mile later, the path crosses the fire lane as it begins heading north through a nice deciduous woods.

Winding its way to the northwest, the trail stays among the hardwoods on high ground for about ½ mile before passing through more pines and crossing two horse trails in quick succession. Now turning toward the north, the trail crosses Evans Ditch, which drains into Swan Creek. This ditch is part of a large network of ditches in Oak Openings, built many decades ago in an attempt to make the land suitable for agriculture.

The path now turns west, with regenerating fields on the right and older woods on the left. After ¼ mile, it reaches and crosses Jeffers Road. Beyond Jeffers Road is a good place to look for badgers, or at least for sign of badger. Seventy-five yards beyond the road, the trail turns south, crosses a small bridge, and makes a large loop through a wet woods. It heads north on slightly higher land, paralleling the west boundary of the park. A fire lane enters from the right after ½ mile, and several hundred feet beyond that the trail makes an abrupt right turn to follow another ditch toward Jeffers Road. After turning left across the ditch, the trail travels the road's edge as it goes west to reach Reed Road near its intersection with Manore Road.

Your hike has now covered about 5 miles. This is a good place to return to the trailhead if you wish to reduce your mileage. To do so, turn right (east) on Reed Road and walk ¾ mile to Oak Openings Parkway. Turn

right and follow the drive ½ mile to the Mallard Lake parking lot, for a total walk of 7½ miles.

Return to the trail another day by reversing the 1¼-mile cutoff described above. To continue walking the Seventeen Mile Trail, angle left across Reed Road to where the yellow-marked trail leaves the road, headed north between a white pine plantation and regenerating old field. As pines blend to hardwoods, the trail angles slightly right for a couple of hundred feet, turns north on the highest land in the park, then turns west, continuing through oak forest. At the edge of the older forest, you cross a north-south fire lane and, ⅛ mile later, cross another. Here, the trail turns north to follow a stream in a curve to the left to the bikeway on the former Norfolk & Western (N&W) Railroad right-of-way. From there, it's only a few feet to the crossing of OH 64 that leads to the Springbrook Lake Picnic Area.

This area is where the park district began its experimentation on stabilizing the sand blowouts of Oak Openings by using pines. Follow the yellow markings onto the path that parallels the tracks headed west. Shortly you will find yourself on a wide fire lane that makes a broad, sweeping curve around the entire area. On the north side, you will pass through one of the three small areas that were still in hardwoods at the time of acquisition. The path returns to OH 64, which it crosses to follow a service road east, then north, to the site of the original dedication monument for the Oak Openings Scout Trail. This area was once used for a midpoint campsite for Scouts but is now closed. On relatively high land above a creek, the woods has one of the largest red maples I have seen in Ohio. Beyond the Scout area, the trail drops to the creek valley, traveling north. Just before the trail reaches Monclova Road, it crosses the

➤ Flowers of the Air

Adult butterflies are considered to be creatures of the summer by most Ohioans, but I have encountered them in forest and field in every month of the year. As cold-blooded creatures, they need heat from an external source to allow them to move about. In nearly every case, that means an ambient air temperature above 60 degrees Fahrenheit and unfiltered sunlight in which to bask. Though the vast majority of the 144 species that are found in Ohio overwinter as pupae or eggs, a few make it through the winter as adults in a condition called reproductive diapause. Instead of breeding shortly after emerging from pupae in late summer or fall, they wait until warm weather the following spring. During one of those rare warm spells in January or February, one of these insects may take to the air. I once saw a Milbert's tortoiseshell along the boardwalk at Cedar Bog State Memorial in January, and I have seen mourning cloaks along the trails at Glen Helen in many February warm spells.

At least two species found in the summer in Ohio, the monarch and the painted lady, do not overwinter here. While some species, notably the cabbage white and the clouded and orange sulphurs, seem to breed continually, with overlapping broods from April through November, most species have only one, two, or three broods. When there is more than one brood, there is usually an overlap. If you are out and about much you will soon come to recognize the peak period of each hatch. To learn more about Ohio butterflies, look for Butterflies and Skippers of Ohio by Iftner, Shuey, and Calhoun (Ohio Biological Survey, OSU, Columbus).

---

stream to the left and goes west along the road for several hundred feet.

For the next 3¼ miles, the Seventeen Mile Trail follows the west bank of Swan Creek. Except for one place where it pulls nearly ¼ mile away from the creek to cross the stream coming in from Swanton Reservoir, the path stays alongside the stream. Crossing side ravines on small bridges, it passes through streambank hardwood forest and more white pine plantations. When the trail reaches OH 2, it stays off the highway berm as it uses the right-of-way to get over Swan Creek. Check phone and power poles and the end of the guardrail for blazes and arrows.

The return route from this point, the northernmost on the trail, provides a diversity of habitat. The trail passes through prairie openings, old fields, mixed black and white oak forest, pin oak swamp, sand dunes, and pine forest. The soil varies from alkaline in the wet prairie to very acidic in the pin oak swamp forest.

At the east end of the OH 2 Swan Creek crossing, the trail turns south into regenerating old fields and old mixed oak woodlands. After crossing almost flat land, the trail begins to swing left as it drops toward Bushnell Ditch. Just before doing so, it splits, with a fire lane going right. Turning left at the ditch, your path travels upstream through more evergreen forest for ¼ mile. Near a property line corner it turns south

---

again, traveling through deciduous woods, brush, and meadow. Where it reaches an east-west-running horse trail, the footpath turns left (east) to share the equestrian path for a couple of hundred yards. Turning south once more, the trail now travels through dry, sandy terrain with prairie grasses and forbs between small stands of oaks. Here and there the mounds of harvester ants can be seen.

After traveling ⅓ mile through mostly open land, the trail enters a large stand of red pine, where it turns left (east) and soon reaches Girdham Road. After crossing the road, you skirt another evergreen planting and continue east through wet deciduous forest. The footpath crosses a fire lane, then makes a left turn and crosses a horse trail, turning right shortly thereafter. After another ⅛ mile of traveling east, the trail swings to the south in a reverse S-curve. This is the flattest area of the preserve. The trail crosses the horse trail once more as it curves right, then left, following the edge of the woods.

South of Monclova Road, cross a horse trail, then swing left (east) on a fire lane alongside deciduous woods for ¼ mile. The trail turns north until Monclova Road is visible through the trees; then it turns right (east), parallel to the road and horse trail. As it approaches Wilkins Road, it crosses the horse trail and turns right (south). Traveling alongside the road, it crosses a small bridge, then passes a lovely stand of cinnamon fern before reaching the bike trail on the N&W right-of-way.

The trail crosses the bike trail and the road together, then shares an old track with a horse trail as both head uphill to the southeast. In traveling through oak woods, the trails split as they reach high land. The horse trail takes the left fork toward a large evergreen forest to the south. Your footpath swings northeast through a wet area, then turns south through very wet pin oak woods. In traveling through this swamp forest, the trail uses corduroy road and boardwalk to keep you dry. Just over 1 mile after the bikeway crossing, the trail emerges from the pin oak swamp forest onto Reed Road.

After a direct road crossing, the trail goes a short distance into a spruce forest, then turns left to continue among the evergreens. When it reaches a fire lane coming in from the left, the trail turns right and soon leaves the spruce stand, headed south through more mixed oak forest. After two jogs to the right, it crosses a horse trail just before curving right to cross Oak Openings Parkway. In the woods just beyond, the trail meets the outbound Seventeen Mile Trail. A right turn onto the ¼-mile trail leads past the Main Group Camp to the lodge. Turn right onto the orange-blazed Evergreen Trail, follow it across the road, and turn left to follow the path around the lakeshore to the Walking Center and Mallard Lake parking lot.

49

Ottawa National Wildlife Refuge

Total distance: 4½ miles (7.25 km)

Hiking time: 2½ hours

Maximum elevation: 575 feet

Vertical rise: Virtually none

Maps: USGS 7½' Metzger Marsh; USFWS Ottawa National Wildlife Refuge Wildlife Foot Trails map

Ottawa National Wildlife Refuge is a special place not only for the hiker but also for more than 265 species of birds. A remnant of the once vast swamp and marshlands that stretched from Sandusky to Detroit prior to settlement, it has been set aside as a haven for wildlife, especially waterfowl, wading birds, and shorebirds. The area has also been used by bald eagles as both a nesting area and a feeding area. America's national bird was once a common nester along the entire Lake Erie shoreline. Unfortunately, the places where eagles like to nest are also choice sites for lakeshore homes. Today, Ottawa is one of the few places in Ohio where you can usually see this majestic raptor.

Here you can also see thousands of Canada geese and ducks, including mallards, blacks, blue-winged teals, wood ducks, American wigeons, and canvasbacks. In late winter, tundra swans pass over the area on their way from the Chesapeake Bay to their nesting grounds near the Arctic Circle.

Any area with standing water suitable for waterfowl and shorebirds is also likely to have a good insect population during the warm months. Such is the case at Ottawa. An ample supply of repellent, a head net, and loose-fitting clothes covering exposed skin are necessary during the summer. A visored cap provides good protection from the sun, and for those especially sensitive to the sun's rays, a protective sunscreen is appropriate.

Though the refuge is operated primarily for the wildlife, facilities have been provided for human visitors. At the parking lot located

Canada geese are common along the trail at Ottawa National Wildlife Refuge.

1 mile from the highway, there is an outdoor exhibit that tells the story of the refuge and delineates four walking trails of varying distances. The Blue Trail takes you past the widest variety of habitats and comes closest to where the eagles are likely to be seen. All of the trails are marked according to their color designation, so the Blue Trail is easy to follow. Trails are open from sunrise to sunset throughout the year.

How to Get There

Ottawa is located about halfway between Port Clinton and Toledo off OH 2; a prominent sign along OH 2 identifies the single public entrance to the lakeshore facility.

The Trail

With binoculars, a bird book, and an area bird checklist from the refuge kiosk in hand, head straight north along the dike. The area across the ditch to the right is known as

Goosehaven, a good place to see nesting Canada geese at the right time of the year. After walking less than ¼ mile, you will reach an intersection where the Blue Heron Trail goes to the left and a sign points to an observation platform. If you are interested in seeing waterfowl or wading birds, turn left and walk the ¼ mile to the observation platform. This fine facility was built in 1995 with financial support from the Ohio Audubon Council (OAC). Return to the dike you were following to continue traveling north. Muskrats are frequently seen in this and other waterways of the refuge.

After 1 mile of traveling due north, the trail swings northwest, then west-southwest. Along this mile-long stretch, eagles might be seen in the distance to the right. During nesting season, one of the adult birds may be seen hunting in this area. At the west end of the trail, which has been following Crane Creek, turn left (south) for

¼ mile, then left again (east) for ½ mile. The area to the right of the trail is drained in the summer so that vegetation can grow. It is then flooded in the fall for waterfowl to feed. The trail turns right (south) for ¼ mile before turning right again (west, then southwest) into a swamp forest. Here you can expect to see wood warblers during the spring and fall migration. Some species, such as the yellow warbler and common yellowthroat, nest in the area, and even the beautiful prothonotary warbler has been seen here during some summers.

After emerging from the woods, the trail turns left (east) along the edge of the woods and then goes right (southeast) through a brushy thicket. It travels back through more swamp forest before returning to the parking lot. There are rest rooms there, but no facilities for picnicking or camping. The latter are available at Maumee Bay State Park near Toledo and East Harbor State Park east of Port Clinton. The refuge office is located just east of the information kiosk. Construction of the bridge to the office was also supported by the OAC.

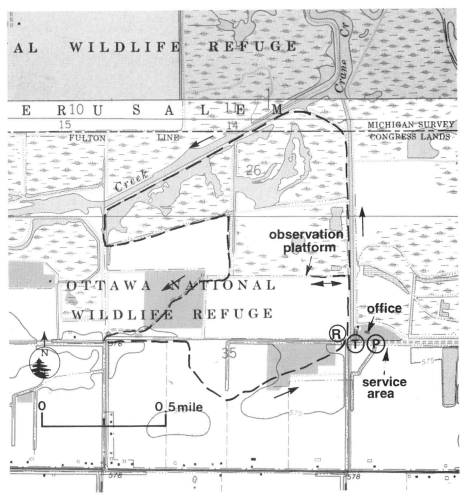

While in the area, be sure to visit Magee Marsh State Wildlife Area just to the east. During much of the year, wildlife is easily seen and photographed from the road there, and a fine interpretive center tells the story of the Lake Erie marshlands. From an observation tower, you can look out over hundreds of acres of marsh. Crane Creek State Park lies to the north of Magee Marsh and shares an entrance road with it. You'll find an excellent beach and picnic facilities there. An elevated boardwalk, Bird Trail, opened in 1989 provides superb birding during spring and fall. It originates from the west end of the beach parking lot. The cooling tower visible to the east of the refuge is part of the Davis-Besse nuclear generating facility. It sits on a limestone outcropping above the marshes and uses water from Lake Erie as a part of the power-generating process. Its operation is closely monitored for signs of thermal or radiation pollution. During the periods of bird migration, the Black Swamp Bird Observatory, based at Oak Harbor, operates a bird-banding station on a beach ridge on a part of the Ottawa National Wildlife Refuge that lies east of the power plant.

50

Providence, Farnsworth, and Bend View/Canal Lands Metroparks

Total distance: 8 miles (12.9 km)

Hiking time: 3½ hours

Maximum elevation: 615 feet

Vertical rise: 10 feet

Maps: USGS 7½' Bowling Green North; USGS 7½' Bowling Green South; USGS 7½' Weston; MPDTA Guide to Farnsworth, Bend View, Canal Lands Metroparks; MPDTA Guide to Isaac Ludwig Mill; MPDTA Guide to Providence Metropark; MPDTA Miami & Erie Canal Restoration; BTA Buckeye Trail Defiance Section map; Buckeye Trail Waterville Section map

The 250-mile Miami and Erie Canal connected Cincinnati on the Ohio River with the Lake Erie port city of Toledo, but it was never a great success. Built in sections over a period of 20 years, it suffered from too little money, too little or too much water, and competition with the new mode of transportation on the scene, the railroads. After 70 years of operation, the 1913 flood dealt the canal system a devastating blow. Destruction of bridges, dams, and the canal itself was widespread. Because the canal was already operating at a deficit, there were no advocates for state funds for repairs. The portion in Cincinnati, including the 10 locks into the river, had been abandoned since 1863, and the Maumee and Manhattan sidecuts at the Toledo end had ceased operation a year later. After 1900, the canal at Providence on the north side of the Maumee River was used only for local commerce. After the 1913 flood, only the pieces that had survived relatively unscathed continued to operate. In 1929 the Miami, Wabash, and Erie Canal, connected to the Miami and Erie near Defiance, finally closed. The Miami and Erie Canal was blocked below Lock No. 30 in 1930, ½ mile downstream from Providence Dam, where a gristmill had been built in 1846 utilizing water rights from the canal. In December 1930, the visionary leaders of the Toledo Metropolitan Park District (now Metropolitan Park District of the Toledo Area) worked out an arrangement to lease the canal lands from Waterville to the Lucas/Henry county line from the state of Ohio. These lands provided the backbone for Farnsworth, Bend View, and Providence

Metroparks.

Until the fall of 1994, the 8-mile section of canal downriver from Providence had not seen a canalboat or heard a muleskinner's shout for over a half a century. Then, with the restoration of Lock 44 complete and the new canalboat *Volunteer* launched, it was again possible to take a trip on the old canal.

With this restoration project came a re-designing of the park, including the addition of a new trailhead at the new Providence Historic Area parking lot. With this construction, a new focus came to the old canal lands. Once trodden only by overworked animals and underpaid men, the towpath is now in use nearly every day of the year for pleasurable recreation purposes. In a part of the state where every acre of good land is in agriculture, the canal lands were the perfect answer to the park district in its early years, for they provided instant parkland along the river and the towpath was an ideal recreational trail. With the addition of the possibility of a canalboat ride, it becomes an even more attractive area for outdoor recreation.

Since this is an end-to-end walk, a two-car shuttle is necessary unless you want to walk it both directions. The shuttle is no problem since there are parking lots at both ends. With a little creative scheduling and an extra mile or two of walking, a railroad buff might want to walk the towpath and

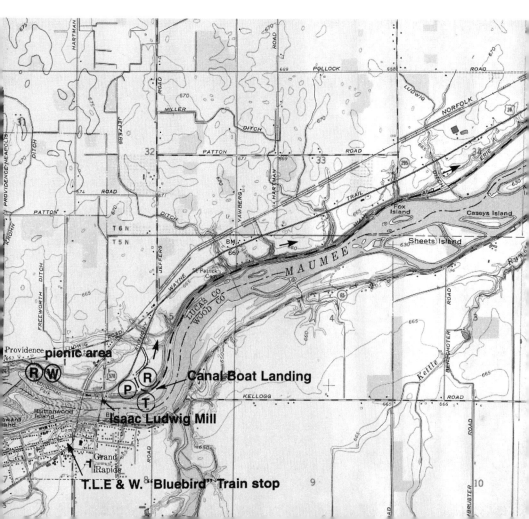

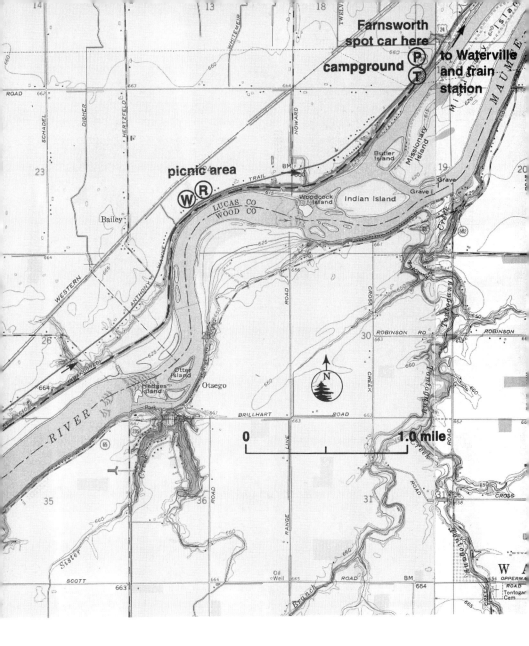

ride the Bluebird Passenger train on the Toledo, Lake Erie & Western Railroad back to near the starting point. A call to the Grand Rapids Area Chamber of Commerce at 419-832-1106 will summon literature about this opportunity.

You may want to take the short trip on the canal boat to the west through Lock 44 and back and visit the restored and operational Isaac Ludwig Mill across OH 578 before or after your walk. And a visit to the dam area at Providence Park along US 24, less than a mile west of the trailhead area, will be worthwhile. There you will see Provi-

Wild turkeys share the former towpath along the old Miami and Erie Canal.

dence Dam, which was originally built in 1838 to water the canal to the east and provide slackwater for navigation to the west. It was rebuilt in 1908. The shelter-house, probably one of the "best by a dam site," was built by the Depression-era Works Progress Administration (WPA) in 1941, just prior to the onset on World War II. Brochures describing these and other facilities and the park district may be obtained by calling 419-535-3050.

How to Get There

To reach the trailhead at Providence Metropark, travel US 24 southwest from Toledo. Turn left (south) at the Providence Historic Area sign. Park there and cross the canal on the bridge to begin your walk. There are rest rooms, drinking water, and outdoor interpretive exhibits here, as well as the ticket booth and boarding area for the canal boat trip.

The Trail

Access to the 8-mile Towpath Trail is to the east from the informational kiosk area. The trail is well marked with the blue hiker symbols of the park district and the blue blazes of the Buckeye Trail. Mileposts are placed along the entire trail so you can answer the "How much farther?" question of young companions. The trail is virtually level the entire route, for there are no locks on this part of the canal. If you wish to, you can walk closer to the river by following the orange-labeled River Bluff Trail downriver until, after about a mile, it intersects the Towpath Trail. It starts at the bottom of a curved trail directly opposite the bridge over the canal.

Along the Towpath Trail, between mile 1 and mile 2, there are two check dams across the canal, one dated 1935 and probably built by the WPA or Civilian Conservation Corps. At one point an earthen dam backs up water in the canal bed for a

Here an authentic reproduction of a 19th-century canalboat is pulled by a team of mules in the waterway next to the hiking trail.

short distance. For the next 4 miles, the trail follows the towpath through the Canal Land Metropark, reachable only on foot. It passes a few houses, new or old, on the left beyond the canal, and by privately owned land between the canal and the river. There are cuts in the canal dike where driveways lead to an occasional trailer or to farm fields. The land alongside the canal and much of the canal bed is forested with sycamore, hackberry, honey locust, redbud, basswood, cottonwood, silver maple, and other hardwoods. Wildlife, including wild turkey and white-tailed deer, is sometimes seen along the trail.

Before reaching mile 7, the trail comes to Bend View Overlook, where there is a small shelterhouse with picnic tables, a waist-high grill, rest rooms, and a Baker pump. These facilities, like those in the other riverside parks, were built during the WPA times. East of the shelter there are a number of homes on the hillside above the canal from which trails run across the canal to private riverfront property. After nearly 2 more miles on the towpath, the trail emerges from the woods at the Towpath Trailhead and boat-launching area, where there are also vault toilets and a drinking fountain. Picnic facilities and canoe rentals are located close by at the Indianola Shelterhouse area of Farnsworth Park.

Pick up your second car here, or turn around and retrace your steps.

Index

Let Backcountry Guides Take You There

Our experienced backcountry authors will lead you to the finest trails, parks, and back roads in the following areas:

50 Hikes Series
50 Hikes in the Maine Mountains
50 Hikes in Southern and Coastal Maine
50 Hikes in Vermont
50 Hikes in the White Mountains
50 More Hikes in New Hampshire
50 Hikes in Connecticut
50 Hikes in Massachusetts
50 Hikes in the Hudson Valley
50 Hikes in the Adirondacks
50 Hikes in Central New York
50 Hikes in Western New York
50 Hikes in New Jersey
50 Hikes in Eastern Pennsylvania
50 Hikes in Central Pennsylvania
50 Hikes in Western Pennsylvania
50 Hikes in the Mountains of North Carolina
50 Hikes in Northern Virginia
50 Hikes in Ohio
50 Hikes in Michigan

Walks and Rambles Series
Walks and Rambles on Cape Cod and
    the Islands
Walks and Rambles in Rhode Island
More Walks and Rambles in Rhode Island
Walks and Rambles in Duchess and
    Putnam Counties
Walk and Rambles in Westchester and
    Fairfield Counties
Walks and Rambles on the Delmarva Peninsula
Walks and Rambles in Southwestern Ohio
Walks and Rambles in Ohio's Western Reserve
Walks and Rambles in the Western
    Hudson Valley
Walks and Rambles on Long Island

25 Bicycle Tours Series
25 Bicycle Tours in Maine
30 Bicycle Tours in New Hampshire
25 Bicycle Tours in Vermont
25 Mountain Bike Tours in Vermont
25 Bicycle Tours on Cape Cod and the Islands
25 Mountain Bike Tours in Massachusetts
30 Bicycle Tours in New Jersey
25 Mountain Bike Tours in New Jersey
25 Bicycle Tours in the Adirondacks
30 Bicycle Tours in the Finger Lakes Region
25 Bicycle Tours in the Hudson Valley
25 Bicycle Tours in the Twin Cities and
    Southeastern Minnesota
30 Bicycle Tours in Wisconsin
25 Mountain Bike Tours in the Hudson Valley
25 Bicycle Tours in Ohio's Western Reserve
25 Bicycle Tours in Eastern Pennsylvania
25 Bicycle Tours in Maryland
25 Bicycle Tours on Delmarva
25 Bicycle Tours in and around Washington, D.C.
25 Bicycle Tours in Coastal Georgia and the
    Carolina Low Country
25 Bicycle Tours in the Texas Hill Country and
    West Texas
The Mountain Biker's Guide to Ski Resorts

We offer many more books on hiking, fly-fishing, travel, nature, and other subjects. Our books are available at bookstores and outdoor stores everywhere. For more information or a free catalog, please call 1-800-245-4151 or write to us at The Countryman Press, PO Box 748, Woodstock, Vermont 05091. You can find us on the Web at http://www.countrymanpress.com.